STARRING **MICHAEL CAINE**

BELOW: Michael Caine in one of his classic roles, as British agent Harry Palmer in *Funeral in Berlin* (1966).

STARRING **MICHAEL CAINE**

DAVID **BISHOP**

REYNOLDS & HEARN LTD
LONDON

TO MY WIFE ALISON, who has seen enough
Michael Caine films to last her a lifetime.

ACKNOWLEDGMENTS

Grateful thanks are due to the staff of the British Film Institute Library, to all those sellers on ebay who made it possible to find and view almost every Caine film since *Zulu*, and to Byron Erickson for supplying a copy of the elusive *Quicksand*. Thanks, too, to John Mackenzie, Nigel Davenport, George Innes and Mike Hodges for agreeing to be interviewed for this volume, and their respective agents for arranging the interviews. Special mention must be made of my publishers, Marcus Hearn and Richard Reynolds, for commissioning the book and guiding it to completion.

Finally, the greatest thanks are due to Sir Maurice Micklewhite himself. He thrilled me as a boy when I went to see *The Man Who Would Be King* at the pictures in New Zealand, and he still makes me laugh and cry when I watch his films. Without him, the film world would have been a poorer place in the last 40 years.

Front and back cover: main images © Rex Features
Subsidiary stills and inside images provided by The Tony Hillman Collection,
The Joel Finler Collection and Rex Features.

First published in 2003 by
Reynolds & Hearn Ltd
61a Priory Road
Kew Gardens
Richmond
Surrey TW9 3DH

A CIP catalogue record for this book is available from the British Library.

ISBN 1 903111 57 9

Designed by James King.

Printed and bound in Great Britain by Biddles Ltd, Guildford, Surrey.

BELOW: A rare
foray into television
for the lavish mini-
series *Jack the
Ripper* (1988).

CONTENTS

INTRODUCTION

MICHAEL CAINE is one of the world's great film actors. He has won two Oscars, three Golden Globes, a BAFTA and numerous career achievement awards. Since his breakthrough role in *Zulu* (1964), he has made 82 movies in 40 years – with more on the way. These films have ranged from the sublime (*Get Carter*, *Sleuth* and *Alfie* to name a few) to the ridiculous (*The Swarm*, *On Deadly Ground* and *Shadow Run*). Caine's remarkable career longevity is underlined by the fact that he is one of only three men to have been Oscar-nominated for acting in five consecutive decades; the others are Laurence Olivier and Jack Nicholson.

He turned 70 in March 2003, an age when most people have already retired. Instead Caine was being feted for giving one of the finest performances of his career in *The Quiet American* (2002). He had another film already in post-production (*Secondhand Lions*) and was about to start work on *The Statement* with acclaimed director Norman Jewison.

Starring Michael Caine is a guide to this iconic actor's feature films. The bulk of the book is devoted to a film-by-film analysis of those 82 movies, including useful information, intriguing facts and a range of opinion. The book's emphasis is placed squarely on Caine's participation and his performances, with extensive quotes by the man himself drawn from hundreds of sources.

Starring Michael Caine is not a biography. There are several of those already available, with Caine's 1992 autobiography *What's It All About?* still the definitive work on the subject. This book is neither a hatchet job nor a hagiography. It is an honest appraisal of Caine's career and the films in which he has appeared. Caine has made foolish choices and has also shown moments

of genius on screen. This volume acknowledges both ends of the spectrum and everything in between. Instead of presenting a chronological career overview, *Starring Michael Caine* concentrates on the films themselves, presenting them in alphabetical order. It tells the behind-the-scenes story of each movie's production, charts critical reactions and helps you sort the gems from the dross.

Lazy critics have frequently written off Caine with the facile suggestion that the actor is merely playing himself. But he has appeared on the big screen as gangsters, journalists, spies, transvestites, murderers, psychopaths, architects, homosexuals, bisexuals, diplomats, racists and assassins, among many other roles. If he was only playing himself, it is unlikely he would carry conviction in all those characterisations. Perhaps Caine's greatest gift is to make what he does look easy, when nothing could be further from the truth.

But how did a South London lad with no formal dramatic training become one of the most respected film actors of the past 40 years? And why has he been so successful for so long? There is no single answer to either question. Certainly he is a pragmatic actor who appears to look upon acting as a craft, rather than an art. He prides himself on being professional and expects others to do the same, because acting is his profession.

To illustrate the many factors that have contributed to Caine's success and longevity, it's necessary, first of all, to briefly examine his life and career.

LIFE BEFORE *ZULU*

Maurice Joseph Micklewhite was born at St Olave's Hospital in London on 14 March 1933. His father was a porter at the Billingsgate fish market, his mother a cleaning lady. The South London family was poor, with Micklewhite Sr frequently unemployed.

At the age of five Maurice Micklewhite developed a lifelong love for films, and began making regular visits to local cinemas. He was evacuated during the Second World War and later recalled being mistreated while billeted away from home. In later life the actor would use such traumatic experiences and injustices as triggers to help him find the necessary emotion for a scene. Caine can cry on demand by reaching back to those painful memories.

After the war the Micklewhite family was relocated to Elephant and Castle, home to vicious criminals and street gangs. Caine based his performances in films like *Get Carter* (1971) on the murderous individuals he encountered at the Elephant. At 15 he joined the drama class at a local youth club to pursue his dream of becoming a film star and to get closer to girls. He left school at 16, becoming an office boy with a small company that made tourist films. Called up for National Service at 18, Micklewhite was later sent to fight in the Korean War. The deaths and carnage he witnessed there had a profound effect on the would-be actor. He subsequently starred in several war films, but almost always chose pictures where the futility of war was made obvious.

Micklewhite left the army in 1952 and talked his way into a job as an assistant stage manager with a small theatre company, adopting the stage name Michael Scott. The young actor started getting walk-on parts, gradually increasing in skill and confidence. When he was offered his first television job, Scott discovered his chosen stage name was already taken. Inspired by *The Caine Mutiny* (1954), the young actor renamed

himself Michael Caine. Over the next decade he continued to perform on stage and in a succession of bit parts in movies. His best hope seemed to be with television, but Caine was determined to succeed in films. He even turned down a regular role in the long-running police series *Z-Cars*. His friends were fast becoming household names, but Caine was approaching 30 without finding a great role. That changed when he was cast in *Zulu* (1964).

Caine showed remarkable resilience during his first 30 years. He determined to become a film star, despite all the odds stacked against him. Men from his background did not aspire to become actors. Such a profession was sneered at and those who chose it were called 'queer'. But Caine persisted with his dream. He did not have the looks of a matinée idol, nor the upper-class accent used by most British actors of the time. He did not have the chance to go to drama school, instead learning to act 'on the job' in repertory theatre, from bits parts in movies and on television. Caine's first marriage to actress Patricia Haines collapsed partly because of his driven ambition to succeed as an actor. Again and again he would tell fellow actors that he was going to be a film star – but nobody believed him.

Timing was another factor in Caine's success. He was ready to make the most of his big break when it came as Lieutenant Gonville Bromhead in *Zulu*. By 1963 he had developed the technical skills to cope with such an opportunity. He did not have much dialogue in the film, but succeeded in giving what he did have far greater impact than a novice could have achieved. Had the chance come sooner, Caine might not have been ready. Equally, a shift in British attitudes by the 1960s made it possible

for creative people from working class origins to break through traditional barriers and become famous. Kitchen sink dramas, angry young men and the rise of rock 'n' roll all helped pave the way for Caine to become a cinema star.

LIFE IN THE 1960s

Luck has played a significant part in Caine's career. His first major roles were all in hit films – *Zulu*, *The Ipcress File* (1965) and *Alfie* (1966). Each helped win him subsequent roles, creating and then enhancing his status. Caine's

performance in *Zulu* secured him the lead in *The Ipcress File* and the financial security of a seven-year contract with producer Harry Saltzman. *The Ipcress File* proved that an actor wearing glasses could be a big screen star – the first time it had happened since Harold Lloyd in the silent era. It also helped win Caine the role of *Alfie* and his first Hollywood picture, *Gambit* (1966), with Shirley MacLaine. *Alfie* brought his first Oscar nomination and, crucially, introduced him to American filmmakers. Had any of these pictures failed, the knock-on effect could have badly derailed his fledgling career.

Other actors have divided their time between cinema, the theatre and television, but Caine has single-mindedly pursued film acting as his career. He abandoned theatre work soon after making *Zulu* and ditched television assignments almost as quickly. He grabbed opportunities to work with established film stars and major directors, always looking to improve his skills and extend his network of industry contacts. But fear of poverty pushed Caine into unwise choices, like a contract with Twentieth Century-Fox that begat two feeble flops, *Deadfall* and *The Magus* (both 1968).

At the end of the 1960s, Caine was stuck in a run of unsuccessful films. Critics wondered if he could ever escape the twin shadows of *Alfie* and Harry Palmer. But another of Caine's strongest assets came to his rescue – professionalism. No matter how bad the film might have been, Caine prided himself on always giving the best performance he could. But his professionalism goes beyond that. Almost everyone who has ever worked with him has said how easy he makes the job for others. In a profession not short of prima donnas, Caine gets on with the job of acting. Producers never lose money because he has thrown a tantrum and refused to come out of his trailer. Directors are delighted to discover he arrives on set already knowing his lines. He is willing to help other actors achieve a good performance, staying behind to feed them lines even when he is not visible in shot. As a result, people are eager to work with him again and again. Caine's professionalism earned him great respect in Hollywood.

THE 1970s

Another reason for Caine's continued success was his willingness to take risks. He played a remorseless hit-man in *Get Carter* (1971), fully endorsing the film's brutally realistic violence.

The picture horrified critics at the time but has since been recognised as a British cinema classic, thanks in no small part to Caine's bleak, chilling performance. In *Sleuth* (1972), he went head to head with Olivier, one of Britain's most respected thespians. The picture offered a unique challenge as it was one of the first movies made with a cast of just two. There was no hiding place for Caine, but he proved himself equal to Olivier as a film actor and both men were nominated for the best actor Oscar.

Many British actors of Caine's generation lost their way in the 1970s due to drink or drugs. In his autobiography Caine recalled that he too was becoming a heavy drinker by the early 1970s, but his relationship with Shakira Baksh changed that. They married in January 1973 and had a daughter later that year. It's impossible for any outsider to know just how influential Caine's 30-year marriage has been upon his career, but it seems likely she has helped him through lean years when others have turned to drink and drugs.

Caine has been in plenty of poor movies, but he has also made many shrewd choices over the years. In the mid-1970s he deliberately began taking roles that would establish him as an international film star. Caine was ready when the British film industry went into near-terminal decline, able to sustain his career by working almost exclusively in Hollywood. After *The Romantic Englishwoman* (1975), he made 15 films in seven years – but only three were British. The actor found himself spending so much time working in Hollywood, he decided to live there. The punitive tax rates imposed on high earners in Britain were another encouragement to leave his homeland.

The transition to America was not easy. To fund the relocation Caine took on ill-advised films like *The Swarm* (1978) and *Ashanti* (1979). But in between them he still managed to impress as a bisexual in *California Suite* (1978). Caine arrived in Hollywood as the 1970s drew to a close but found himself back at the bottom of the ladder when it came to getting the best scripts and the best parts. It was like starting all over again. But he still had to earn a living and threw himself into what work was available, even if it meant the movie disaster *Beyond the Poseidon Adventure* (1979).

THE 1980s

Caine's struggle to re-establish himself as a credible actor in Hollywood continued in the early 1980s. He made three horror films in succession, with only Brian De Palma's controversial *Dressed to Kill* (1980) giving Caine a credible platform to display his talents. It took all the actor's powers of persuasion to secure the lead in *Deathtrap* (1982), a minor film by Sidney Lumet that nevertheless raised Caine's profile. Ironically, he went back to British films to prove himself once and for all. *Educating Rita* (1983) reunited him with *Alfie* director Lewis Gilbert and secured Caine another best actor Oscar nomination.

Caine was never afraid of hard work, appearing more comfortable on a soundstage than a golf course. His fierce work ethic reached new heights in the mid-1980s, which saw him appearing in 12 films between 1985 and 1988. Caine was determined to prove his range. Widely perceived as a dramatic actor, he took on as many comedies as possible. Some were sublime, such as his Oscar-winning role in *Hannah and Her Sisters* (1986) or co-starring with Steve Martin in *Dirty Rotten Scoundrels* (1988), some were fitfully funny (*Sweet Liberty* in 1986), and others simply fell flat (*Water* in 1985). By the end of this prolific period Caine and his family had returned to live in England.

When he turned 55 Caine reversed a long-standing policy of refusing all offers to act on television. He was paid a seven-figure sum to star in a TV mini-series, *Jack the Ripper* (1988). The project was a ratings hit and Caine was persuaded to make another, *Jekyll & Hyde* (1990). Deciding it was time to take stock, he stepped off the treadmill of constant filming and began writing his autobiography, *What's It All About?*

THE 1990s

When Caine tried to get back into acting after a year off, it proved harder than he expected. He set up a production company with American Martin Bregman to make small British thrillers, but the venture failed when their first film, *Blue Ice*, flopped in 1992. A year later he found himself in Alaska making *On Deadly Ground* (1994) with martial arts action hero Steven Seagal. Caine's career was in trouble and he knew it.

For years the actor had sworn he would never make another Harry Palmer film, having hung up his NHS frames after *Billion Dollar Brain* (1967). But in 1994 Caine made two Harry Palmer films back-to-back in Russia, both doomed to go straight to video. It seemed Caine's time had passed. He was over 60 and could only find worthwhile scripts for TV projects. The actor decided to concentrate on running his restaurants, opening a new one in Miami, Florida. Just when he was thinking of retiring altogether, his lucky streak returned with the arrival of Jack Nicholson and director Bob Rafelson.

The pair were making a movie in Florida called *Blood and Wine* (1997). They invited Caine to play a dying safecracker. It was only a supporting role but got him back on the big screen. Within a year Caine had joined the cast of *Little Voice* (1998), establishing a fruitful relationship with America's powerful Miramax studio. This led to his supporting role in *The Cider House Rules* (1999) and a second best supporting actor Oscar. Caine was being taken seriously again by Hollywood – the comeback was complete.

THE 2000s

In the past four years Caine has played a mixture of lead and supporting roles, balancing lightweight comedies like *Miss Congeniality* (2000) and *Austin Powers in Goldmember* (2002) with dramatic films such as *Last Orders* (2001) and *The Quiet American* (2002). The latter earned him a sixth Oscar nomination, largely thanks to Caine's own efforts to get a film perceived as anti-American released in a hostile political climate. He didn't win the Oscar, but just getting his name among the five nominees was a testament to his talent, perseverance and networking skills.

So what's next? *Secondhand Lions* is already in post-production and should be released soon after this book is published. Considering the harsh response of British critics to Caine's New England accent in *The Cider House Rules* (1999), it'll be interesting to see what reviewers have to say about his Texan drawl. Shooting is underway on *The Statement*, a potential Oscar contender, judging by its cast and crew.

Caine is hopeful that two other projects will come to fruition. Production was due to start on *Boswell for the Defence* in 2001 but financing fell apart just before shooting began. Plans are afoot to try again towards the end of 2003, with Caine in the lead. Also being nursed towards production is a new film version of the stage play *Sleuth*, featuring Caine and rising star Jude Law. Both make for intriguing prospects.

STARRING MICHAEL CAINE

This book details all the feature films Caine has appeared in from his breakthrough role in *Zulu* (1964) up to *The Actors* (2003), his most recently released picture when this volume was going to

press, and including, for good measure, two further productions currently awaiting release. These 82 movies are presented in alphabetical order, rather than chronological, for several reasons. Firstly, ease of reference – the casual reader can find the entry for a particular movie much more easily in an alphabetical format. Secondly, it enables each film to receive due consideration on its own merits, rather than solely within the context of Caine's career. Lastly, and least importantly, it creates delightful juxtapositions for those who choose to read this volume from cover to cover. For example, the letter 'I' throws together the bizarre trio of espionage thriller *The Ipcress File* (1965), schlock-horror pirate picture *The Island* (1980) and crime caper classic *The Italian Job* (1969).

Mention must be made here of the criteria used to determine inclusion and exclusion from these pages. None of Caine's films that pre-date *Zulu* get an entry in this book. The actor is believed to have made his cinema debut as early as 1950 in the British feature *Morning Departure* and went on to appear in more than a dozen movies during the next 13 years, popping up in a succession of bit parts and uncredited roles. None brought him any meaningful recognition, the roles are of little significance and Caine himself has dismissed his cinema work before *Zulu* as irrelevant. For the record, there is a full listing of all the actor's confirmed feature film appearances at the back of this book.

Several films have been included that are yet to be seen in the UK or US, and which may never be released in either territory. *The Debtors* (1999) is the subject of a long-running legal battle that keeps the picture in limbo, having only been screened for one day at the Toronto Film Festival. The fascinating story of the movie's making and the acrimony that followed is included here. Also featured is *Quicksand* (2002), the film Caine made just before shooting his Oscar-nominated role in *The Quiet American* (2002). *Quicksand* has been released on DVD in some European territories but remains unavailable in the UK or US. In an exclusive interview, director John Mackenzie details what happened to this film.

Missing from the main listings are Caine's appearances in documentary films (eg, *Tonight Let's All Make Love in London*, 1967), clips from his movies used in compilation features (eg, *Terror in the Aisles*, 1984) and all Caine's TV projects. He is reputed to have featured in more than 100 television dramas before making *Zulu*. Once he began to get leading roles on film, he effectively abandoned the small screen for a quarter of a century. A $1 million fee persuaded Caine to reverse his antipathy towards television acting in 1988 for the mini-series *Jack the Ripper*. As his film roles dried up during the 1990s, he found himself doing more TV projects, such as *Jekyll & Hyde*, *World War II: When Lions Roared, Mandela and de Klerk* and *20,000 Leagues Under the Sea*. But Caine's career resurgence in the late 1990s has restored the actor to his natural habitat – the big screen.

One exception to the no-TV criteria has made it into this book. *Midnight in St Petersburg* (1997) was shot over four weeks in Russia during 1994. Filmed back-to-back with *Bullet to Beijing* (1996), *Midnight in St Petersburg* was made for TV and ought to be excluded from these pages on that basis. However, it is a Harry Palmer film and thus has strong links with four other films already included here. Its production and release mirror those of *Bullet to Beijing*, making it almost an identical twin of that picture. So the criteria have been relaxed to let *Midnight in St Petersburg* sneak in.

The year attached to each movie relates to when the film was first released, rather than the year it was made. Most features are shot a year before they are released to cinemas, but some

pictures are held up for longer due to problems with finance, distribution or other issues.

The cast listings only feature the first 12 actors billed and the characters they played, with their spellings and order taken from the closing credits where possible. Some listings have more than a dozen cast members, some fewer, as was deemed appropriate. The crew listings use standardised titles for some jobs. For example, cinematography is used to describe a role variously credited as photographer, director of photography, lighting cameraman and cinematographer in different films. The writer credit lists those officially billed as having written the screenplay for each feature. Where appropriate, the names of those who contributed to the script in other ways (eg, Cornelius Ryan wrote the book *A Bridge Too Far*) are noted within the body of the listing.

Each film entry includes a brief synopsis of the plot. The summaries are not exhaustive, but some contain story details that may spoil your enjoyment of the film if you have not already seen it. For example, if you don't wish to know the twist ending to *Dressed to Kill* (1980), you're best to watch the movie before reading its entry in this book.

Where available the budgets and box-office grosses for each film have been included. Accurate box-office figures are the stuff of news items these days, with companies declaring how much a film has taken down to the last pound or dollar. It was not always thus and so figures from before 1980 are limited. A similar situation applies to determining the budget of each film. Where any of these facts or figures could not be confirmed, they have been omitted.

Lastly, I give my personal verdict on each film, as viewed today. This section is determined by my own tastes and prejudices, but it also tries to give a measured view of the merits and failings of each Caine movie.

RIGHT: Caine's performance as Lieutenant Gonville Bromhead in *Zulu* (1964) served notice of a film star in the making.

A few final thoughts before moving on to consider Caine's 82 films since *Zulu*. There are only two major genres this versatile actor has yet to tackle – the Western and science fiction. The former is perhaps not surprising, as the Western has been out of favour with filmmakers for most of Caine's career, and the British industry doesn't produce many Westerns anyway. Then there is the fact that Caine has an oft-stated antipathy for horses, having been unseated and unsettled by the animals on almost every occasion he has acted with them. 'I'll never be in a Western,' Caine told *GQ* in 1997, 'because I hate horses, I don't like wide open spaces, and I'm not very keen on baked beans.'

As for science fiction, it's difficult to imagine Caine slipping into a spacesuit these days. Most of his film roles have been resolutely contemporary when they were made, with only a handful set before the 20th century. The closest he ever got to a science fiction picture was facing the killer bees of *The Swarm* (1978). The fall-out from that almighty flop probably persuaded him science fiction was a genre best left to others.

It seems unlikely that Caine will retire soon. He received the best notices of his life for *The Quiet American* and is still hungry to win a best actor Oscar after four unsuccessful nominations. More importantly, Caine is still hungry to act. Many of his friends and colleagues have been content to retire, but Caine wants to stretch himself. Since turning 65 the actor has produced some of his best work. Hopefully there's more to come…

RIGHT: An evocative shot of Caine from the late sixties television documentary *Film Star*.

THE ACTORS (2003)

Cast: Michael Caine (Anthony O'Malley),
Dylan Moran (Tom), Michael Gambon
(Barreller), Lena Headey (Dolores Barreller),
Miranda Richardson (Mrs Magnani), Michael
McElhatton (Jock), Aisling O'Sullivan (Rita),
Ben Miller (Clive), Abigail Iversen (Mary),
Michael Colgan (audition director),
Deirdre Walsh (camcorder girl),
Bill Hickey (stage doorkeeper).
Crew: Conor McPherson (director),
Stephen Woolley, Neil Jordan and Redmond
Morris (producers), Conor McPherson (writer),
Michael Nyman (music), Seamus McGarvey
(cinematography), Emer Reynolds (editor),
Mark Geraghty (production designer).

Ageing actor Anthony O'Malley befriends
a minor Dublin crook, Barreller, who owes
money to Magnani, a London gangster whom
he's never met. O'Malley concocts a scheme
to dupe Barreller out of the cash and enlists the
aid of a struggling young actor called Tom. The
plan works fine until Magnani sends a henchman
to Dublin for the money. Tom and O'Malley are
forced to adopt various disguises to maintain
the pretence they have begun, a situation
complicated by Tom falling in love with
Barreller's daughter Dolores. Finally, Magnani
flies to Dublin to resolve the situation and
O'Malley gives her the money. He ends up
in traction but wins a theatrical award for his
performance in a ludicrous production of
Richard III set in Nazi Germany. Tom
and Dolores become a couple and she
gets her first acting job in a TV
commercial for sausages...

'THE REASON TO SEE THIS FILM, OF
COURSE, IS MICHAEL CAINE ... [WHO]
CAMPS IT UP BRILLIANTLY IN EVERY
SCENE HE APPEARS IN.' *EMPIRE*

'CONOR MCPHERSON EVIDENTLY
DIDN'T REALISE THAT WHEN WE
SAID WE WANTED COMEDIES LIKE
THEY USED TO MAKE THEM, WE
DIDN'T MEAN *ON THE BUSES*.
IT'S RESOLUTELY MISGUIDED
AND MISTIMED AND SO CHILLINGLY
UNFUNNY NOT EVEN THE ... SIGHT OF
CAINE IN DRAG WITH HIS HAIR ON FIRE
CAN SAVE IT.' *SUNDAY TELEGRAPH*

The Actors began life as a story written by film
director Neil Jordan in the early 1990s. 'It was a
kind of challenge to see if I could come up with
a plot which forced an actor to imitate as many
different people as possible,' he claimed. Jordan
worked on the idea off and on for several years,
considering whether to turn it into a novel.
He admired the work of fellow Irishman
Conor McPherson, a young playwright and
film director. 'I showed him what I'd written
and asked would he be interested in writing a
screenplay,' Jordan continued. McPherson agreed
and began developing the story: 'Conor wrote
this wonderfully funny script and the idea of
him directing it was a natural progression.'
Jordan remained attached as producer.

It was McPherson who suggested
approaching Caine for the role of theatrical
has-been O'Malley. 'I couldn't believe it
when ... he wanted to do it,' McPherson told
the film's website. 'I'd be lying if I said I wasn't
intimidated. But you have to realise one of the
things that makes Michael so popular is his
common touch. He is really an authentically
down-to-earth guy. Ultimately what I liked about
working with Michael was his professionalism.

He knows what to do, he arrives prepared and just does it.'

Filming on the $5million project took place on location in Dublin and County Wicklow between March and May 2002. It was the second feature Caine had made in Ireland's capital city; 20 years earlier he had starred in *Educating Rita* on location in and around Dublin. *The Actors* reunited him with Sir Michael Gambon, with whom he had co-starred in two Harry Palmer films shot in Russia eight years earlier, *Bullet to Beijing* and *Midnight in St Petersburg*. The star had also worked with Jordan before, having been directed by him in *Mona Lisa*.

Caine told the *East Anglian Daily Times* that *The Actors* reminded him of his early days in repertory during the 1950s: 'I based my role on every old character actor I had ever worked with. I must have known about 50 of these guys. They did the same old plays year after year and never realised just how dreadful they were. My character is a combination of all those people – totally pompous, vain and terrific to watch and fun to play.'

In 2002 the actor told *Hello* magazine that he simply couldn't refuse the script. 'It's set around a very run-down theatre company and they're doing *Richard III*, so I get to play the worst Richard III you've ever seen. He's a fascist and runs around on a motorcycle. I couldn't turn that down. It was a lot of fun … a lunatic film.' Photographs of the actor from some of his

ABOVE: Veteran thespian Anthony O'Malley tries to inspire his sidekick Tom (Dylan Moran) in *The Actors* (2003). The low budget Irish comedy was a flop with critics and audiences.

previous film roles are used in theatrical posters on O'Malley's dressing room walls.

The Actors was released in British and Irish cinemas on 16 May 2003, receiving mediocre reviews from most critics, although many praised Caine's performance. The picture grossed more than $500,000 in its first week of release, but longer term prospects did not look promising. But after a month in UK cinemas the movie was struggling to reach a box office total of $750,000. The film's North American distribution rights are held by Miramax, but no US release date had been confirmed as this book was going to press. During 2002 Caine threatened to withdraw from all promotional work for *The Actors* unless Miramax released *The Quiet American* (2002) in time for Oscar consideration. His threat secured that release,

helping earn Caine a Best Actor nomination.

The Actors tries to combine theatrical satire and crime caper but only succeeds in falling between two stools. The problems stem from McPherson's script, which at best provokes no more than a few wry smiles. The crime caper fails to involve because there is never any sense of jeopardy and the theatrical satire is surprisingly thin, considering McPherson's background as a playwright. Caine gives a solid performance but, like the rest of a talented cast and crew, he cannot compensate for the absence of jokes in whatis supposed to be a comedy.

ALFIE (1966)

Cast: Michael Caine (Alfie), Shelley Winters (Ruby), Millicent Martin (Siddie), Julia Foster (Gilda), Jane Asher (Annie), Shirley Anne Field (Carla), Vivien Merchant (Lily), Eleanor Bron (doctor), Denholm Elliott (abortionist), Alfie Bass (Harry Clamacraft), Graham Stark (Humphrey), Murray Melvin (Nat).

RIGHT: 'She's in beautiful condition!' East End wide boy Alfie Elkins woos American bombshell Ruby (Shelley Winters) in *Alfie* (1966).

Crew: Lewis Gilbert (director and producer), Bill Naughton (writer), Sonny Rollins (music), Otto Heller (cinematography), Thelma Connell (editor), Peter Mullins (art direction).

Alfie is a man of many lovers, playing the field in swinging 1960s London. His philosophy is have fun and avoid emotional attachment if you want to avoid pain. When standby lover Gilda gives birth to his son, Alfie can't help enjoying being a father. But he refuses to commit, so Gilda marries another man. Alfie is diagnosed with tuberculosis and spends six months in a sanatorium. After leaving he sleeps with Lily, the wife of another patient. Alfie acquires two further lovers – a Northern girl called Annie who cooks and cleans for him and a lively American

called Ruby. But he drives Annie away, fearful of commitment. Lily gets pregnant from her fling with Alfie and he procures an illegal abortion for her. Ruby takes a younger lover and casts Alfie aside. He is left on his own, haunted by the consequences of his actions…

'*ALFIE* PULLS FEW PUNCHES … BEHIND ITS ALLEY-CAT PHILOSOPHY, THERE'S SOME SHREWD SENSE, SOME POINTED BARBS AND A SHARP MORAL.' *VARIETY*

'MICHAEL CAINE … TENDS TO BE MONOTONOUS. BOTH HE AND DIRECTOR GILBERT SEEM AS LITTLE CONSCIOUS OF THE CHARACTER'S

PSYCHOLOGICAL UNDERTONES
AS ALFIE HIMSELF.' *MONTHLY*
FILM BULLETIN

Alfie began life as *Alfie Elkins and His Little Life*, a radio play written by Bill Naughton. It subsequently became a stage play, with Caine auditioning unsuccessfully for the lead. Several years later Lewis Gilbert acquired the film rights. But finding an actor willing to play the lead proved difficult, according to Caine. 'Everyone who was right for the role turned it down, based on the fact it would ruin them. They wouldn't play a part where the leading man procured an abortion. I didn't give a damn about it because I just wanted to do the part.' Among those who turned down *Alfie* was Caine's flatmate at the time, Terence Stamp. Instead he suggested Caine for the role.

On the DVD commentary for *The Ipcress File*, editor Peter Hunt explains how he helped influence the casting. Gilbert met Hunt during post-production of the first Harry Palmer film and they discussed who would play Alfie. 'He said he didn't know. He was very worried about it,' Hunt recalls. 'He asked, "What's this boy like that you're working with, Michael Caine?"' Hunt gave Gilbert a secret preview of *The Ipcress File* while it was still being edited. 'I think the next day he signed up Michael to do *Alfie*.'

Even when the director was convinced, he still had to sell the actor to Paramount Pictures. 'The original choice for *Alfie* was Tony Curtis and he was very hot at the time,' Gilbert told *Films and Filming* in 1985. 'I said it had to be a Cockney and, as it wasn't a very big budget film, could I have Michael Caine? The reaction then was "Who is Michael Caine?"' Gilbert eventually got his way and the part went to Caine. Also in the cast was young English actress Jane Asher, then the girlfriend of Paul McCartney. The Beatle visited the set and insisted Asher wear a less revealing shirt during a bedroom scene with Caine. The film was shot on location around London and at Twickenham Studios for a budget of $500,000.

In the late 1980s Caine gave a televised masterclass in film acting. In the published transcript, Caine revealed he had based his performance as Alfie on a friend called Jim Slater, who was very successful with women. 'In *Alfie* my character spoke to the audience through the camera, a bit like the technique of 'asides' in the theatre. I used Jim as the person to whom I was talking. When I first spoke directly to the camera, I treated it like a large audience.' Gilbert directed Caine to perform the speeches as if to a single person. 'I played the moment as though I were talking to Jim. He would have especially appreciated remarks like "She's in beautiful condition" when Alfie was running his hands over a woman's bum, because Jim used to say things like that. That confidence in Jim's appreciation is what won me the collusion of the cinema audience, even when they didn't really approve of Alfie's goings-on.'

Gilbert told *Film Review* that *Alfie* was an audience participation movie. 'In many of the key scenes Alfie turns to the audience and talks quite frankly and intimately to them. They must respond. In fact the success of the film will depend largely on the viewer going along with Alfie and feeling to be part of his life.'

Alfie was presented to the British Board of Film Censors (BBFC) in January 1966, which passed the picture uncut with an X certificate. At the time this excluded children under the age of 16. The most contentious part of the movie was the abortion, with Gilbert battling US distributor Paramount to keep it in. The director had already trimmed the sequence after five secretaries fainted at a preview screening. Eventually the studio relented, although the scene was subsequently deleted in some countries.

ABOVE: Caine poses with four of his female co-stars Vivien Merchant, Jane Asher, Julia Foster and Shelley Winters during a photo call for *Alfie* (1966).

Alfie was a box-office smash in Britain and earned Vivien Merchant a BAFTA award as most promising newcomer, along with nominations for best British film, actor (Caine), screenplay, editing and cinematography. The theme song to *Alfie* by Hal David and Burt Bacharach was sung on screen by Cher but became a British Top 10 hit for Cilla Black. In France the film received a special jury prize at the Cannes Film Festival and was nominated for the Golden Palm.

Despite this success, Caine felt sure his accent and the film's subject matter would prevent it doing well in America. Paramount had him loop more than a hundred lines of dialogue, softening his accent and changing words like 'fag' to 'smoke' to avoid confusion. *Alfie* opened in the US during August 1966 and became a huge hit, reportedly grossing about $15 million and introducing Caine to American audiences. The movie was nominated for five Oscars – best picture, actor (Caine lost to another British actor, Paul Scofield, in *A Man for all Seasons*), supporting actress (Merchant), adapted screenplay and song. Caine was also nominated for a Golden Globe as best actor in a drama film and won the best actor award from America's National Society of Film Critics.

In interviews Caine has listed *Alfie* among his favourite roles, because it took his name around the world. 'That film struck a chord,' he told *Loaded* in 1999, 'because men all over the world would watch it and think they could pull all the birds, just like Alfie. People would assume I was just like the character. But I wasn't really.'

In 1975 a less successful sequel called *Alfie Darling* was released. Alan Price replaced Caine in the lead role with Ken Hughes taking over as director. In 1996 pop group Divine Comedy had a Top 30 hit in Britain with the single 'Becoming More Like Alfie'. The film *Austin Powers in Goldmember* (2002) initially featured a new version of the *Alfie* theme song but this was cut after poor reactions at test screenings. The sequence can be seen on the DVD release and includes footage from *Alfie*. In September 1999 the British Film Institute (BFI) took a poll of 1000 people within the industry to find the Top 100 British movies of the 20th century. *Alfie* won the third highest place of seven Caine pictures on the list, being voted 33rd.

In 2002 *Alfie* was among several Caine films mooted for a remake. Actors Ewan McGregor and Brad Pitt were both tipped to play the lead. Caine described the idea as flattering: 'We can't have done a bad job of it the first time if they want to remake them now.' In April 2003 *Variety* reported that Paramount was negotiating with Jude Law to star in the remake, directed by Charles Shyer with a script by Shyer and Elaine Pope.

Some 40 years after it was made, *Alfie* now looks like a period piece from an era before the Pill or AIDS – at least on the surface. Despite this, *Alfie* remains fresh and enjoyable. The balance of power has shifted in the battle of the sexes since the mid-1960s, but this film still has much to say about the way men and women interact. Caine gives a bravura performance, all the more remarkable for being only his second leading role. He makes Alfie completely likeable, despite the way the Cockney Casanova uses everyone around him. The device of having a character talk directly to the audience is over-familiar these days from its frequent use on television sitcoms, but here it is compelling, drawing you into Alfie's mindset. Caine's finest moment is the quiet horror he displays when looking down at the aborted foetus that would have been his child. Gilbert directs Naughton's funny, poignant script with a light touch, aided by Heller's rich cinematography. *Alfie* is a restrained, thoughtful film and well worth seeing.

ASHANTI (1979)

*Cast: Michael Caine (Dr David Linderby),
Peter Ustinov (Suleiman), Kabir Bedi (Malik),
Beverly Johnson (Dr Anansa Linderby), Omar
Sharif (Prince Hassan), Rex Harrison (Brian
Walker), William Holden (James Sandell),
Zia Mohyeddin (Djamel), Winston Ntshona
(Ansok), Tariq Yunus (Faid), Tyrone Jackson
(Dongaro), Akosua Busia (Senofu girl).
Crew: Richard Fleischer (director),
Georges-Alain Vuille (producer), Stephen Geller
(writer); Michael Melvoin (music); Aldo Tonti
(cinematography); Ernest Walter (editor),
Mario Chiari, Aurelio Crugnola and
Kuli Sander (art direction).*

Doctors David and Anansa Linderby are
travelling around West Africa on behalf of the
World Health Organisation. Anansa's ancestors
were members of the Ashanti tribe, but she was
educated in America before marrying her white
English husband. Anansa is abducted by slave
traders led by a ruthless Arab, Suleiman. David
pursues Suleiman's caravan of slaves for 3000
miles across Africa to the Red Sea. He is aided
by Malik, an Arab who has sworn vengeance
after Suleiman abducted and sold Malik's family
as slaves. The duo finally confront Suleiman,
but he has already sold Anansa into slavery.

He agrees to say more only if Malik swears not
to slay him. Suleiman says Anansa was bought
by an Arab royal, Prince Hassan, who has
already set sail. David murders Suleiman.
The doctor and Malik get aboard the
prince's ship and rescue Anansa, but
Malik is killed by the prince's bodyguards…

'A DESERT SAGA, THE MOVIE IS GIVEN
AN ADDED EDGE BY FLEISCHER'S
PROFESSIONALISM AND BY A FULLY-
RIGGED, LUSH PRODUCTION … THE
TENDENCY HERE TO VIOLENCE AND
CLICHÉS CAN BE OVERLOOKED WHEN
ACTORS OF THE STATURE OF MICHAEL
CAINE, REX HARRISON, WILLIAM
HOLDEN AND OMAR SHARIF ARE
ON HAND.' *FILMS IN REVIEW*

'IT IS A TOSS-UP AS TO WHETHER
USTINOV OR THE CAMELS HAVE
THE BEST LINES.' *THE GUARDIAN*

Ashanti was based on Alberto Vasquez-
Figueroa's 1976 novel *Ebano*, about slave
trading in Africa during the 1970s. The film's
production, which began on 24 April 1978,
was troubled, with the original director
(Richard C Sarafian), female lead and several
crew members leaving after the first week.
Work resumed a fortnight later, with the film
shot on location in Kenya, Israel and Sicily, with
the Sinai Desert doubling for the Sahara. 'Of the
films I've made *Ashanti* was by far the hardest,'
Caine told the *Sunday Express* in 1978. Filming
took place in 130 degree heat: 'The Egyptians
can have the Sinai Desert back as far as I'm
concerned. The camels were fainting from
the heat and they still expected me to act.'

Two years later Caine told *Film Comment*
that *Ashanti* was the only film he'd ever made
just for the pay cheque. He was moving to

BELOW: Dr David Linderby is stunned to be told that his wife has probably been captured by slave traders in *Ashanti* (1979).

Hollywood and needed cash. 'I did *Ashanti* solely for the money, and I have never been so unhappy in my career. I swore I would never do it again, no matter how broke I was. That was the one and only time. Though I did what I could with the part, I hated and loathed every second on it.'

Neither critics nor the public were impressed when *Ashanti* was released in Britain early in 1979. The Council for the Advancement of Arab-British Understanding was incensed by the movie, issuing the following statement: '*Ashanti* is one of the most virulent examples of Israel's supporters attempting to prejudice Western opinions against the Arabs.' In the US, *Ashanti* was released in April.

In his autobiography, Caine calls *Ashanti* the worst, most wretched movie he ever made. He certainly seems to have had a terrible time during shooting, but there are worse pictures in his long career. Nevertheless, this film is blander than a blancmange and twice as lifeless. Geller's script never rises about routine, introducing characters with potential and then dismissing them minutes later. As the slave trader, Ustinov gets all the best lines and hams like crazy, but Caine merely alternates between anger and frustration. A particular low point is when he spends two minutes trying to get on a camel in what is presumably meant to be a comic interlude. Fleischer's flat, flabby direction leaves you begging for the end, but the finale is perfunctory at best. *Ashanti* is best watched with the fast-forward button close to hand – or not watched at all.

AUSTIN POWERS IN GOLDMEMBER (2002)

Cast: Mike Myers (Austin Powers, Dr Evil, Fat Bastard, Goldmember), Beyoncé Knowles (Foxxy Cleopatra), Seth Green (Scott Evil),
Michael York (Basil Exposition), Robert Wagner (Number Two), Mindy Sterling (Frau Farbissina), Verne Troyer (Mini-Me), Michael Caine (Nigel Powers), Fred Savage (Number Three), Diane Mizota (Fook Mi), Carrie Ann Inaba (Fook Yu), Nobu Matsuhisa (Mr Roboto). Crew: Jay Roach (director), John S Lyons, Mike Myers, Eric McLeod, Demi Moore, Jennifer Todd and Suzanne Todd (producers), Mike Myers and Michael McCullers (writers), George S Clinton (music), Peter Deming (cinematography), Jon Poll and Greg Hayden (editors), Rusty Smith (production designer).

British secret agent Austin Powers captures his arch-enemy, Dr Evil, who is sentenced to 400 years in prison. Austin gets knighted but his father, superspy Nigel Powers, misses the ceremony. Soon afterwards Nigel is kidnapped by a Dutch madman called Goldmember and taken to the year 1975. Austin time-travels to 1975 where he teams up with US agent Foxxy Cleopatra. But Goldmember flees to 2002, taking Nigel with him. Dr Evil escapes prison and shifts operations to a submarine off the coast of Japan. Goldmember and Dr Evil join forces, hatching a plan to flood the world unless an enormous ransom is paid. Austin and Foxxy rescue Nigel but Goldmember and Dr Evil escape. Austin and Foxxy infiltrate Dr Evil's sub. Just as Austin is about to shoot his nemesis, Nigel walks in and reveals that Dr Evil and Austin are brothers. Dr Evil joins the good guys and helps them thwart Goldmember. Dr Evil's own son Scott runs off, vowing revenge.

'IT'S STRICTLY MORE OF THE SAME FROM THE GROOVIDELIC SHAGMEISTER ... USUALLY FUN EVEN IF IT'S NOT TERRIBLY FUNNY. CAINE AS DAD WAS AN INSPIRED CASTING IDEA...' *VARIETY*

'EXTRAVAGANT, UNEVEN, RETRO-HAPPY CELEBRATION OF THE MOVIES AS INTERNATIONAL SETTERS OF INDELIBLE STYLE ... THE MOVIE IS REMARKABLY SPRY AND INSPIRED...'
ENTERTAINMENT WEEKLY

Austin Powers: International Man of Mystery was a minor hit in 1997, before developing a cult following on video. Two years later a sequel, *Austin Powers: The Spy Who Shagged Me,* was a box-office smash, grossing more than $200 million in the US. Another sequel was inevitable and work began on the script in March 2001.

Mike Myers wrote a long letter to Caine, asking him to play England's most famous spy, Nigel Powers. The creation of Austin Powers had been much inspired by Caine films from the 1960s. 'The very first time I saw *Austin Powers*,' Caine told interviewers, 'I realised Mike had based it on a character I played many years ago. The 1960s, the glasses, and the accent – I knew it was me. Not only was I ideal to play it, I felt I was the only person who could play it.' The actor accepted the role, having taken several months off after filming his exhausting role in *The Quiet American* (2002).

Production began in November 2001 and the film was shot predominantly on studio lots. Advance promotional material announced the film's title, but this was withdrawn in January 2002 following court action by the owners of another spy character, James Bond. It was alleged that *Goldmember* was trading on the Bond franchise without permission. The film was temporarily renamed *Austin Powers III* but the original title was eventually reinstated.

The main cast were encouraged to ad-lib during filming, creating considerably more material than was required. Director Jay Roach's first cut lasted three hours – double the length of the final picture. A brief excerpt of Caine

from *Hurry Sundown* (1967) appears in the film during a flashback. On the *Austin Powers in Goldmember* DVD commentary track, Roach says the hardest cut was removing a sequence where the main characters sing along with a version of the theme song to Caine's 1966 film *Alfie*. 'We were all sure it was going to be one of the highpoints ... the audience just felt it slowed the movie down. We tried it in two previews and the movie took a big dip in momentum. It was brutal to cut something like that.' The sequence is featured among more than 20 minutes of deleted scenes and out-takes on the DVD release.

Austin Powers in Goldmember was simultaneously released in the US and the UK on 26 July 2002 – four days after its premiere. The film proved even more successful than its predecessor, grossing $213 million in the US and another $36 million in Britain. Bulging with cameos from famous faces, it featured at least half-a-dozen Oscar winners in the cast. Among those making fleeting appearances was musician Quincy Jones, who provided the music for *The Italian Job* (1969).

This is a broad comedy stuffed full of slapstick, in-jokes and hilarious homages. The opening superstar cameo sequence is the highpoint of the film, but *Austin Powers in Goldmember* doesn't outstay its welcome. Director Roach keeps the action moving while the script by Myers and McCullers is laden with juvenile japes. But this movie is not just fart jokes and scatological humour. It also features a density of media cross-references matched only by the better episodes of TV sitcom *The Simpsons*. Caine steals his scenes as the oldest swinger in town, performing a parody of a parody of himself. In the midst of all this, the film examines father-son relationships with surprisingly heartfelt care.

BELOW: Caine spoofed his own 1960s screen personas as shagadelic superspy Nigel Powers in *Austin Powers in Goldmember* (2002). He is pictured here with co-stars Mike Myers and Beyoncé Knowles.

BATTLE OF BRITAIN (1969)

Cast: Laurence Olivier (Air Chief Marshal Sir Hugh Dowding), Robert Shaw (Squadron Leader Skipper), Christopher Plummer (Squadron Leader Colin Harvey), Susannah York (Section Officer Maggie Harvey), Michael Caine (Squadron Leader Canfield), Ian McShane (Sergeant Pilot Andy), Kenneth More (Group Captain Baker), Trevor Howard (Air Vice Marshal Keith Park), Patrick Wymark (Air Vice Marshal Trafford Leigh-Mallory), Ralph Richardson (British minister in Switzerland), Curt Jürgens (Baron von Richter), Harry Andrews (senior civil servant). Crew: Guy Hamilton (director), Harry Saltzman and Benjamin Fisz (producers), James Kennaway and Wilfred Greatorex (writers), Ron Goodwin (music), Freddie Young (cinematography), Bert Bates (editor), Maurice Carter (supervising art direction).

In June 1940 advancing German forces drive the retreating British troops out of France and back across the English Channel. But rather than attempting an immediate invasion, the Germans pause – giving British forces time to regroup. The Royal Air Force (RAF) prepares for the next phase, the Battle of Britain. German planes outnumber those of the RAF by four to one. The Luftwaffe strikes on 10 August, attacking vital radar stations and blowing up RAF airfields. The bombing runs continue for weeks, with British planes winning the dogfights in the air but losing a war of attrition. In September Reichmarschall Goering arrives in France to take charge of the campaign. After Berlin is bombed, he directs the Luftwaffe to attack London. This gives an advantage to the RAF and the Luftwaffe suffers heavy losses. The planned invasion is postponed – the Battle of Britain is over…

'ONCE THEY ARE AIRBORNE AND COVERED WITH GOGGLES AND OXYGEN MASKS, IT IS IMPOSSIBLE TO DISTINGUISH BETWEEN ANY OF THE ACTORS.' *TIME*

'ON THE GROUND AN IMPRESSIVE ASSEMBLAGE OF STARS APPEAR AND DISAPPEAR. BUT THAT IS ALL THEY ARE GIVEN A CHANCE TO DO … HUMAN INTEREST IS KEPT TO AN ABSOLUTE MINIMUM.' *THE TIMES*

Battle of Britain sought to recreate one of the most famous aerial conflicts in history, using material from a 1961 book, *The Narrow Margin* by Derek Wood and Derek Dempster. To ensure authenticity, ten technical directors who had fought in the battle were on set – including several former Luftwaffe pilots. Dozens of planes that survived the Second World War were gathered to recreate the aerial skirmishes. Producer Harry Saltzman boasted he had assembled the eleventh largest air force in the world for his film.

More than a dozen of Britain's most respected actors were cast in the principal roles, led by Laurence Olivier. Caine had been under contract to Saltzman but the producer had recently released him from the deal as a birthday present. Caine agreed to help fill out the cast of *Battle of Britain*, spending two weeks with the production in the role of Squadron Leader Canfield. The film was shot on location in Spain, England and France, with studio work at Pinewood near London. Helming the picture was Guy Hamilton, who had just directed Caine in *Funeral in Berlin* (1966).

Battle of Britain was released in the UK in September 1969, with US release following a month later. The film was dismissed by the critics and ignored by audiences, reportedly losing $10 million. Unfortunately, the VHS version is only available as a full-screen edition, hampering the visual impact of the many aerial sequences. A widescreen DVD edition was released in North America in May 2003.

Battle of Britain means well but drains all drama and suspense from what should be a gripping story. Striving for authenticity, it becomes a crashing bore. The script tries to create poignant character moments but evokes bathos, not pathos. The film's big selling point is also its great weakness. The aerial conflicts are spectacular at first but take up far too much screen time. Few things date a film like special effects and *Battle of Britain* has some

that would provoke laughter from a modern audience. Caine's role is strictly a bit part, despite his prominent credit. File this film under noble failure.

BEYOND THE LIMIT (1983)

See THE HONORARY CONSUL (1983)

BEYOND THE POSEIDON ADVENTURE (1979)

Cast: Michael Caine (Captain Mike Turner), Sally Field (Celeste Whitman), Telly Savalas (Stefan Svevo), Peter Boyle (Frank Mazzetti), Jack Warden (Harold Meredith), Shirley Knight (Hannah Meredith), Shirley Jones (Gina Rowe), Karl Malden (Wilbur Hubbard), Slim Pickens (Tex), Veronica Hamel (Suzanne Constantine), Angela Cartwright (Theresa Mazzetti),

BELOW: Captain Mike Turner gets that sinking feeling in the ill-advised sequel *Beyond the Poseidon Adventure* (1979).

STARRING **MICHAEL CAINE**

Mark Harmon (Larry Simpson).
Crew: Irwin Allen (director and producer),
Nelson Gidding (writer), Jerry Fielding (music),
Joseph Biroc (cinematography), Bill Brame
(editor), Preston Ames (production designer).

The luxury cruise ship *Poseidon* is capsized by
a massive wave during a storm. Nearby, Captain
Mike Turner keeps his tugboat *Jenny* from
flipping, but loses his cargo. A bank will
foreclose on Turner's boat if he returns to
shore. A coast guard helicopter leads him to
discover the *Poseidon*, upside down but still
afloat – just. Turner wants salvage rights
to the ship. Another vessel arrives, captained
by Stefan Svevo. He claims to be a doctor.
Turner and his two crew members, Wilbur
and Celeste,

BELOW: Mike Turner and Celeste Whitman (Sally Field) in *Beyond the Poseidon Adventure* (1979).

30

climb down into the *Poseidon*, accompanied by Svevo and three paramedics. As they descend, their escape route is cut off. Moving through the corridors, the group finds eight passengers still alive. Turner discovers that Svevo is intent on recovering plutonium, not saving lives. Drowning and shootings
claim several passengers. Turner succeeds in getting four passengers and Celeste away safely, but loses nearly all the loot he had salvaged. The *Poseidon* explodes, killing Svevo and his henchman…

'MORE A MOVIE DISASTER THAN A DISASTER MOVIE…' **SUNDAY EXPRESS**

'A VIRTUAL REMAKE OF THE 1972 ORIGINAL, WITHOUT THAT FILM'S MOUNTING SUSPENSE AND EXCITEMENT.' **VARIETY**

The Poseidon Adventure, based on a novel by Paul Gallico, was a smash hit in 1972. It grossed more than $80 million in the US, garnered three Oscar nominations and a win for best song. It also created a new genre, the disaster movie.

The formula was simple – gather a dozen stars in one location, give them just enough character to make audiences care what happens next, then trap the lot in a disaster with lavish special effects and maximum thrills. Producer Irwin Allen was the master of disaster movies, but by the end of the 1970s the genre had gone out of fashion.

Allen decided to make a sequel to the film that started the trend. Most sequels either show what happened next or simply remake the story with a fresh cast. Nelson Gidding's script opted for the latter. Allen chose to direct the picture himself, despite the critical backlash suffered by his previous effort, *The Swarm* (1978). Returning from that film was Caine. 'I made it for a friend of mine,' he told *Film Comment* in 1980. 'I liked the idea of it. I had never been in a big Hollywood special effects picture before, and I thought the experience would be interesting. Trying to make something of the rather cardboard characters in those movies is quite difficult. Also, I wanted pictures in America. I was just moving there, I needed to start making a living. That was a very important consideration.'

Caine had moved to Hollywood in early 1979. In February he told the *Daily Mirror* that Britain's crippling tax rates for high earners were not his only reasons for shifting. 'When I left London last month it was freezing, there were strikes everywhere. If I hadn't already decided to go and live in California, that would have been enough to make me. Besides the sunshine and only 50 per cent maximum tax, hardly any of my films are made in Britain.'

Beyond the Poseidon Adventure was shot predominantly at Burbank Studios in California. The hull of the capsized ship was constructed on a barge and then floated in the Pacific, south of Malibu. Cast members were flown out by helicopter to the barge for filming at sea. Caine overcame his claustrophobia in learning how to scuba dive for the underwater sequences. But all the effort counted for little. Released across America in May 1979, *Beyond the Poseidon Adventure* was savaged by critics and audiences stayed away. Several months later it reached the UK, where the BBFC required minor cuts before rating the film A.

'I obviously didn't read the script for either *Beyond the Poseidon Adventure* or *The Swarm* and say "This'll get me an Academy Award,

I must do it at all costs,"' Caine told *Film Comment*. 'Frankly, I thought both of these movies would be much better than they were. I had tremendous thoughts about the special effects possibilities … but the effects in *Poseidon* were so much smaller than in the original. Kind of chintzy, really.'

Disaster movies made a comeback in the late 1990s with the success of *Independence Day* (1996) and *Titanic* (1997), but Allen didn't live to see this resurgence, having died in 1991.

Cheap and cheerless, *Beyond the Poseidon Adventure* is an exercise in futility. The lacklustre script shamelessly recycles the original film's plot, adding a mediocre villain. Caine is the lead but rarely gets to do more than spout exposition and grit his teeth. What little action there is grinds to a halt so the supporting cast can each have a moment in the spotlight. Convenient explosions either endanger or rescue the cast, depending upon plot requirements, while Allen's direction is joyless and dreary, never coming close to attaining the original film's suspense. The explosion that finally sinks the Poseidon best resembles a firecracker let off in a bathtub. This film isn't bad enough to be entertainingly awful, merely dull and mediocre.

BILLION DOLLAR BRAIN (1967)

Cast: Michael Caine (Harry Palmer), Karl Malden (Leo Newbigen), Ed Begley (General Midwinter), Oscar Homolka (Colonel Stok), Françoise Dorleac (Anya), Guy Doleman (Colonel Ross), Vladek Sheybal (Dr Eiwort), Milo Sperber (Basil), Stanley Caine (G P O Special Delivery boy), Donald Sutherland (scientist at computer), Susan George (Russian girl on train).
Crew: Ken Russell (director), Harry Saltzman

(producer), John McGrath (writer),
Richard Rodney Bennett (music), Billy Williams
(cinematography), Alan Osbiston (editor),
Syd Cain (production designer).

British spy Harry Palmer has resigned from
MI5 and set up his own detective agency.
An anonymous phone call offers Harry £400 to
deliver a package to Helsinki. When he arrives,
Palmer is met by a woman called Anya.
She takes him to her lover, Leo Newbigen,
a former CIA agent and old acquaintance of
Harry's. Leo invites Palmer to work with him
for a covert organisation, Crusade for Freedom.
Harry's former boss, Colonel Ross, coerces him
into rejoining MI5. The colonel says the package
contained eggs filled with a deadly virus stolen
from a British research laboratory. Palmer is
assigned to get the eggs back from Crusade
for Freedom.

Palmer travels to Latvia for a meeting with
local Crusade for Freedom agents. During the
night he is visited by Russian General Stok,
who warns him about Crusade for Freedom's
boss, General Midwinter. Stok says Midwinter is
planning to create an anti-communism revolution
in Latvia. Harry discovers the local agents are
just gangsters. Harry and Leo travel to Texas
where Midwinter shows off his super-computer,
the Billion Dollar Brain. Leo is faking the
existence of 300 agents in Latvia and
pocketing their pay. Palmer convinces
Midwinter of Leo's duplicity.

Harry returns to Helsinki and locates Anya
when she collects the virus eggs. Anya leads
Palmer to Leo, but she escapes with the eggs.
Midwinter launches an invasion of Latvia from
Finland, leading his army across the frozen water
between the two countries. Harry and Leo try
to stop the Crusade for Freedom forces. But the
Russians are expecting the army and blow up

the ice. Everyone drowns except Harry. Stok and
Anya arrive by helicopter. She was Stok's agent
in Finland. The colonel gives Palmer the eggs
back as a gift for Ross…

'I LIKED MUCH OF *THE IPCRESS FILE*,
SOMETHING OF *FUNERAL IN BERLIN*,
BUT LITTLE OF THIS SCARCELY
COMPREHENSIBLE RIGMAROLE
EXCEPT, PERHAPS, THE SNOW-
COVERED FINNISH SCENE AND
OSCAR HOMOLKA AS A GENIAL
OLD COMMUNIST.' ***DAILY TELEGRAPH***

'OSCAR HOMOLKA INHABITS,
INIMITABLY, A LITTLE FILM OF
HIS OWN IN THE MIDDLE …
AND MICHAEL CAINE'S
PRESENCE COUNTS FOR
A LOT. BUT EVERYONE ELSE
SINKS WITHOUT TRACE.'
MONTHLY FILM BULLETIN

The first Harry Palmer film, *The Ipcress File*,
had been a hit for producer Harry Saltzman in
1965. A sequel, *Funeral in Berlin*, followed a
year later. In 1967 the third film in the series
was made, with Ken Russell as director. John
McGrath was hired to adapt Len Deighton's
complex thriller into a screenplay. '*Billion
Dollar Brain* was a complicated and difficult
novel,' Russell told *Films and Filming* in 1970.
'When one came to analyse it and try to make
a film script, it just didn't add up. Probably
one should have abandoned it then and there,
but I was promised I could do other films …
if I made *Billion Dollar Brain*.'

Russell had been a television director for a
decade and shot only one previous feature film,
French Dressing (1963). *Billion Dollar Brain*
had a budget of $3 million, the biggest yet for

ABOVE: Harry Palmer hitches a ride with deadly double agent Anya (Françoise Dorléac) in *Billion Dollar Brain* (1967). Sadly, the actress died before the film's release.

a Harry Palmer film. Caine returned as the reluctant spy. Also back were Guy Doleman as his British boss and Oscar Homolka as Stok.

Almost all the location work was shot around Finland in sub-zero temperatures. In 1997 Caine told *GQ* about working with Russell: 'British movie crews have a way of sussing things out. By the third day he was known as Rasputin.' Studio work was completed at Pinewood, with Caine rushing away to Paris for filming of his short sequence in *Woman Times Seven* (1967) with Shirley MacLaine. Leading lady Françoise Dorleac died in a car crash not long after the Palmer film wrapped.

Billion Dollar Brain was released in the US in December 1967. In Britain the BBFC required minor cuts before granting an A certificate. The film hit UK cinemas in January 1968, accompanied by scathing notices from critics. 'The worst reviews I've seen for one of my own films for a long time were those for *Billion Dollar Brain*,' Caine told *Films and Filming* the following year, adding that the movie still made quite a lot of money. Three years later Caine criticised the picture in an interview with the *Radio Times*: 'Ken Russell, who directed it, is a friend of mine. But he lost the story somewhere, and no one could care a damn about what was going on because they couldn't follow what *was* going on.'

In 1968 Caine announced he was giving up the role of Harry Palmer. 'After three films

ABOVE: Did you want ice with that? Harry Palmer narrowly escapes drowning in *Billion Dollar Brain* (1967).

I don't think the Palmer character holds anything for me any more. The films have helped me a lot. I hope some new actor can give his interpretation of Harry Palmer and have the help I did.' Plans were announced for a fourth Palmer film, based on the Deighton novel *Horse Under Water*, but nothing came of it. The character stayed in retirement until the 1990s when Caine returned for two ill-fated films made in Russia.

Billion Dollar Brain was released on rental video in Britain with a PG rating in 1985. But this tape was withdrawn soon afterwards and is now almost impossible to find. All the other Harry Palmer films are available but a problem with musical clearance rights for the Beatles' song *A Hard Day's Night* means an imminent VHS or DVD release for *Billion Dollar Brain* seems unlikely.

Three cameo appearances are worth spotting. Caine's brother Stanley makes his acting debut as a postman in the opening scene. A young Susan George shows up as 'Russian girl on train', eating an orange and offering Harry a newspaper as he travels to Latvia. Most noteworthy is Donald Sutherland getting one line as 'scientist at computer', asking Leo 'What's going on?' in Midwinter's HQ. Sutherland would become a major film star within three years thanks to films like *The Dirty Dozen*, *M*A*S*H* and *Kelly's Heroes*. He later appeared with Caine in *The Eagle Has Landed* (1976) and takes Noël Coward's role in the 2003 remake of *The Italian Job*.

As you can tell from the synopsis above, *Billion Dollar Brain* is a film with an overly complicated plot. Ultimately, this gets in the way of everything else and makes the lavish spectacle difficult to enjoy. Russell's direction has deft visual touches but suffers from sluggish pacing. Caine's performance as Harry remains consistent, despite this film's more baroque flavour. Previous pictures were determinedly

small scale, but this veers dangerously close to 007 territory with massive sets and globe-trotting adventures. How much you enjoy it will depend on which style of spy film you prefer.

THE BLACK WINDMILL (1974)

Cast: Michael Caine (Major John Tarrant), Donald Pleasence (Cedric Harper), Delphine Seyrig (Ceil Burrows), Clive Revill (Alf Chestermann), John Vernon (McKee), Joss Ackland (Chief Superintendent Wray), Janet Suzman (Alex Tarrant), Catherine Schell (Lady Julyan), Joseph O'Conor (Sir Edward Julyan), Dennis Quilley (Bateson).
Crew: Don Siegel (director/producer), Leigh Vance (writer), Roy Budd (music), Ousama Rawi (cinematography), Antony Gibbs (editor), Peter Murton (art direction).

RIGHT: British spy John Tarrant carries half a million pounds of stolen diamonds in *The Black Windmill* (1974).

RIGHT: Tarrant takes a crucial call in *The Black Windmill* (1974).

Major John Tarrant is an MI6 operative trying to infiltrate a ring of saboteurs run by Ceil Burrows and a man called McKee. They kidnap Tarrant's young son David and demand a ransom of £517,057 in uncut diamonds. That's exactly the amount purchased earlier by Tarrant's boss, Harper. The only people with knowledge of the diamonds are Tarrant, Harper and the General Purposes Committee, headed by Sir Edward Julyan. Burrows and McKee plant evidence to frame Tarrant. The government refuses to pay the ransom so Tarrant steals the diamonds and takes them to a rendezvous in Paris.

The major is knocked out and drugged, losing the diamonds. Tarrant is found by French police, lying unconscious beside Burrows' corpse. He is charged with her murder. McKee helps Tarrant escape custody and tries to have him killed. Tarrant returns to London and traces his son to a black windmill in Sussex. Realising one of the committee members must be involved, Tarrant calls all of them with a message that will lure the traitor to Sussex. Sir Edward takes the bait. Tarrant storms the windmill, kills McKee and rescues his son…

'DON SIEGEL'S FILMMAKING TAKES A DIP IN *THE BLACK WINDMILL* … THE PRODUCTION FIZZLES IN ITS FINAL HALF HOUR.' *VARIETY*

'*THE BLACK WINDMILL* IS AN ENGAGING FAILURE BUT … THE IMPORTANT THING TO SAY ABOUT ITS 106 MINUTES IS THAT FEW OF THEM ARE DULL. QUITE A FEW ARE SILLY. BUT NOT DULL.' *FILMS ILLUSTRATED*

The Black Windmill began life as *Seven Days to a Killing*, a 1973 novel by Clive Egleton. Leigh Vance adapted it into a screenplay for American director/producer Don Siegel, who came to England in 1973 to make the film after 30 years helming high-calibre action movies like *Invasion of the Body Snatchers* (1956) and *Dirty Harry* (1971). In *The Black Windmill* pressbook, Siegel stated that his first and only choice for the part of Tarrant was Caine. 'There are actors who are tougher, more handsome, more emotive, but there was only one with a centre solid enough to convey the very complex undertones of this role.'

Caine took the role for the opportunity to work with Siegel. 'I grew up with his films,' the actor said in his pressbook interview. '*The Black Windmill* is a dramatic, suspense plus love story.' The 11-week shoot began in August 1973, using the working title *Drabble*. Filming was predominantly location-based at sites in England and France, with some studio work at Twickenham. The picture reunited Caine and Donald Pleasence, who had worked together on *Kidnapped* (1971).

The Black Windmill was released in the summer of 1974. Critics considered it one of Siegel's lesser works. Emma Andrews' 1978 book *The Films of Michael Caine* quotes the actor on why the picture did not live up to its promise: 'I think the gentility of England rubbed off on Don Siegel … It became too sentimental and convoluted.'

The Black Windmill is a routine espionage thriller that never surprises. Siegel's direction is efficient and workmanlike, while Caine gives a taut, controlled performance as Tarrant. But the film's attempts to create suspense and misdirect the viewer's suspicions never grip or convince. The Roy Budd music strongly evokes a later TV espionage series, *The Professionals*; Bodie and Doyle would not have looked out of place in *The Black Windmill* and might well have enlivened the film. This is a minor work in the careers of almost everyone involved.

BLAME IT ON RIO (1984)

Michael Caine (Matthew Hollis), Joseph Bologna (Victor Lyons), Valerie Harper (Karen Hollis), Michelle Johnson (Jennifer Lyons), Demi Moore (Nicole Hollis), José Lewgoy (Eduardo Marques), Lupe Gigliotti (Signora Botega), Michael Menaugh (Peter), Tessy Callado (Helaine). Crew: Stanley Donen (director and producer), Charlie Peters and Larry Gelbart (writers), Kenneth Wannberg (music), Reynaldo Villalobos (cinematography), George Hively and Richard Marden (editors), Marcos Flaksman (art direction).

The marriage of Matthew and Karen Hollis is in trouble. The couple are due to leave for a holiday in Rio de Janeiro with their teenage daughter Nicole, Matthew's best friend Victor Lyons and his teenage daughter Jennifer. But Karen goes to a Club Med resort at Bahia instead, saying she needs time alone. Jennifer has always had a crush on Matthew. She seduces him, despite their 25-year age difference. Matthew keeps trying to end the affair but fails. When he does stop it, Jennifer confesses to her father about the affair – but doesn't name Matthew as her lover. An enraged Victor hunts for the mystery man. Eventually Matthew confesses all. Nicole

ABOVE:
John Tarrant gets frustrated by his spymaster Cedric Harper (Donald Pleasence) in *The Black Windmill* (1974).

STARRING **MICHAEL CAINE**

She's the hottest thing on the beach...
She's also his best friend's daughter...

Blame it on RIO 15
A new tropical comedy

summons her mother from Club Med. Matthew learns that Karen and Victor were having an affair. Jennifer tries to commit suicide but soon recovers. Karen gives Matthew a second chance…

'CAINE IS A TALENTED ENOUGH AND LIKEABLE ENOUGH PERFORMER TO CREATE THE ILLUSION OF A MATURE IRONY AT WORK ON CATCHPENNY MATERIAL.' *VOICE MAGAZINE*

'WHAT IS OBJECTIONABLE IS NOT THE AFFAIR ITSELF … BUT THE WAY THAT THE FILM MILKS ITS EVERY COMIC OR

SEXUAL POSSIBILITY, TRADING ON THE
HUMBERT HUMBERT IN ALL OF US.'
THE TIMES

Blame it on Rio was a remake of a French
comedy, *Un moment d'egarement* (1977).
The American version's director and producer
was Stanley Donen, whose previous credits
included classic musicals like *Singin' in the Rain*
(1952), *Seven Brides for Seven Brothers* (1954)
and *Funny Face* (1957). He shifted the story's
location to South America and commissioned
screenwriter Charlie Peters to revise the script,
using the working titles *Only in Rio* and *Love,
Rio*. TV sitcom scribe Larry Gelbart later joined
the project. He had co-written the screenplay for
a previous Caine movie, *The Wrong Box* (1966).

Caine told *Screen International* that he and
Donen had wanted to work together for years:
'Stanley knew I wanted to do a comedy as I
haven't done that many. The film is no great
political or social thing, it's just a romantic
comedy in a lush place. It's completely escapist
entertainment. You should come out of it laughing.'

Caine was unconcerned that playing a man in
his 40s having an affair with a teenage girl might
have a detrimental effect on his image. 'I don't
give a monkey's about all that,' he told *News of
the World*. 'It doesn't worry me if the character is
a swine. I take chances with my work because it
gets boring playing [in] adventure films all the
time. And this script was something different.'
Caine had piled on weight for his previous films,
Educating Rita (1983) and *The Honorary Consul*
(1983). He went on a crash diet, shedding 37
pounds in six weeks, so that *Blame it on Rio*'s
romance would be more credible.

For the crucial role of Caine's teenage lover,
Donen chose a 17-year-old with no previous
acting experience. The director auditioned
400 actresses before he saw Michelle Johnson's
picture in a fashion magazine. He flew her to

Hollywood for a screen test. 'I wanted a young
girl who was forward and outgoing – sexually
open, but not heavily so,' Donen told *News of
the World*. 'It's not a movie for the raincoat
crowd. In Michelle we found someone who
could arouse the audience and at the same
time make them laugh.'

The $10 million film was shot on location
in Rio over 14 weeks. Caine was impressed by
the young actress playing his daughter, Demi
Moore. Previously she had only played bit parts
in movies. In a 1999 interview with *Premiere*
magazine, Caine recalled working with her:
'We did a pretty intense scene, and at the end of
her close-up I said, "Demi, I think you will be a
big star one day." And she said to me, "Michael,
you're full of shit."' But Caine's prediction
proved accurate. Within a decade Moore was
one of the highest paid actresses in the world,
commanding fees of several million dollars
a film. More recently she has moved into
producing, including *Austin Powers in
Goldmember* (2002)

Blame it on Rio was released in the US in
February 1984, reaching the UK later that year.
The film took a hammering from critics made
uncomfortable by the storyline and the age
difference between the lovers. Donen was
unrepentant: 'The film might offend some
people, but it will make a lot of people laugh
because it strikes very close to that funny bone,
the real truth.' *Blame it on Rio* grossed £18.6
million in the US and remains Donen's last
feature film to date. Johnson was nominated
as worst new star at the Razzie Awards in 1985.

Blame it on Rio took a lot of stick from
critics who perceived it to have sleazy overtones
of *Lolita* and incest. But that's to damn the film
for crimes it does not commit. The biggest
problems are the awful acting of Michelle
Johnson, Donen's willingness to let the camera
linger on her ample charms and a tendency for

ABOVE: Caine's late career comeback began with his role as dying jewel thief Victor Spansky in *Blood and Wine* (1997).

"(RAFELSON'S) BEST FILM IN A DECADE
... A TRUE FILM NOIR."
THE PREMIER

"...A BRILLIANTLY-ACTED, VICIOUS THRILLER..."
THE GUARDIAN

"...VERY STYLISH AND HUGELY ENTERTAINING."
EMPIRE ENQUIRES

J A C K   N I C H O L S O N

There is no honour
amongst thieves.

Blood & Wine.

STEPHEN
DORFF

JENNIFER
LOPEZ

JUDY
DAVIS

and MICHAEL
CAINE

15

the script to have everyone wisecracking at every opportunity. Characters in sitcoms may speak only in zingers but films require more subtlety. Caine proves himself an able comedian, striking a balance between farce and the forlorn. Mention must also be made of the excruciating theme song that recurs throughout the film. *Blame it on Rio* is not as bad as you might expect, but all too often it leaves the viewer wincing.

BLOOD AND WINE (1997)

Cast: Jack Nicholson (Alex Gates), Stephen Dorff (Jason), Jennifer Lopez (Gabriela), Judy Davis (Suzanne), Michael Caine (Victor Spansky), Harold Perrineau Jr (Henry), Robyn Peterson (Dina Reese), Mike Starr (Mike), John Seitz (Frank Reese). Crew: Bob Rafelson (director), Jeremy Thomas (producer), Nick Villiers and Alison Cross (writers), Michal Lorenc (music), Newton Thomas Sigel (cinematography), Steven Cohen (editor), Richard Sylbert (production designer).

Miami wine dealer Alex Gates plans to steal a diamond necklace worth $1 million from a wealthy family. He is having an affair with their illegal immigrant nanny, Gabriela. Alex's relationship with his wife Suzanne and adult stepson Jason is falling apart. Aided by English safecracker Victor, Alex steals the necklace. Jason gets romantically involved with Gabriela. Alex hides the necklace in a suitcase and, before he can leave, gets into a fight with Suzanne. She beats him with a cane, knocking him out. Suzanne flees, taking Jason and the suitcase. Jason finds the necklace and uses a stone from it to buy a fishing boat. Alex and Victor pursue Suzanne and Jason. Suzanne dies in a car crash and Alex murders his partner in crime. Jason has a final meeting with Alex and Gabriela on the boat. Jason gives the necklace to Gabriela, who leaves. Alex beats his stepson, but Jason uses the boat to crush Alex's legs. Gabriela returns and gives the necklace to Alex, keeping one diamond for herself. Jason leaves in the boat while Gabriela drives away. Approaching sirens are closing in …

'WHEN YOU HAVE TWO PROS LIKE JACK NICHOLSON AND MICHAEL CAINE, CAN MUCH GO WRONG? OF COURSE NOT. WHAT THE FILM LACKS IS ANY REASON WHY WE SHOULD CARE FOR ANYONE IN IT.' ***EVENING STANDARD***

'CAINE HASN'T BEEN AS WATCHABLE FOR AGES AS THE WHEEZING OLD CROOK … EVERYONE'S GOOD, BUT IT'S LESS THAN THE SUM OF ITS WATCHABLE PARTS.' ***THE GUARDIAN***

Blood and Wine started life as a story written by director Bob Rafelson and Nick Villiers. Rafelson had worked with Jack Nicholson on several previous movies, most notably the Oscar-nominated *Five Easy Pieces* (1970). But he never intended for Nicholson to appear in *Blood and*

BELOW:
Alex Gates (Jack Nicholson) and Victor Spansky in *Blood and Wine* (1997).

Wine. 'I didn't have Jack in mind, I just had the idea for the script,' the director told *Time Out* in 1997. 'I wanted to do it as a very low-budget movie and I knew I couldn't afford Jack. So I asked him, as a friend, to read with other actors and tell me what he thought.' Eventually Nicholson put himself forward for the leading role.

Caine was semi-retired by the mid-1990s. 'I took a lot of time out and wrote my autobiography,' he told *Candis* magazine in 2000. 'I got lazy and I didn't want to go back to making movies. And then when I did, nobody knew who the hell I was. I couldn't get a job – not a good one, though I knew I could make money by doing bad scripts. I'm sent a lot of those.' Between 1993 and 1996 only one film featuring Caine got a cinema release – the Steven Seagal vehicle *On Deadly Ground* (1994). 'Finally I got *Blood and Wine.* It was a movie I wasn't ashamed of.'

'If you're an actor and you don't act for a long time you sort of think, I wonder if I can still do it?' Caine said during a public interview with Barry Norman at the National Film Theatre in 1998. Frustrated by the quality of the scripts he was getting, Caine appeared in two historical TV projects as Joseph Stalin and F W de Klerk to test his acting abilities. He was nominated for an Emmy award for both performances. 'Then I got *Blood and Wine* … I did that as another little test.'

Caine had opened a restaurant in Miami; Nicholson and Rafelson visited and asked him to play safecracker Victor. 'I've known them for 20, 30 years,' Caine told *Hello* in 1999. 'They walked into the restaurant one day and said, "Well, you're here. Do you want to be in the movie?" It wasn't a very big part, but Jack and I had never worked together, and I love Bob's work. So I agreed. And I had so much fun. Work became a joy again.' The $26

million film was shot on location in Florida.

Released in the US in February 1997, *Blood and Wine* grossed a disappointing $1 million. A month later it opened in Britain and received mixed reviews from the critics, though Caine's performance was widely praised. The picture's biggest success was in Spain, where it grossed nearly $1.4 million. Caine won the Best Actor award at the San Sebastián Film Festival, despite only having a supporting role.

Blood and Wine would pass without much notice if it didn't have such a great cast. The film looks great, with Lorenc's subtle score underlining the ominous, downbeat mood. Caine is excellent, giving his best performance for nearly a decade as the wheezing, flailing Victor. He communicates the character's desperation and fear through every gesture. Sadly, he is the best thing about *Blood and Wine.* Anaemic and polite, the film lacks the vitality and flavour of its respective namesakes.

BLUE ICE (1992)

Cast: Michael Caine (Harry Anders), Sean Young (Stacy Mansdorf), Ian Holm (Sir Hector), Bobby Short (Buddy), Alun Armstrong (Osgood), Sam Kelly (George), Jack Shepherd (Stevens), Philip Davis (Westy), Bob Hoskins (Sam Garcia). Crew: Russell Mulcahy (director), Martin Bregman and Michael Caine (producers), Ron Hutchinson (writer), Michael Kamen (music), Denis Crossan (cinematography), Seth Flaum (editor), Grant Hicks (production designer).

Harry Anders is a former spy who runs a jazz club. He meets an American woman, Stacy Mansdorf; they become friends and then lovers. Harry discovers that Stacy is married to the American ambassador. She asks Anders to find her ex-lover, Kyle, and Harry enlists the aid of Osgood, a detective at New Scotland Yard. They

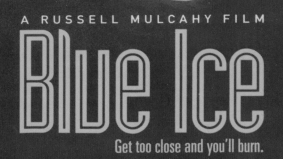

If Harry's past ever catches up with him, he won't live long enough to regret it.

MichaelCaine SeanYoung

A RUSSELL MULCAHY FILM

Blue Ice

Get too close and you'll burn.

trace Kyle to a seedy hotel near London Bridge. But Kyle gets murdered and the killer also slays Osgood. Next morning Kyle's body is removed from the morgue by American soldiers. Anders is approached by his former boss, Sir Hector, who warns him to be careful. Stacy reveals that Kyle worked for US military intelligence, tracing illegal weapons shipments from the docks of London. Harry arrives as the latest shipment is being loaded. Sir Hector is the mastermind and Harry kills his old boss in a shootout. Stacy returns to America with her husband…

BELOW:
There was a conspicuous mismatch in ages between Caine and his on-screen lover Sean Young in *Blue Ice* (1992).

'MICHAEL CAINE RE-DONS SPYCATCHER DUDS IN *BLUE ICE*, A DETERMINEDLY OLD-FASHIONED ACTIONER THAT'S TERMINALLY LIGHT ON REAL THRILLS.' ***VARIETY***

'IT IS A TESTAMENT TO MICHAEL CAINE'S SCREEN PRESENCE AND SHEER PROFESSIONALISM THAT … HE ALMOST SINGLE-HANDEDLY CARRIES THIS ROUTINE BRITISH THRILLER.' ***TIME OUT***

In 1992 Michael Caine and American film producer Martin Bregman formed M & M Productions, a company dedicated to making mainstream movies in Britain. Financing help for the venture came from US cable channel HBO. 'The idea was to start a new commercial cinema, make smaller British action movies,' Caine told *Empire* magazine. 'HBO knew that Marty was a friend of mine, and they said to him, "You know what we'd like to see? Michael Caine with a gun in his hand again,

and a woman in the other arm." That was the whole premise. So we bought these really hard, seedy, gritty detective books and made an incredibly tough film, all action. This is a bit of a Dirty Harry Palmer.'

The character of Harry Anders had been created by a former British spy, Ted Allbeury. In 1992 Bregman told *Time Out* that he hoped to make a series of Harry Anders movies: 'I wanted to develop something where I could use Michael's abilities. He's a touch weathered, which most women find extremely attractive. You never see a romantic man on screen who's over 40.' Bregman had strong credentials as a producer, including several of Al Pacino's best films – *Dog Day Afternoon* (1975), *Scarface* (1983) and *Sea of Love* (1989). He also produced *Sweet Liberty* (1986), starring Caine and Bob Hoskins.

The director of *Blue Ice* was Russell Mulcahy, best known for helming the action-packed *Highlander* films. Caine wooed Sharon Stone for the part of Stacy, but the sudden success of *Basic Instinct* (1992) meant she became unavailable. Instead the role went to Sean Young, an actress with a formidable reputation among Hollywood gossip-mongers. 'Everybody cringed with horror,' Caine told *Empire*, 'and said "She'll be sending things through the post and leaving dead rats on your doorstep." But I don't believe everything I read in the press ... she wasn't an ounce of trouble, she charmed everyone on set, down to the last technician.'

The $7 million film was shot on location around London and at Ealing Studios. Joining the cast in a cameo role was Bob Hoskins, returning the favour Caine did him on *Mona Lisa*

(1986). Other familiar faces included Alun Armstrong, who made his film debut with Caine in *Get Carter* (1971), and US jazz pianist Bobby Short, who had a cameo in Woody Allen's *Hannah and Her Sister*s (1986).

Caine told the *Sunday Times* that there was a market for nice little thrillers: 'There's no money for huge crowd scenes or incredible jumbo jets crashing through hotels or something. So what we lack in money, we have had to make up in style, wit and invention.' HBO retained the right to veto a cinema release, but Caine hoped that wouldn't happen.

'We're not making a television movie, we're making a cinema movie with television money. When we're finished, they will look at it and decide whether it is worth releasing as a picture that can hold up at the box-office against the big ones.'

Blue Ice was released in the UK in October 1992. The picture grossed just over $350,000 and received mediocre reviews. HBO decided against a cinema release in the US, premiering the movie on cable instead and then putting it out on VHS.

Casting Caine as a retired British spy was always going to invite comparison with *The Ipcress File* – a comparison *Blue Ice* will never win. Aside from a hallucination sequence in the middle of the movie, Mulcahy abandons his usual flashy directing style for something duller and drearier. It's a bad sign when a British movie shows Londoners explaining Cockney rhyming slang – to each other. Caine tries his best, but the dialogue lurches from clichéd to cringe-inducing. Put simply, *Blue Ice* is a poor film with few distinguishing features.

A BRIDGE TOO FAR (1977)

Cast: Dirk Bogarde (Lieutenant General Browning), James Caan (Staff Sergeant Dohun), Michael Caine (Lieutenant Colonel J O E Vandeleur), Sean Connery (Major General Urquhart), Edward Fox (Lieutenant General Horrocks), Elliott Gould (Colonel Stout), Gene Hackman (Major General Sosabowski), Anthony Hopkins (Lieutenant Colonel Frost), Hardy Kruger (Major General Ludwig), Laurence Olivier (Doctor Spaander), Ryan O'Neal (Brigadier General Gavin), Robert Redford (Major Cook), Maximilian Schell (Lieutenant General Bittrich), Liv Ullman (Kate Ter Horst). Crew: Richard Attenborough (director), Joseph E Levine and Richard P Levine (producers), William Goldman (writer), John Addison (music), Geoffrey Unsworth (cinematography), Antony Gibbs (editor), Terence March (production designer).

In a bid to end the Second World War in Europe by Christmas 1944, the Allies launch Operation Market Garden. Thirty-five thousand troops are dropped behind enemy lines in Holland with orders to take and hold a series of vital bridges. Meanwhile ground forces are ordered to smash through the German lines and link up with the paratroopers, travelling 63 miles in just two days. The goal is to secure Arnhem Bridge, giving the Allies direct access to the heartland of Germany. But weather conditions, technical problems and tactical errors bedevil the operation. It takes the ground troops nine days instead of two to reach Arnhem and the armoured advance fails one mile short of the bridge. The Allies are forced to pull back...

'WHEN CELLULOID DEATH IS SO RANDOM AND SO SPECTACULAR, SO MECHANISED AND SO GROTESQUE … THEN IT IS IMPOSSIBLE NOT TO FILL THE SCREEN, INTERMITTENTLY, WITH PICTURES WHICH STUN THE MIND AND BRUISE THE CONSCIENCE.'
SUNDAY TIMES

'SO WEARILY, EXPENSIVELY PREDICTABLE THAT BY THE END THE VIEWER WILL IN ALL LIKELIHOOD BE TOO ENERVATED TO NOTICE ATTENBOROUGH'S PROSAIC MORAL EPILOGUE.' *MONTHLY FILM BULLETIN*

Operation Market Garden was one of the Second World War's most heroic failures. It was the largest airborne operation ever mounted and cost the lives of thousands of soldiers. Cornelius Ryan turned these events into an international bestseller, *A Bridge Too Far*, first published in 1974. Film rights were optioned by independent producer Joseph E Levine, who came out of retirement for this project. Levine had helped make such diverse movies as *Zulu* (1964), *The Graduate* (1967), and *Carnal Knowledge* (1971).

A Bridge Too Far was a massive endeavour, with a cast of thousands and 14 major actors in starring roles. It was reportedly the most expensive British production ever made at the time, with a budget estimated between $22 million and $45 million. To finance the project, Levine hired a superstar cast to pre-sell the film to distributors worldwide. The producer paid his stars between $500,000 and $1 million a week each.

British actor-director Richard Attenborough was chosen to helm the picture, while Oscar-winning screenwriter William Goldman turned the sprawling epic into a three-hour screenplay, later including a fascinating chapter about the production of the film in his seminal book, *Adventures in the Screen Trade*. Filming took place over six months on location in Holland and England, with interiors at Twickenham Studios. Despite the massive scope of the project, it finished on schedule and under budget.

Caine played Lieutenant Colonel J O E Vandeleur, leading the armoured ground forces on their charge towards Arnhem. Caine arrived on location only two days after finishing another WWII film, *The Eagle Has Landed* (1976). But while that picture merely purported to have some basis in fact, *A Bridge Too Far* was firmly reality-based. Caine sought advice from the real Vandeleur, who was a technical advisor on set. The veteran was full of praise for his film incarnation. 'Michael Caine was first class,' Vandeleur told the *Daily Express*. 'I think it will be a marvellous film. Dickie Attenborough is a great director.'

The picture was released on 15 June 1977 across America, rated PG; the MPAA had initially branded it an R but this was changed after an appeal by Levine. The film grossed more than $50 million in the US but received mixed reviews; American critics found elements of the story unbelievable, despite the factual source material. The British release followed a week later, with the BBFC requiring cuts before granting an A rating. UK reviewers were also unsympathetic, some paying as much attention to the cost of the film as to the content. Despite this, *A Bridge Too Far* was nominated for eight BAFTA awards in 1978 and won four – best supporting actor (Edward Fox), music, soundtrack and cinematography. A DVD version was released in 2001 with a two-disc special edition announced for 2003.

Like *Battle of Britain*, this film is a Second World War epic based on real events, encrusted with big name actors in small roles. But *A Bridge Too Far* is the more successful of the pair, keeping its focus on the war and not getting diverted by attempts at human interest. This is an accomplished feat of filmmaking by Attenborough, with stunning imagery and a stirring score. Goldman's screenplay succeeds in making sprawling events easy to follow, while familiar faces help the viewer keep track of who's who. Caine's role is relatively minor and mainly involves sitting atop an armoured vehicle. This film is superior to *Battle of Britain*, but the failure of Operation Market Garden necessitates a downbeat ending that may leave you unsatisfied.

BULLET TO BEIJING (1996)

Cast: Michael Caine (Harry Palmer), Jason Connery (Nick), Mia Sara (Natasha), Michael Gambon (Alex), Michael Sarrazin (Craig), Lev Prygunov (Colonel Gradsky), Anatoly Davidov (Yuri Stephanovich), Sue Lloyd (Jean), Burt Kwouk (Kim Soo).
Crew: George Mihalka (director), Alexander Goloutva, John Dunning and André Link (producers), Peter Welbeck [pseudonym for Harry Alan Towers] (writer), Rick Wakeman (music), Peter Benison and Terence Cole (cinematography), François Gill (editor), Yuri Pashigorie (production designer).

British secret agent Harry Palmer witnesses a Russian scientist being assassinated at a demonstration outside the North Korean embassy in London. Before he can investigate the case, Palmer is given accelerated retirement – effective immediately. Harry is offered $5000 to fly to St Petersburg. As soon as he arrives, people try to kill him. The former spy is taken to meet Alex, a wealthy Russian who employs him to find a missing biological weapon called Red Death. After surviving another attempt on his life, Harry boards a train to Beijing. He discovers half a dozen people on board, all working for Alex. They are supposed to deliver Red Death to the North Korean embassy in Beijing, in exchange for heroin. But the samples are fakes. When everyone returns to St Petersburg there is a shootout at the train station. Despite much treachery and double-crossing, Harry survives and the heroin is destroyed. Palmer makes a

mortal enemy of Alex but decides to stay in Russia, going into business for himself …

'CAINE WORKS OVERTIME TO SET THE MOOD AMONG AN OTHERWISE DULL CAST. PALMER WAS PRETTY WORLD-WEARY DECADES AGO AND NOW HAS SLOWED TO AN APPROPRIATELY IRONIC SNAIL'S PACE.' *VARIETY*

'COMPARED WITH SUCH PRECISION-TOOLED HOLLYWOOD THRILL MACHINES AS *THE FUGITIVE* AND *SPEED*, THE [FILM'S] LOW BUDGET, MEANDERING SMALL TALK AND PEDESTRIAN PACING ARE ODDLY REFRESHING … WITH NO HELP FROM HIS COLOURLESS SIDEKICK JASON CONNERY, OR HIS INDIFFERENT DIRECTOR GEORGE (*MY BLOODY VALENTINE*) MIHALKA, CAINE NONETHELESS GETS THE STORY UP ON ITS FEET.' *SIGHT AND SOUND*

In 1992 Caine told *Empire* that he steadfastly refused to make another Harry Palmer film. Two years later he found himself in Russia making not one but two Harry Palmer movies, shot back-to-back between August and November 1994 under the aegis of legendary wheeler-dealer Harry Alan Towers. [See *Midnight in St Petersburg* for more information about the other half of this pair.] Caine's presence was an essential ingredient to secure the use of author Len Deighton's insubordinate spy. 'I told the producers to come back when Michael had agreed,' Deighton told the *Sunday Times* in 1995, 'thinking he never would.'

Caine told the *Mail on Sunday* that returning to the role was amazing. 'After all this time, the moment I put on those heavy glasses, the character of Harry Palmer came back to me whole – the voice, the walk, the lot. I felt it was only yesterday that I had hung up Harry's props.' The actor spent time with KGB officers, learning about the reality of espionage. 'They showed me their headquarters. I said it was a bloody ugly building but not particularly sinister. They said "Yeah, but there are eight storeys underground..."'

Post-production on *Bullet to Beijing* was completed in 1995. An article in the *Sunday Times* suggested that the film might reach British cinemas that autumn. Instead the movie received a limited release in Canada during 1996 and was nominated for an award by the Canadian Society of Cinematographers.

In January 1997 the *Sunday Times* reported that the film had been killed off by bosses at Disney, at a cost of $9 million. The success of James Bond's comeback in *GoldenEye* (1995) was cited as a factor in cancelling a cinema release for *Bullet to Beijing*. Instead, the movie made its US debut on cable network The Movie Channel, premiering on 5 April 1997, with a video release later that month. The film went straight to video in Britain during 1997 and has since been deleted. A DVD was released in Canada, incorporating 20 minutes of extra footage.

Bullet to Beijing gives a prominent acting credit to Sue Lloyd as Jean, reprising her role as the female agent from *The Ipcress File* (1965). 'We brought her back for five minutes in the new one for old times' sake,' Caine told the *Sunday Times* in 1995. But the character did not appear on screen in the UK video release; Lloyd's cameo can be found only on the extended Canadian DVD version. Harry and Jean meet for dinner. Jean left the secret service to get married years earlier, but her rich husband recently died. Palmer asks if she will marry him, but Jean refuses. They begin making love.

In 1998 Caine talked about *Bullet to Beijing* during his public interview at the NFT. 'It was one of those things when it seemed like a good idea at the time. It was interesting to do, but kind of boring at the same time. I'll tell you what it was like. It was like a holiday romance. It wasn't so good once you got back home. She didn't look as hot as she did on the beach, when you'd had eight sangrias!'

Caine's film career has been through many peaks and troughs, and the first half of the 1990s was most definitely a trough. This is the better of the two Harry Palmer films shot in 1994, but that's to damn it with the faintest of praise. The clumsy script is packed with pointless action sequences and occasional nods to *The Ipcress File* (1965). These only reinforce how badly this film compares with its predecessor. Harry spends the first 30 minutes asking stupid questions to elicit exposition from the other characters. After that, things go downhill. Mihalka's flaccid direction has the hallmarks of a journeyman, while the cast look ready to shoot their agents. Caine tries his best but has precious little to work with. It's no surprise this film went straight to video in most countries.

BULLSEYE! (1990)

Cast: Michael Caine (Sidney Lipton, Doctor Daniel Hicklar), Roger Moore (Gerald Bradley-Smith, Sir John Bevistock), Sally Kirkland (Willie), Deborah Barrymore (Flo Fleming), Lee Patterson (Darrell Hyde), Mark Burns (Nigel Holden), Derren Nesbitt (Inspector Grosse), Deborah Leng (Francesca), Christopher Adamson (Death's Head), Steffanie Pitt (Donna Dutch).
Crew: Michael Winner (director, producer), Leslie Bricusse and Laurence Marks & Maurice Gran (writers), John Du Prez (music), Alan Jones (cinematography), Arnold Crust [pseudonym for Michael Winner] (editor), John Blezard (production designer).

American scientist Dr Hicklar is in Britain working for Sir John Bevistock, developing cold fusion as a cheap source of energy. When they make a breakthrough, the pair decide to sell their secret to the highest bidder on the black market. The auction is taking place on a tour of stately homes. Two small-time British conmen, Sidney Lipton and Gerald Bradley-Smith, are almost identical doubles of the treacherous scientists. Sidney and Gerald are persuaded to replace Hicklar and Bevistock on the tour. Both MI5 and the CIA want the crooks to find the formula for cold fusion. But the secret agencies have a hidden agenda. They send the real Hicklar and Bevistock after the impostors. After much double-crossing and confusion, Sidney and Gerald find the formula and sell it to the British government for £10 million. The pair retire to Barbados, hoping to live happy every after...

'*BULLSEYE!* IS A GALUMPHING FARCE PLAYED BY TWO AGEING AND OUT-OF-CONDITION TALENTS IN THE OVERWEIGHT SHAPES OF MICHAEL CAINE AND ROGER MOORE. A SHOT OF TWO DOGS COPULATING IS FUNNIER BY FAR THAN ANYTHING 'THE TWO STARS MANAGE.' *EVENING STANDARD*

'AN ABSOLUTE MESS, WITH GAGS THAT WOULDN'T PASS MUSTER IN A *CARRY ON* FILM AND TWO STARS THAT MAKE ABBOTT AND COSTELLO LOOK LIKE MODELS OF SOPHISTICATION.' *EMPIRE*

Producer Menahem Golan wanted Roger Moore and Michael Caine to star in an epic remake of the classic action-adventure film *Gunga Din* (1939). But the actors declined, pointing out they were far too old to be credible as corporals in the Indian Army. Instead Moore's agent submitted a script called *Train of Events* by Oscar-winning songwriter Leslie Bricusse. Nine different scribes contributed to rewriting it. The story was eventually credited to Leslie Bricusse, Michael Winner and Nick Mead, while the screenplay was attributed to Bricusse and British TV sitcom stalwarts Laurence Marks and Maurice Gran.

Winner was appointed director and producer of the $10 million project, with Golan as executive producer. Filming began in October 1989, predominantly on location around London and Scotland, with a short sequence filmed in Barbados. Jerry Pam was Caine's American publicist at the time. In Michael Freedland's biography *Michael Caine*, Pam says he didn't

want Caine to make the picture. 'I tried to talk him out of it, but he was determined. I think what he really liked was a chance to work with Roger Moore.'

The three-month shoot proved enjoyable, with Caine telling the *Sun* newspaper how much fun he was having. 'Roger in particular is quite a trickster. He plays jokes on me all the time. I have to keep watching my back. He has also started on Michael Winner who has quite a short temper, but luckily he has taken it all in good form.' For one of his dual roles, Caine adopted an American accent that became a running joke on screen.

The film arrived in British cinemas in November 1990. Critics were savage and the movie bombed at the box-office, grossing less than $200,000. A video release followed in 1991. *Bullseye!* went straight to VHS in America, making its debut in August 1991. The film has long since been deleted and has not yet been released on DVD.

Caine rarely discusses this movie. When doing publicity for his Oscar-winning roles in *The Cider House Rules* (1999), the actor often talked about how tough it was tackling an American accent. He would sometimes recall developing his Southern accent for *Hurry Sundown* (1967) but never mentioned the American accents he used in *Bullseye!* or *On Deadly Ground* (1994).

The actor did talk about his lesser films during a public interview at the NFT in 1998: 'Stinkers creep up on you. You're sort of doing it and it's going along, it's going along, and then one day you go, "Oh God! What am I doing here?" And you think I better make the best of it. I know what I'll do – this is the review I'll get for this: the picture stank but as usual Caine gave a good performance.'

What do you call an unfunny comedy? *Bullseye!* That joke may be bad, but it's infinitely funnier than anything to be found in this dreadful mess. Put aside the ludicrous, unbelievable plot. Ignore the feeble attempts to evoke the sort of saucy double entendres on which Benny Hill built a career. Close your ears to Caine's ponderous, pointless voiceover narration that redundantly explains the plot over and over again. Instead, look at the desperation in Caine's eyes as he watches his career sailing away towards the sunset. Even in his most excruciating films, Caine rarely gives a bad performance. *Bullseye!* is an exception. His American accent is the stuff of amateur dramatics, while both Caine and Moore invest their dual roles with zero charisma. Avoid.

ABOVE:
Dangerous villains Sir John Bevistock (Roger Moore) and Dr Daniel Hicklar (Caine) threaten Willie (Sally Kellerman) and her secret agent daughter Flo (Deborah Barrymore) in Michael Winner's 1990 comedy *Bullseye!*

C

CALIFORNIA SUITE (1978)

Cast: Jane Fonda (Hannah Warren), Alan Alda (Bill Warren), Maggie Smith (Diana Barrie), Michael Caine (Sidney Cochran), Walter Matthau (Marvin Michaels), Elaine May (Millie Michaels), Herbert Edelman (Harry Michaels), Denise Galik (Bunny), Richard Pryor (Dr Chauncey Gump), Bill Cosby (Dr Willis Panama), Gloria Gifford (Lola Gump), Sheila Frazier (Bettina Panama). Crew: Herbert Ross (director), Ray Stark (producer), Neil Simon (writer), Claude Bolling (music), David M Walsh (cinematography), Michael A Stevenson (editor), Albert Brenner (production designer).

Five couples arrive at the Beverly Hills Hotel in California. New York journalist Hannah Warren is meeting her ex-husband Bill. Their 17-year-old daughter Jenny ran away to California to stay with Bill. Hannah wants her daughter to come home but eventually relents. Diana Barrie is nominated for best actress at the Academy Awards. She arrives at the hotel with her bisexual husband, Sidney Cochran. Diana does not win the Oscar and gets drunk. In the aftermath she and Sidney have a bitter argument, but manage to renew their love for each other. Marvin Michaels travels to Los Angeles for his nephew's bar mitzvah. Marvin's brother Harry pays for a prostitute to spend the night with Marvin. Next morning Marvin's wife Millie arrives and discovers the hooker. Millie forgives her husband but vows to spend all his money. Two doctors from Chicago drive across the country with their wives on what is supposed to be the holiday of a lifetime. But the vacation is one long argument that finally turns violent...

'THE ONLY STORY THAT IS REMOTELY SUCCESSFUL IS THAT CONCERNING AN OSCAR NOMINATED ACTRESS COMING TO TERMS WITH HER HUSBAND'S BI-SEXUALITY, TOUCHINGLY CONVEYED BY MICHAEL CAINE WHO'S BETTER THAN HE HAS BEEN FOR MANY FILMS...'
SUNDAY TELEGRAPH

'NEIL SIMON AND HERBERT ROSS HAVE GAMBLED IN RADICALLY ALTERING THE SUCCESSFUL FORMAT OF *CALIFORNIA SUITE* ... VEERING FROM POIGNANT EMOTIONALISM TO BROAD SLAPSTICK IN SUDDEN SHIFTS.'
VARIETY

Playwright Neil Simon had great success in 1968 with *Plaza Suite*, a collection of one-act plays all set in the same New York hotel room. The play became a successful film in 1971, starring Walter Matthau. Five years later Simon returned to the formula for *California Suite*, this time relocating events to the Beverly Hills Hotel. In 1978 director Herbert Ross collaborated with Simon on adapting the play into a film. Rather than simply presenting the stories one after the other (as in *Plaza Suite*), they opted to intersperse them.

The project attracted a high-calibre cast with six of the actors having previously won, or been nominated for, Oscars. Caine played Sidney Cochran, his first performance as a gay man on film. 'It was quite a difficult role but fascinating,' he told the *Daily Mirror* in 1979. 'I really don't know what it will do to my image. The homosexuals will probably say, "I always knew he was one" and the heterosexuals will say, "I always wondered about him."'

BELOW: Never one to shy away from unconventional roles, Caine played Maggie Smith's bi-sexual husband in the film of Neil Simon's hit play *California Suite* (1978).

ABOVE: When Maggie Smith won an Oscar for her role in *California Suite* (1978), she said half the golden statuette belonged to her co-star Caine.

In a 2002 interview with *Venice* magazine, Caine recalled an encounter with Neil Simon on set during shooting: 'One day he said to me, "You can really do my stuff. I've been watching the rushes." I said, "Yeah, do you know what the secret to doing Neil Simon is? You can never stop moving." You can't do it standing still. It's like Groucho Marx.'

California Suite received its US premiere in December 1978. The picture got mixed reviews, with the sequence starring Caine and Maggie Smith getting the best notices. But the film still grossed nearly $30 million, aided by a strong showing at the awards ceremonies. Smith won for best actress in a musical or comedy at the Golden Globes, and the picture was nominated as best musical or comedy film. Smith was also nominated at the BAFTAs. She won an Oscar as best supporting actress – ironically for playing an actress who *doesn't* win an Oscar. The film also received nominations for Simon's screenplay and art direction. In her acceptance speech Smith thanked Caine, saying he deserved half her statuette: 'It should be split down the middle.'

The film opened in the UK in March 1979. Again, reviews praised Caine and Smith. In 1980 Caine considered his performance in *California Suite* among his best. 'The timing was everything,' he told *Film Comment*. 'Doing that character was like walking on a razor blade. Very, very difficult and enervating.'

In 1994 Simon wrote *London Suite*, completing his trilogy of hotel-based plays. The characters played by Caine and Smith in *California Suite* returned in the new stage show. Caine declined an invitation to perform in the play, but offered his services if *London Suite* ever became a film.

Transferring a successful stage play to the screen is a tricky business. Taking a show made up of four small plays and turning *that* into a movie is even harder. Despite having a great cast, an acclaimed writer and an Oscar-nominated director, *California Suite* doesn't work as a cohesive movie. Cutting the four stories together simply heightens the disparities between them, rather than creating a meaningful contrast. Best of the quartet is the pairing of Caine and Smith as husband and wife, their scenes together proving both funny and moving. While Alan Alda and Jane Fonda get funnier dialogue in their segment, the British duo display far greater finesse. The bedroom farce with Walter Matthau is mildly amusing but the slapstick antics of Bill Cosby and Richard Pryor are just annoying. *California Suite* is the filmic definition of something being less than the sum of its parts.

THE CIDER HOUSE RULES (1999)

Cast: Tobey Maguire (Homer Wells), Charlize Theron (Candy Kendall), Delroy Lindo (Mr Rose), Paul Rudd (Wally Worthington), Michael Caine (Dr Wilbur Larch), Jane Alexander (Nurse Edna), Kathy Baker (Nurse Angela), Erykah Badu (Rose Rose), Kieran Culkin (Buster), Kate Nelligan (Olive Worthington), Heavy D (Peaches), K Todd Freeman (Muddy), Paz de la Huerta (Mary Agnes).
Crew: Lasse Hallström (director), Richard N Gladstein (producer), John Irving (writer), Rachel Portman (music), Oliver Stapleton (cinematography), Lisa Zeno Churgin (editor), David Gropman (production designer).

St Cloud's Orphanage in Maine takes unwanted babies. During the 1940s the resident physician, Dr Wilbur Larch, also performs illegal abortions. One of St Cloud's children, Homer Wells, is twice adopted and returned. As Homer grows up Dr Larch teaches him how to be an obstetric and gynaecological surgeon. Homer starts delivering babies but refuses to perform abortions. In 1943 Wally Worthington brings his girlfriend Candy Kendall to St Cloud's for an abortion. Homer leaves with them, wanting to see the outside world. He becomes an apple picker at the Worthington family orchard, sleeping in the bunkhouse with the migrant workers. The migrants are led by Mr Rose, whose daughter Rose Rose is one of the pickers. Wally goes off to war as a pilot.

The board of the orphanage want another physician to help Larch. He forges credentials indicating that Homer is fully qualified, then uses these to dupe the board. Larch also sends Homer a doctor's bag containing surgical instruments. Homer and Candy fall in love. When the migrant workers return after the winter, Rose is pregnant and Homer offers to help her have an abortion. Candy learns that Mr Rose is the father, while Wally's mother hears that her son has been paralysed from the waist down. Homer performs the abortion on Rose. She leaves that night after stabbing her father, after which Mr Rose commits suicide by stabbing himself repeatedly in the wound Rose made. Dr Larch dies of an accidental ether overdose. When Homer hears this, he returns to St Cloud's and becomes the new doctor…

'THIS COMING OF AGE TALE ACHIEVES A KIND OF MELANCHOLY POIGNANCY DESPITE NEVER FULLY CHARGING ITS DRAMATIC ENGINES. CAINE SCORES IN AN UNCHARACTERISTIC ROLE AND EASILY THE FILM'S MOST MEMORABLE SUPPORTING TURN, BRINGING LARCH A RICH, DISARMING HUMANITY.'
VARIETY

'THE STORY SLIPS TOUGH AND EVEN INCENDIARY SUBJECT MATTER INTO AN OLD-FASHIONED YARN. WITH HIS TART ADAPTATION OF *THE CIDER HOUSE RULES*, JOHN IRVING GETS TO THE CORE OF HIS FANCIFUL NOVEL.'
ENTERTAINMENT WEEKLY

John Irving's novel *The Cider House Rules* was first published in 1985. It took 14 years and four directors before the book was successfully transformed into a film. It was planned to go into production during April 1997 but was delayed because no actor of sufficient stature could be found for the part of Dr Larch; Paul Newman had read an early version of the screenplay and turned it down. In 1998 Sweden's Lasse Hallström was attached as director. The movie began production in September that year, with

a budget of $24 million. Irving has written a fascinating memoir of the long journey his novel went through to reach the screen, called *My Movie Business*.

Before accepting the part of Larch, Caine hired a dialect coach to work with him on developing a New England accent. The actor recalled the process in an interview with reel.com: 'I told him, "Be brutally frank with me. I don't want to make a fool of myself. Let's work for two weeks and if at the end of two weeks, you don't think I can do this, tell me." I didn't want to be a British actor doing an American accent, and have people go, "That is fantastic, that American accent."' Caine wanted the accent to be imperceptible. 'I had this extraordinarily difficult thing to do before I even started doing this extraordinarily difficult part.'

The Cider House Rules was shot on locations in the US states of Vermont, Maine and Massachusetts. Caine started work on the film in November 1998, flying back to London a few days later for a public interview at the NFT. Caine told the audience he might win an Academy Award as best supporting actor for the film, despite having only spent three days on set. 'It's one of those pictures where you think, "Oh, I might get an Oscar for this."'

He also said the script was very emotional. 'The day before yesterday, I was doing this scene and the director stopped it. He said, "Michael, the others are supposed to be crying, not you." I realised there were tears streaming down my face and I didn't even know. So we had to re-apply all the make-up and start again. It's a tough picture, and it's a fascinating script.' Caine had not read the original novel when he accepted the script, so he bought a copy. 'I started to read it. I thought, "You can't make a script out of this," but over on the table I could see it. Irving has got a great script out of it, he's quite ruthless.

TOBEY MAGUIRE
CHARLIZE THERON
DELROY LINDO
PAUL RUDD
& MICHAEL CAINE

7 ACADEMY AWARD®
NOMINATIONS
including
BEST FILM
BEST SUPPORTING ACTOR - MICHAEL CAINE
BEST DIRECTOR - LASSE HALLSTRÖM
BEST ADAPTED SCREENPLAY - JOHN IRVING

BRITISH ACADEMY FILM
AWARD® NOMINATION
for
MICHAEL CAINE
BEST SUPPORTING ACTOR

"MICHAEL CAINE HAS NEVER
BEEN BETTER THAN HE IS IN
'THE CIDER HOUSE RULES.'"
The Independent - David Thomson

"MAKES GOING TO
THE MOVIES A JOY."
The Today Show

a film by
LASSE HALLSTRÖM
THE CIDER
HOUSE
RULES

*A story about how far we
must travel to find the place
where we belong.*

I've never seen an artist be so ruthless with his own work.'

After appearing at film festivals, *The Cider House Rules* went on limited release in America during December 1999. Critical reaction was strong, particularly regarding Caine's performance and Irving's screenplay. Both were nominated for Golden Globe awards and Caine won the Screen Actors Guild Award for best supporting actor. When the Oscar nominations were announced in February 2000, *The Cider House Rules* was named in seven categories. All this recognition and positive word of mouth increased public interest in the film. It eventually grossed nearly $60 million in the US.

Anti-abortion protestors demonstrated outside the Academy Awards ceremony in March 2000. Inside, the protests went unheeded as Irving and Caine both won in their categories. For the actor it was his second Oscar triumph, but the first time he was present to collect his trophy. Caine gave an emotional speech and was close to tears when he left the stage. In subsequent interviews he emphasised the significance of the film in reviving his career. '*The Cider House Rules* was important, it reminded people that I was still around,' he told the *San Bernadino County Sun* in 2002. 'The Oscar didn't hurt, either. I think I got *The Quiet American* (2002) because of *The Cider House Rules*. I'll always be grateful to Lasse.' The award also had the effect of pushing up his fee for subsequent pictures.

The film opened in the UK in March 2000. Reviews in Britain were less sympathetic to Caine, with several criticising his American accent, but the picture still grossed more than $2.5 million. It was a bigger hit in Germany, taking more than $6.5 million. At the BAFTAs Caine missed out on an award for best supporting actor. But he did receive the British Academy's highest honour, the BAFTA Fellowship. Caine used his speech to strike back at critics, saying it felt as though he had been invited in from the cold. His remarks created controversy in some newspapers and magazines.

'People misunderstood that speech,' Caine told the *Radio Times* in 2002. 'When you read about it afterwards it sounded like I'd been vehemently sitting in a room for 40 years

thinking, "No one cares about me." I know how appreciated I am in Britain, and it's great.' Caine said his outburst was a reaction to terrible reviews of the film. 'When I did *The Cider House Rules* I got an Academy Award, but I got fucking slaughtered in Britain.'

The actor also discussed the speech in a 2000 interview with *Time Out*: 'For me, criticism should be informed, constructive and impersonal. Critics here always seem to review me from a deeply personal, almost savage viewpoint. They said my accent stank! The *New York Times* and the *New England Gazette* said it was a perfect New England accent, so how uninformed can you be? And then you start to think what is their agenda?'

The remarkable thing about *The Cider House Rules* is that the film ever got made. Turning a 500-page book about illegal abortions and incest into a heart-warming, life-affirming film can have been no easy feat. Previous attempts to adapt John Irving novels failed to find an audience. But the author's own screenplay is a marvellous and surprisingly funny distillation of his novel. Hallström's restrained, delicate direction keeps the film just the right side of sentimentality, aided by lush cinematography and a strong cast. Caine gives one of his most affecting performances, with an impeccable New England accent – particularly in the wry voiceover. It's not hard to see why he won an Oscar.

CURTAIN CALL (1998)

Cast: James Spader (Stevenson Lowe), Polly Walker (Julia), Michael Caine (Max Gale), Maggie Smith (Lily Marlowe), Buck Henry (Charles Van Allsburg), Sam Shepard (Will Dodge), Frank Whaley (Brett Conway), Marcia Gay Harden (Michelle Tippet), Frances Sternhagen (Amy), Peter Maloney (Maurice),

*Nicky Silver (Lee), Phyllis Somerville (Gladys).
Crew: Peter Yates (director), Andrew Karsch
(producer), Todd Alcott (writer), Richard Hartley
(music), Sven Nykvist (cinematography),
Hughes Winborne (editor), Stuart Wurtzel
(production designer).*

Stevenson Lowe is a publisher of literary
novels in New York. When his family business
is acquired by a corporation, Lowe finds himself
fighting to retain his integrity. Stevenson's
personal life is also in crisis, as he is unable
to commit to his long-term girlfriend Julia.
Stevenson buys an old brownstone building
haunted by the ghosts of a theatrical couple
from the 1920s, Max and Lily, who are
constantly bickering with each other.
Only Stevenson can see the ghosts.
Romantic complications ensue, with Julia getting
involved with a senator and Stevenson dodging
the attentions of an old flame. Finally, Stevenson
resigns himself to starting his own publishing
company and asks Julia to marry him. Max
and Lily are reconciled and slowly fade away…
Curtain Call was based on a story by producer
Andrew Karsch, whose previous credits included
producing the Oscar-nominated Barbra Steisand
vehicle *Prince of Tides* (1991). Actor James Spader
was going to make his directing debut with this
film, but had to step aside due to scheduling
difficulties. Experienced director Peter Yates was
brought in as a replacement two weeks before
shooting began. British-born Yates had been
Oscar-nominated for *Breaking Away* (1979) and
The Dresser (1985), and also directed the much-
loved Steve McQueen action picture *Bullitt* (1968).

Curtain Call began production on 10
February 1997, shooting on location in New
York City and Washington DC with a budget of
just under $20 million. The picture's title went
through several permutations during filming,
including *Later Life* and *Trouble with Stevenson*.

The picture reunited Caine and Maggie Smith,
who had previously appeared together as
husband and wife in *California Suite* (1978).
'When I saw this script I went nuts,' Caine told
Premiere magazine in 1997. 'I mean, we're two
old actors and ghosts. We could just do what
we liked – camp it up and do it over the top.'

Yates told *Premiere* that the supernatural
comedy was not an outright farce: 'It's a comedy
that doesn't rely on any reaction from 12-year-
old boys. Nowadays, unfortunately, that passes
for sophistication.' The film disappeared into
limbo for more than a year after completing
post-production.

In November 1998 *Curtain Call* was one of
six films acquired by the Encore Media Group
(EMG) for its Starz pay-TV network in America.
EMG's senior vice president of programming,
Bob Leighton, told *Variety* that Starz was buying
pictures that had been denied a theatrical release
because box-office returns might not offset the
additional $3 million minimum cost for film prints
and advertising. 'These are not the kinds of movies
in favour at the box-office right now,' Leighton
said. The pay-TV network paid an average of
$750,000 for each film. *Variety* reported that
Curtain Call would get its world premiere
on Starz in December 1998.

Two years later the film was released in
full-screen format on VHS and DVD in the US.
Curtain Call has never been released in the UK,
making it one of Caine's harder to find films.

Curtain Call is a gentle romantic comedy that's
guilty of recycling too many ideas from better
stories, like Noël Coward's play *Blithe Spirit*. The
script is all too predictable, with a subplot (about a
literary publishing firm having its reputation strip-
mined) that has little connection with the rest of the
film. Caine and Smith give the script more class
than it deserves, but they are swimming upstream
against a torrent of banalities. *Curtain Call* offends
nobody and excites even less.

D

DEADFALL (1968)

Cast: Michael Caine (Henry), Giovanna Ralli (Fe), Eric Portman (Moreau), Nanette Newman (the girl), David Buck (Salinas), Leonard Rossiter (Fillmore), Carlos Pierre (Antonio), Vladek Sheybal (Dr Delgado), John Barry (orchestra conductor), Renata Tarrago (solo guitarist).

Crew: Bryan Forbes (director/writer), Paul Monash (producer), John Barry (music), Gerry Turpin (cinematography), John Jympson (editor), Ray Simm (production designer).

Henry Clarke is an outstanding jewel thief who plans to steal diamonds from a rich man called Salinas. Henry poses as an alcoholic in order to enter a Spanish clinic where Salinas is a patient. Henry is approached by a beautiful woman called Fe on behalf of her ageing husband Moreau; the couple want to collaborate with Henry on stealing Salinas' diamonds. The thief agrees and moves in with them. Henry and Moreau burgle a private home as a test of how well they work together. Henry begins an affair with Fe, but she refuses to leave her husband – even though Moreau is gay. Fe says that Moreau betrayed a lover during the war to save himself from the Nazis. Moreau reveals he is Fe's biological father, as well as her husband. Henry attempts the Salinas job on his own, but is shot by a guard and falls to his death. Moreau commits suicide. Fe is taken away by the police…

FAR RIGHT:
Caine and Giovanna Ralli spoof the art of scene stealing between takes on *Deadfall* (1968).

'THE PRINCIPAL PROTAGONISTS MOVE LIKE SO MANY SOMNAMBULISTS THROUGH THE TURGID LABYRINTH OF BRYAN FORBES' LATEST FILM, WITH MICHAEL CAINE'S PERFORMANCE …

DIRECTLY BELYING THE EMOTIONAL EXCESSES ATTRIBUTED TO HIM IN THE SCRIPT.' *MONTHLY FILM BULLETIN*

'AN APPARENT ATTEMPT TO PULL OFF AN ALFRED HITCHCOCK SUSPENSER, WITH ADDED FREUDIAN SCHLEPS, *DEADFALL* FALLS DEAD AS LITTLE MORE THAN PONDEROUS, TEDIOUS TRIVIA.' *VARIETY*

Director Bryan Forbes wrote the screenplay for this £1 million feature, adapting a 1965 novel by Desmond Cory. Production began in the autumn of 1967, with location shooting in Spain and studio work at Pinewood. For Caine, the feature provided a reunion with Forbes and the director's wife, actress Nanette Newman – the three had worked together on *The Wrong Box* (1966). It was the first half of a disastrous two-picture contract Caine had agreed with Twentieth Century-Fox; the other half was *The Magus* (1968).

During filming in Majorca Forbes described *Deadfall* as a horror story in sunlight. 'I didn't want to move into the Hitchcock field, all shadows and gloom,' the director told *Nova* magazine. 'I wanted everything clear and nasty under the sun – horrible because of that. The story's about a jewel thief, but it's also about the darker side of human nature: homosexuality and incest. It's all good clean family fun.' Forbes predicted that Caine's career would be altered by the movie. 'This film could open up an entirely new landscape for him. He's got to escape through one trapdoor to find the next one.'

Caine also felt *Deadfall* marked a change. 'This is what I call my first handsome part,' he told *Nova*. 'Alfie and Harry Palmer were either downtrodden or treading on themselves. This character is tougher, more subtly brutal. More like me. I don't let anyone take liberties

with me. Filming's all right when it's going well, but when it's going badly, it's a bastard. Now I don't let it bother me – after all the film's being built round me. It's how I feel that counts.'

Deadfall's music was composed by John Barry, a frequent contributor to Caine movies in the 1960s. Unusually, Barry also appeared on screen as conductor of an orchestra. Forbes wrote about this in his 1992 autobiography, *A Divided Life*. 'For *Deadfall* I asked him [Barry] to give me a guitar concerto of concert-platform standard, for it had to be performed in its entirety by Renata Tarrago and at the same time underline the drama of a robbery – the film being cross-cut between the concert and the working out of the crime.'

The film was released in the UK in November 1968. It received an X rating from the BBFC, restricting entry to those aged 16 and over. *Deadfall* was panned by critics and a failure at the box-office. Its reception was just as harsh in the US, where it was rated R. The film has never been released on VHS or DVD.

Deadfall makes two hours seem so much longer. The three central characters talk and talk without saying anything of consequence. Since Forbes wrote and directed this, he must take the blame. Cinema is a visual art form, yet this film constantly has people talking about events instead of showing them. Everyone answers questions with more questions and melodrama crushes any real drama. Whenever the 'action' flags, Forbes cuts away to an image of waves crashing on a stony beach or seagulls squawking overhead. In the midst of all this Caine is lost, unsure of how to pitch his performance and – unusually – unable to create even a hint of empathy for his character. This film comes alive only during the cross-cut sequence of theft and concerto, which owes much to the classic French caper film *Rififi* (1954). Otherwise, *Deadfall* is a dead loss.

FAR RIGHT:
Caine starred as murderous gay playwright Sidney Bruhl in *Deathtrap* (1982). He had to fight for the role after four years of appearing in flops and horror films.

DEATHTRAP (1982)

Cast: Michael Caine (Sidney Bruhl), Christopher Reeve (Clifford Anderson), Dyan Cannon (Myra Bruhl), Irene Worth (Helga ten Dorp), Henry Jones (Porter Milgrim), Joe Silver (Seymour Starger), Tony DiBenedetto (Burt, the bartender), Al LeBreton (handsome actor).
Crew: Sidney Lumet (director), Burtt Harris (producer), Jay Presson Allen (writer), Johnny Mandel (music), Andrzej Bartkowiak (cinematography), John J Fitzstephens (editor), Tony Walton (production designer).

Sidney Bruhl used to write smash-hit comedy thrillers for Broadway. But his last four plays have flopped and he is getting desperate. The playwright receives a wonderful script from a former pupil, Clifford Anderson. Sidney decides to murder the budding scribe and steal the play for himself. Sidney's weak-hearted wife Myra is not sure whether he is being serious. When Clifford arrives, Myra tries to talk Sidney out of murdering the young writer, but Sidney chokes Clifford and buries him in a shallow grave.

The Bruhls are visited by Dutch psychic Helga ten Dorp. She warns them there will be violence and pain in their house. That night Clifford reappears and terrifies Myra so much she dies of a heart attack. Sidney and Clifford are lovers. They staged their elaborate charade with a fake play to frighten Myra to death. After her funeral Clifford becomes Sidney's secretary. But the veteran playwright discovers Clifford is turning their crime into a play called *Deathtrap*. Sidney decides he must murder his lover, fatally wounding Clifford with a crossbow. Helga reappears and accuses Sidney of murder. A storm cuts off the electricity. In the confusion Clifford kills Sidney. Several months later the events are replayed on Broadway in the opening night of *Deathtrap* – a play by Helga ten Dorp.

'CAINE … IS THE MAIN PLEASURE OF A CONCOCTION THAT OTHERWISE DEPENDS FOR ITS EFFECT ON A SUCCESSION OF EVER MORE UNLIKELY SURPRISES.'
THE GUARDIAN

'THE CHIEF SURPRISE IS MICHAEL CAINE. HERE AS BELEAGUERED BRUHL, FIRING OFF INCENSED APHORISMS AT ALL PASSERS, HE'S A JOY.' **FINANCIAL TIMES**

In the early 1980s Ira Levin's *Deathtrap* held the record as Broadway's longest-running thriller. The creative pairing of screenwriter Jay Presson Allen and director Sidney Lumet collaborated on adapting the play to film. The duo had been Oscar-nominated for the screenplay of their previous project, *Prince of the City* (1981). Caine wanted to play the lead in *Deathtrap* but Allen had doubts about his suitability. The actor had been stuck in horror films and disaster movies for four years. Caine eventually persuaded Allen at a dinner party arranged by the actor's agent.

Caine described his preparations for the part to interviewer W J Weatherby: 'You look at what the character does and says, and then try to figure out what kind of person he is. What came out for me in studying *Deathtrap* was that my character was simply criminally insane. Just crazy. That was the only way to translate the theatrical quality into a realistic medium – make his behaviour crazy. But I also try to play this insane character as a real person with human quirks. I see him as a born nut. He's been under terrific pressure … the pressure has brought out things that were already in him but were under control, until separated failures turn him more and more into a desperate character. It's a study of a menopausal nut case.'

Caine was keen to highlight the macabre comedy elements: 'The theatricality has been toned down, but the humour's still there. I'd forgotten just how funny it is, a comedy hidden inside a thriller. The thing I really enjoy doing is comedy, but nobody gives anything to me that's funny.'

The film was shot in the spring of 1981, almost entirely on studio sets in New York's East Harlem. A few exterior sequences were added to open out the play, with scenes set in a Broadway theatre book-ending the movie. Lumet also shot exteriors of a converted windmill house in East Hampton as the Bruhls' home in the country.

Deathtrap featured a gay kiss between Caine and his on-screen lover Christopher Reeve. 'Neither of us had kissed a guy on the lips before,' Caine told *Premiere* in 1999. 'We had a pact that neither of us would loosen our lips. We practised the scene over and over again so we wouldn't blow the lines or anything, it was the most well-rehearsed scene – except for the kiss. It's one of those things that if you don't want to do it again, you have got to throw yourself into it with tremendous enthusiasm so everyone thinks it wonderful.' The scene was completed in a single take. 'If you're gay, that's fine, but if you're not, it's bloody difficult to kiss a man.'

The film opened in the US in March 1982. Initially rated R by the MPAA, this was reduced to PG on appeal. The picture received a muted reaction from critics, although Caine and Reeve were praised for their performances. *Deathtrap* grossed nearly $20 million in America. In Britain the movie was given an A rating. Again, reviews were mixed but Caine got good notices. After appearing in the likes of *Victory* (1981), *The Island* (1980) and *Beyond the Poseidon Adventure* (1979), *Deathtrap* was seen as a return to form for the actor.

Deathtrap is an adequate thriller with

plenty of plot twists and turns, but it suffers by comparison with the superior *Sleuth* (1972). Both are adaptations of hit stage plays featuring Caine, both revolve around two men trying to outsmart each other and both feature murderous machinations and intrigues. *Sleuth* wins out thanks to its stronger, tauter script and the presence of Laurence Olivier. Reeve is good, but no match for one of Britain's finest actors. *Deathtrap* never escapes its stage origins, with Lumet's attempts to open it out cursory at best. The climactic ending is fumbled, as choppy editing renders the denouement unclear. Caine gives a strong performance as Bruhl, giving the character unwritten depth and believability. But the gay kiss looks more like two friends trying to avoid sharing a cold sore. *Deathtrap* is worth watching – but only once.

THE DEBTORS (1999)

Cast: Michael Caine, Randy Quaid, Catherine McCormack, Jamie Kennedy, Udo Kier.
Crew: Evi Quaid (director), Kara Meyers and Evi Quaid (producers), Jordan Roberts, Jeremy Pikser and Evi Quaid (writers), Simon Boswell (music), Eric Edwards (cinematography), Jon Gregory, William S Scharf (editor), Patricia Norris (production designer).

A sex fiend, a compulsive gambler and a shopaholic meet when they join the same counselling group. The trio go on a road trip to cure their addictions.

'DESPITE STRONG PERFORMANCES BY RANDY QUAID AND MICHAEL CAINE AND SOME TRULY FUNNY MOMENTS, THE FILM ALSO VEERS INTO SELF-INDULGENCE AND VULGARITY.' *PREMIERE*

'I WOULDN'T RECOMMEND THIS MOVIE TO ANYONE. THAT WOULD BE EVIL!' *EXTRACT FROM RESPONSE CARD AT TEST SCREENING*

In March 1998 would-be film director Evi Quaid met Microsoft billionaire Charles Simonyi, who was interested in film investment. She persuaded him to spend $12.8 million on making an independent movie called *The Debtors*, a screwball comedy about addictions. Quaid had never directed a film. She was a production assistant on *Bloodhounds of Broadway* (1989), an associate producer on *Curse of the Starving Class* (1995) and had read scripts for her husband, actor Randy Quaid.

Production began in Los Angeles during August 1998, with Randy Quaid as one of the three leads. The other key roles went to Caine and Catherine McCormack, reportedly replacing Burt Reynolds and Joan Cusack just before shooting began. Within a month the film's line producer quit. The director favoured unorthodox methods of working, such as scribbling new dialogue on scraps of paper and handing them to the actors just before a take. 'It was great,' she told *Premiere* magazine. 'Nobody knew what I was shooting from one day to the next. And I never had a record of it.' Quaid spent close to a million dollars of her own money on last-minute changes.

A climactic scene in a ballroom with 200 extras in expensive couture clothes created special problems. German industrial band Rammstein was hired to perform its stage show, including simulated anal sex. The lead singer pretended to sodomise another band member with a plastic penis, before spraying a mixture of milk and water that spattered the face of a female extra.

After his Oscar talk regarding *The Cider House Rules*, Caine discussed the film at his NFT interview in 1998: 'I just did a comedy in LA for which I know *nobody's* going to get an Oscar, but which you make for box-office. And I had a great deal of fun with it. I was up in Las Vegas, and LA, and New York, and doing scenes up and down Madison Avenue, with beautiful women and bright times. You think, we're not going to get an Oscar here, but let's have a great time making the movie.'

In February 1999 Caine told *Hello* magazine why he decided to make the film with a first-time director: 'Because she's nuts. Because she wrote it. Because she believes in it. And because I'd never worked with a woman director. And it was really smashing. She had lots of women on set so the testosterone was down to a very low level, which pleased me. It's tiring being macho all the time. As to whether it's any good, your guess is as good as mine. Comedy's a bit like parachute-jumping … sometimes nothing happens. There's no such thing as a mediocre comedy. It's either very funny or it sinks like a stone. We'll see.'

In April 1999 Quaid set up a preview screening of an early cut of the film in Seattle, with Simonyi in attendance. Response cards from the 300 test-audience members were vitriolic. Soon afterwards legal battles began for possession of the movie. The director was ordered by a federal judge not to screen *The Debtors* while the court case was being resolved. Quaid took the movie to England in June where she hired *Four Weddings and a Funeral* editor Jon Gregory to help her re-cut it. She showed the new version to the head of the Toronto Film Festival, who agreed to publicly screen it. Quaid also screened the film for Caine. The actor's publicist said Caine had reservations about it.

The Debtors was screened at the Toronto Film Festival on 13 September 1999 under the temporary title *High Expectations*, despite American court orders that prohibited Quaid from showing it. The director's own legal representatives resigned. In January 2000 Evi and Randy Quaid filed for bankruptcy, with debts of more than $1 million. The fate of *The Debtors* remains in limbo and it seems unlikely the film will ever be released. No verdict can be passed on the movie, but two published opinions are quoted above.

THE DESTRUCTORS (1974)
See THE MARSEILLES CONTRACT (1974)

DIRTY ROTTEN SCOUNDRELS (1988)

Cast: Steve Martin (Freddie Benson), Michael Caine (Lawrence Jamieson), Glenne Headly (Janet Colgate), Anton Rodgers (Inspector Andre), Barbara Harris (Fanny Eubanks), Ian McDiarmid (Arthur), Dana Ivey (Mrs Reed), Meagen Fay (lady from Oklahoma), Frances Conroy (lady from Palm Beach). Crew: Frank Oz (director), Bernard Williams (producer), Dale Launer and Stanley Shapiro & Paul Henning (writers), Miles Goodman (music), Michael Ballhaus (cinematography), Stephen A Rotter and William Scharf (editors), Roy Walker (production designer).

Lawrence Jamieson is a high-class con-man in the South of France who poses as an exiled prince to take money from rich women. A boorish, small-time American grifter called Freddie Benson arrives in town and threatens to spoil Lawrence's operation. Newspapers mention a clever young American con-artist called the Jackal whom Lawrence believes is Freddie. After failing in attempts to get rid of Freddie, Lawrence agrees to tutor him, hoping to drive the interloper away. They make a wager – whoever is first to con $50,000 from a rich young American woman called Janet Colgate can stay, but the other must leave. When Lawrence discovers Janet is not rich, the bet is changed. Now the wager is whether Freddie can get Janet into bed with him. Janet leaves before Freddie can succeed, but she also takes $50,000 of Lawrence's money. The two men realise Janet is the Jackal. Several days later she reappears, inviting them to join her latest scam. They agree…

'THOUGH CAINE DOESN'T QUITE HAVE THE SOPHISTICATION OF NIVEN, HIS SKILL AND TECHNIQUE CONVINCE YOU HE DOES … IT'S A SUBTLE, BEAUTIFULLY CONTROLLED PERFORMANCE.' *SUNDAY EXPRESS*

'MARTIN IS AN ACKNOWLEDGED COMIC TALENT, BUT CAINE TOO IS WELL UP TO THE TASK … BETWEEN THEM THE FILM BECOMES A COMPULSIVELY WATCHABLE EXERCISE IN REFINED VULGARITY ' *DAILY TELEGRAPH*

Bedtime Story (1964) was a comedy about two con-men competing with each other on the French Riviera. The film was a flop, with one review calling it the most vulgar, embarrassing film of the year. Nearly a quarter of a century later the original script by Stanley Shapiro and Paul Henning was updated by Dale Launer for Frank Oz to direct. US comedian Steve Martin was attached to play the younger con-man,

BELOW:
Lawrence Jamieson and Freddie Benson (Steve Martin) face off in *Dirty Rotten Scoundrels* (1988).

ABOVE: Lawrence
Jamieson begins
transforming
loudmouth
American grifter
Freddie Benson
(Steve Martin) into
a suave conman
in *Dirty Rotten
Scoundrels* (1988).

Marlon Brando's role in the original.

Oz was uncertain about casting Caine as
the character originally played by David Niven.
'I saw Michael as a great dramatic actor,' Oz
says on the film's DVD commentary. 'He
volunteered to read for the part. It worked out
just perfectly.' Caine's on-screen appearance
was inspired by Niven's look. 'Michael and
I agreed his hair should be slicked back,' Oz
recalls, 'not like Michael Caine is usually
seen – and he should have a little moustache.'

Dirty Rotten Scoundrels was shot between
June and August 1988 at locations in the South
of France, and at La Victorine Studios in Nice.
Oz says he wanted the film to look and feel like
a 1950s movie: 'I needed to create a world with
a 1950s sheen where you'd believe these two

characters would live up to their bargain over
$50,000.' The director and Martin did a lot of
work on the script during production, particularly
the final scene at the airport. 'We had no idea of
how to end this movie. We shot for two months
with no ending.' Oz and Martin wrote the finale,
with help from Caine.

'That's probably the most fun I've ever had
doing a film,' Caine told *Venice* magazine in
2002. 'It's funny, Steve is such a serious guy.
People would come on the set and expect Steve
to be wild and crazy, when in fact I was the nutty
one and he was the serious one. We're exactly
the opposite of what each of us was on screen.
But it was one of those films where everyone
was giggling. Glenne Headly especially was
a big giggler.'

Caine said the comedy in *Dirty Rotten Scoundrels* was much harder to carry off than his role in *Get Carter* (1971). '*Get Carter* required such a controlled performance. It was all about the stillness … like a room with minimalist furniture. *Dirty Rotten Scoundrels* was not quite over-the-top Victorian, but it came close. Slightly over-furnished. You have to time comedy to silence, you see. The crew can't laugh. So comedy is much more difficult.'

The film was released in America in December 1988. It was critically praised and proved popular with audiences too, grossing more than $40 million in the US. Caine was nominated as best actor in a comedy or musical at the Golden Globe awards, losing to Tom Hanks' performance in *Big* (1988). *Dirty Rotten Scoundrels* reached UK cinemas in June 1989 and grossed more than $4 million. The film was issued on DVD in 2001, but the US version is superior. It includes Oz's audio commentary and other extras. In 2000 Caine talked about his hopes of making a sequel but said efforts had been stalled by the bankruptcy of Orion Pictures, the studio behind *Dirty Rotten Scoundrels*.

An April 2003 poll of Blockbuster Video customers named the duo of Caine and Martin as the top film comedy pairing of all time, just ahead of Laurel and Hardy.

Dirty Rotten Scoundrels is a thoroughly enjoyable comedy that keeps you guessing until the end. Even if you deduce the identity of the Jackal before the finale, the film is executed with such panache it doesn't matter. Martin's physical comedy skills run riot while Caine provides the perfect foil, elegance and charm contrasted with brash and bluster. The supporting cast is just as good, with not one performance out of place.

BELOW: The team of Caine, Glenne Headly and Steve Martin helped turned *Dirty Rotten Scoundrels* (1988) into a smash hit comedy, despite it being a remake of the flop *Bedtime Story* (1964).

The music is playful and wry, the production design sumptuous, the lensing a joy to the eye. *Dirty Rotten Scoundrels* is a little gem and proof, if proof were needed, of Caine's comedy prowess.

DRESSED TO KILL (1980)

Cast: Michael Caine (Dr Robert Elliott), Angie Dickinson (Kate Miller), Nancy Allen (Liz Blake), Keith Gordon (Peter Miller), Dennis Franz (Detective Marino), David Margulies (Dr Levy), Ken Baker (Warren Lockman), Susanna Clemm (Betty Luce), Brandon Maggart (Cleveland Sam).
Crew: Brian De Palma (director/writer), George Litto (producer), Pino Donaggio (music), Ralf Bode (cinematography), Jerry Greenberg (editor), Gary Weist (art direction).

Middle-aged New Yorker Kate Miller is seeing a psychiatrist, Dr Robert Elliott, for help dealing with her loveless second marriage. She asks Elliott if he wants to have sex with her, but he declines. Kate goes to a museum and gets picked up by a stranger. They have sex at his apartment. As Kate leaves, she is murdered by a blonde woman wielding a cut-throat razor. The killer is

seen by a high-class escort girl, Liz Blake. Elliott receives a message from Bobbi, a transsexual who wants to have a woman's body. Bobbi confesses to taking Elliott's razor and using it to kill Kate. The case is investigated by Detective Marino, who summons Dr Elliott to the police station. There Elliott meets Kate's teenage son Peter, who overhears Marino asking Elliott if one of the psychiatrist's patients could be the killer.

Peter positions a camera to take photos of everyone visiting Elliott's office. Liz is stalked by a blonde woman. The escort is attacked on the subway, but Peter rescues her. He shows Liz photos of the blonde leaving Elliott's office. Liz tells Marino but he is unable to act without proof. Liz gets an appointment with Elliott and makes a pass at him. She leaves the room to look in his appointment book for the blonde's name. When she returns, Liz is attacked by the razor-wielding blonde. But the killer is shot from outside by another blonde woman. The killer is revealed to be Dr Elliott, dressed as a woman. Elliott is Bobbi the transsexual. He killed Kate and tried to murder Liz because both women aroused his male sexuality. Liz was rescued by a blonde police woman who had been following her for Marino…

BELOW:
Psychiatrist Dr Robert Elliott counsels his patient Kate Miller (Angie Dickinson) in *Dressed to Kill* (1980).

'BRIAN DE PALMA GOES RIGHT FOR THE AUDIENCE JUGULAR IN … A STYLISH EXERCISE IN ERSATZ-HITCHCOCK SUSPENSE-TERROR. CAINE … IS EXCELLENT AS THE SUAVE SHRINK.' *VARIETY*

'IT DOESN'T MATTER THAT THE PLOT HAS MORE FLAWS THAN A SECOND-HAND SUIT … THIS IS A MASTERLY PIECE OF FILMMAKING WITH THE GRIP OF A HANGMAN'S NOOSE.' *DAILY EXPRESS*

Director Brian De Palma wrote a screenplay based on the book *Cruising* by Gerald Walker, but was unable to secure the rights. (The book was made into a 1980 film by William Friedkin, starring Al Pacino.) Instead De Palma recycled some of the elements from his script and melded them with other ideas to create the suspense thriller *Dressed to Kill*. The $6 million film was mostly shot at locations around New York and in a city studio, with a Philadelphia museum used for interiors set inside New York's Metropolitan Museum, when permission could not be gained to shoot inside the real building.

In his acting masterclass Caine recalled making the film: 'Brian De Palma has a bit of a chilly personality, but I admire him as a director and technician. So when he offered me *Dressed to Kill*, I figured this was a gamble that might pay off. He was very demanding. I remember one nine-page sequence that incorporated a 360-degree swing of the camera and required 26 takes (a record for me) … That one sequence took a whole day to shoot.'

The part required Caine to be in drag for his sequences as Bobbi. 'I had never done it before, and I thought, suppose I like it?' he told *Premiere* in 1999. 'I hated it. I couldn't wait to get the damn stuff off. I think it's the most

uncomfortable form of dress. If you're a man, it's terrible.' Caine had to shave his legs every morning and found it very difficult to walk in high heels. In many of the stalking scenes his place was taken by Susanna Clemm, the actress who also played the policewoman mistaken for Bobbi.

In *The Making of Dressed to Kill* documentary, co-star Karen Allen recalls the first time she saw Caine as Bobbi. He was in the full costume and make-up, smoking a big cigar. 'Michael looked around at the crew and said, "I always knew if I worked long enough and hard enough I'd get to play me mum."'

When first presented to the MPAA, the film was given an X rating. This guaranteed commercial failure as many cinema chains refused to screen X-rated movies. De Palma was enraged that he had to cut his film to get an R rating and complained to the news media. But the picture was still trimmed to secure the less damaging rating.

Released in America in June 1980, *Dressed to Kill* was praised by many critics. The controversy about its rating and content helped fuel public interest, and the film grossed more than five times its budget. But the movie was attacked by some reviewers as being misogynistic. De Palma also faced accusations of imitating the work of filmmaker Alfred Hitchcock. *Dressed to Kill* featured several elements seen in *Psycho* (1960), such as a transvestite killer and a female lead character who gets killed off after 30 minutes. 'Hitchcock's story ideas are the best that exist,' De Palma says in *The Making Of Dressed to Kill*. 'If you're going to work in this genre, Hitchcock's done it all. If you're going to be good, you are going to use some of his ideas.'

The picture's notoriety earned it several nominations at the dreaded Razzie Awards, including one for Caine as worst actor.

The nomination also made mention of his performance in *The Island* (1980).

In Britain the film was dogged by controversy for different reasons. Released while the Yorkshire Ripper was still at large, it became one of several films targeted by 'Reclaim the Night' feminist pickets; in Bradford (centre of the Ripper's territory), protestors threw a bucket of animal blood over a cinema screen where *Dressed to Kill* was playing. Tabloids jumped on the story, further contributing to the film's notoriety. It got an X rating, but in the UK that only banned anyone under 18 from seeing the movie.

A DVD version was issued in the US in 2001, including an uncut version of the film and several documentaries. The 2002 DVD release in the UK has only minimal extras.

Dressed to Kill explores its twin themes of sexuality and violence with style, contrasting them to sometimes terrifying effect. De Palma's use of devices like split-screen, showing the same scene from multiple points of view, and lingering tracking shots all help heighten the picture's mood. The plot relies too much on coincidence and contrivance but the suspense generated helps overcome these problems. Yes, the story parallels to *Psycho* are particularly strong, but a nine-minute wordless museum sequence also evokes memories of *Vertigo*, as does Pino Donaggio's score. Caine's performance is remarkably subtle, the repression his character suffers only obvious on repeat viewing. If you can forgive the story's flaws and have a taste for terror, *Dressed to Kill* will serve you well.

E

THE EAGLE HAS LANDED (1976)

Cast: Michael Caine (Colonel Steiner), Donald Sutherland (Liam Devlin), Robert Duvall (Colonel Radl), Jenny Agutter (Molly), Donald Pleasence (Himmler), Anthony Quayle (Admiral Canaris), Jean Marsh (Joanna Grey), Sven-Bertil Taube (Captain von Neustadt), John Standing (Father Verecker), Judy Geeson (Pamela), Treat Williams (Captain Clark), Larry Hagman (Colonel Pitts).

Crew: John Sturges (director), Jack Wiener and David Niven Jr (producers), Tom Mankiewicz (writer), Lalo Schifrin (music), Anthony Richmond (cinematography), Anne V Coates (editor), Peter Murton (production design).

In 1943 Adolf Hitler commissions a feasibility study into kidnapping British Prime Minister Winston Churchill. Colonel Radl believes the plot may be possible after learning that Churchill is to visit a small Norfolk village. Radl selects an IRA dissident, Liam Devlin, to parachute into England to make preparations. For the kidnapping, Radl selects a disgraced war hero, Colonel Steiner, and his squad of 16 paratroopers. The insurgents enter the village posing as Polish troops. But their true identities are discovered when one of the Germans dies saving a local child from drowning.

Steiner and his men take the villagers hostage in the church. The priest's sister escapes and alerts a nearby company of American troops, whereupon their foolhardy leader, Colonel Pitts, leads a disastrous attack against the church. Steiner escapes the church but his men volunteer to stay behind, giving him more time. They all die in the next attack. That night Steiner finds

ABOVE:
German war hero
Kurt Steiner and his
men try to protect
a Jewish girl from
the Gestapo in
*The Eagle Has
Landed* (1976).

ABOVE:

Colonel Radl
(Robert Duvall,
second left) offers
Steiner a chance
to end the Second
World War by
kidnapping Winston
Churchill in *The
Eagle Has Landed*
(1976). Watching
are IRA terrorist
Liam Devlin
(Donald Sutherland,
left) and Captain
von Neustadt
(Sven-Bertil Taube).

Churchill and assassinates the British leader, before being gunned down himself. But the real Churchill is at a secret meeting in Persia – the man Steiner killed was a variety artist pretending to be Churchill. Radl is executed by firing squad for the mission's failure.

'THE FILM MANAGES THE REMARKABLE FEAT OF BEING BOTH FAR-FETCHED AND DULL AT THE SAME TIME. CAINE, SUTHERLAND AND A HOST OF STALWART BRITISH CHARACTER ACTORS GO THROUGH THEIR PACES WITH UNBLENCHING PROFESSIONALISM.'
FINANCIAL TIMES

'SINCE MOST MOVIEGOERS PROBABLY KNOW THAT GERMAN FORCES DID NOT KIDNAP WINSTON CHURCHILL DURING WORLD WAR II *THE EAGLE HAS LANDED* IS IN THE UNENVIABLE POSITION OF BEING A THRILLER WITHOUT THRILLS.' *NEWSWEEK*

The Eagle Has Landed began life as a best-selling novel by Jack Higgins, claiming its story had some basis in reality. The book was quickly optioned for the cinema, with Tom Mankiewicz adapting it for the big screen. US director John Sturges was attached to the project, having previously helmed such classic films as *Bad Day at Black Rock* (1955), *The Magnificent*

Seven (1960) and *The Great Escape* (1963).

The leading role of Colonel Kurt Steiner went to Caine, who developed several different variations of accent for his performance. 'At first we thought that Steiner should have a German accent when he's in Germany and an English accent when he comes to England,' the actor told *Photoplay* in 1976. 'But then we decided that the German characters wouldn't have an accent when they're talking amongst themselves, because they wouldn't sound foreign to each other. So I used a clipped military accent for the scenes when Steiner's giving orders to his men in German.'

One of Caine's reasons for accepting the part was a chance to be directed by Sturges. 'I've never worked with John before but I admire his work very much,' the actor said. The film also reunited him with Donald Sutherland: 'Donald's an old mate. We first worked together years ago on an early episode of *Dixon of Dock Green*.' Sutherland had also made a brief appearance in the third Harry Palmer film, *Billion Dollar Brain* (1967).

The Eagle Has Landed was shot over 12 weeks in the summer of 1976. For the first week the production went to Rovaniemi in Finland, the biggest town in the Arctic Circle. Caine had sworn off ever returning to Finland after the making of *Billion Dollar Brain*, but went back for Sturges. That was followed by a week in Cornwall, which doubled for the Channel Islands. The bulk of filming took place in the Berkshire village of Mapledurham. Among the extras was a young Ray Winstone, who co-starred with Caine in *Last Orders* (2001) a quarter of a century later.

The film was released across Britain at the end of 1976, receiving harsh reviews from many critics. It reached America early in 1977 and proved to be the swan-song of Sturges' career. A budget price DVD version was issued in Britain in 2000, but this full-screen edition suffers from poor picture quality and cannot be recommended. A widescreen DVD is available in the US.

The Eagle Has Landed could have been lifted straight from the pages of war comics like *Battle Picture Weekly* or *Commando*. More mature minds will reject it as fanciful nonsense. The mission must fail because history tells you the Nazis did not kidnap Churchill, thus limiting any suspense. The film's pace feels too languid for a thriller, while an attempt to develop a romantic subplot is cursory at best. But Caine succeeds in making his character sympathetic, aided by a clever variation of accent and manner. Your enjoyment will depend entirely upon how far you are willing to suspend your disbelief.

EDUCATING RITA (1983)

Cast: Michael Caine (Dr Frank Bryant), Julie Walters (Rita), Michael Williams (Brian), Maureen Lipman (Trish), Jeananne Crowley (Julia), Malcolm Douglas (Denny).
Crew: Lewis Gilbert (director/producer), Willy Russell (writer), David Hentschel (music), Frank Watts (cinematography), Garth Craven (editor), Maurice Fowler (art direction).

Rita is a 26-year-old hairdresser who wants to better herself. She enrols in an Open University course on English literature and begins taking tutorials with Dr Frank Bryant, a drunken lecturer who used to be a poet. Rita's husband Denny wants children but she wants to discover herself first. When Denny gives Rita an ultimatum, she chooses learning ahead of him. Rita begins flat-sharing with Trish, a glamorous woman who seems to have all the answers.

Frank receives a final warning from the college after trying to deliver a lecture while drunk, and, though Rita is now able to recite poetry from memory and will pass her exams with ease, Frank dismisses her progress, saying she has just swapped one sham existence for another. When Trish tries to commit suicide, Rita realises what her own odyssey has been about. She now has choices. Rita sits the exam and passes with distinction. Frank is leaving for a two-year sabbatical in Australia. Rita declines the chance to accompany him, but gives Frank a haircut as a going-away present.

'THIS IS A MASTER FILM ACTOR'S PERFORMANCE. THE GOAL OF CAINE'S TECHNIQUE SEEMS TO BE TO DISSOLVE ALL VESTIGES OF "TECHNIQUE". HE LETS NOTHING GET BETWEEN YOU AND THE CHARACTER HE PLAYS.' *THE NEW YORKER* 'CAINE'S UNSELFISH PARTNERING OF THE NEWCOMER [JULIE WALTERS] DOESN'T CONCEAL THE FINESSE THAT NOW SHADES HIS EVERY APPEARANCE ON THE SCREEN…' *EVENING STANDARD*

Educating Rita started out as a stage play by Willy Russell, with Julie Walters originating the leading role. Director-producer Lewis Gilbert acquired the film rights, hiring Russell to adapt his own script for the cinema. When the project was turned down by all the major studios, Gilbert raised the $6 million budget from bankers in the City of London. He began shooting the film without a distribution deal in place, a move that gave him the freedom to cast whomever he wanted in the two main roles.

'The stories about Dolly Parton are true,' Gilbert told *Films and Filming* in 1985. 'The studios wanted her to play Rita and the film to be set in America.' Executives also wanted Rita and Frank to end up in bed together. Gilbert retained Walters from the original stage production and chose Caine for the role of drunken lecturer Frank. The pair had worked together on *Alfie* (1966), a film that won international acclaim and earned Caine his first Oscar nomination. 'Michael has matured and progressed as an actor,' Gilbert said. 'He was well cast in *Alfie*, but there are things in *Educating Rita* he couldn't have done 16 years previously. He just gets better and better.'

To prepare for the part, Caine transformed himself physically, putting on weight and growing a full beard. 'When I played Frank, I based him on two people I know,' Caine said in his acting masterclass. 'While I knew what it was like to be drunk, alcoholism was another thing; and I had no concept of how a university lecturer behaves – I'd never been to a university. I based Frank-the-lecturer partly on a writer friend of mine named Robert Bolt [author of *The Royal Hunt of the Sun*, among others], who was a great teacher. I'd seen him talking and explaining, I knew his manner. And for Frank-the-alcoholic I imagined myself to be another friend of mine named Peter Langan [notorious restaurateur], someone who behaved like an alcoholic of truly historic proportions. I amalgamated the two people to make Frank.'

Caine said it would have been a cliché for Rita and Frank to fall into bed with each other. 'I felt very strongly that although Frank does fall in love with Rita, it's never spoken about and is totally unrequited. I gained 35 pounds and grew a beard because there should never have been the possibility of Rita's being sexually attracted to this fat old drunk.'

Educating Rita was filmed entirely on location in the Republic of Ireland during the summer of 1982. For five weeks the production was based in Dublin's Trinity College while all the students were away on holiday. Another

BELOW: Drunken English professor Dr Frank Bryant tries to teach working class hairdresser Rita (Julie Walters) about William Blake in *Educating Rita* (1983). Both actors were Oscar-nominated for their roles in this hit film.

five weeks followed, shooting in and around the capital city. Fake snow was used on the college quad to simulate winter.

Caine has frequently said the film is among his favourite performances. 'It was a big character change for me,' he told *Venice* magazine in 2002. 'Up until that point I'd been playing Michael Caine-ish in everything. The most extraordinary thing about that role for me was that I could find nothing of myself in it. He was the farthest away from myself I'd ever been with a character, which is the ideal place for an actor to be. Julie Walters really helped to make me look good. She'd never done a movie before. She'd done the play, so she was very into the characters, but I thought she played down, into the style of film acting, just beautifully. A lot of theatre actors would have gone over the top with it.'

The film was released across Britain with a 15 rating in April 1983, attracting rave reviews and grossing nearly $4 million at the box-office. It reached America in September that year; initially rated R, this was reduced to PG on appeal. Again, critical reaction was overwhelmingly positive and it grossed nearly $15 million during a six-month run in cinemas. At the end of 1983 *Educating Rita* was included in many critics' Top Ten film lists for the year, leading to a strong showing in the major cinema awards.

Caine and Walters both won Golden Globe awards as best actor and actress in a musical or comedy. The pair also won acting awards at the BAFTAs and Gilbert received the best film trophy. At the Oscars, Caine, Walters and Russell were all nominated but left empty-handed. Best Actor went to Robert Duvall for *Tender Mercies* (1983) – the only American among the five nominees. Caine would have to wait nearly 20 years before receiving another Best Actor nomination.

In the BFI's 1999 poll to find the Top 100 British movies of the 20th century, *Educating Rita* was one of seven Caine pictures on the list, voted 84th. In 2002 there were rumours of a remake starring Oscar winners Denzel Washington and Halle Berry.

Educating Rita is an exceptional film, blessed by fine performances from the two leads. On the surface the plot has echoes of Bernard Shaw's *Pygmalion* and its musical adaptation *My Fair Lady*, but this film covers more than matters of class or accent. *Educating Rita* is also about self-worth, personal freedom and making choices. Caine stretches himself, showing how far he had grown as an actor. It's not just the

physical transformation that is startling, but the depth of emotion on display in the eyes and the voice. Compare that with the lazy kickabout that was Caine's performance in *Victory* (1981) just two years earlier. Walters shines as Rita, giving no hint that this is her first major film role. Gilbert directs with deft simplicity, giving Russell's poignant and funny script a fitting vehicle. You only need to imagine a Hollywood remake of the story to realise how restrained and sensitive this version is. The only sour note comes from the grating, cod-classical synthesiser score. It badly dates what should be a timeless film. Otherwise, *Educating Rita* is close to perfect.

ESCAPE TO VICTORY (1981)
See VICTORY (1981)

RIGHT: John Preston keeps a close watch on the activities in a Greek café in *The Fourth Protocol* (1987).

F

THE FOURTH PROTOCOL (1987)

Cast: Michael Caine (John Preston),
Pierce Brosnan (Petrofsky), Ned Beatty
(Borisov), Joanna Cassidy (Vassilievna),
Julian Glover (Brian Harcourt-Smith),
Michael Gough (Sir Bernard Hemmings),
Ray McAnally (General Karpov),
Ian Richardson (Sir Nigel Irvine),
Anton Rodgers (George Berenson).
Crew: John Mackenzie (director),
Timothy Burrill (producer), Frederick Forsyth
(writer), Lalo Schifrin (music), Phil Meheux
(cinematography), Graham Walker (editor),
Allan Cameron (production designer).

The Cold War is finally thawing. To maintain his power-base as chairman of the KGB, General Govershin launches a covert operation to break the fourth protocol of a nuclear arms treaty; this prohibits the smuggling of atomic weapons. Major Petrofsky is sent to Britain and takes up residence beside a US air base. Couriers bring him the components to assemble an atomic bomb. But one courier is intercepted, alerting British agent John Preston to the operation. Govershin's deputy, General Karpov, also discovers what is being planned. A Russian operative is spotted entering Britain and Preston follows the operative to a Greek café outside London. This leads British intelligence to Petrofsky's residence. Preston and special forces gunmen storm the house and prevent Petrofsky from detonating the bomb. The Russian is murdered to prevent him talking. Preston realises it was Karpov who sent the operative, leading the British agents to Petrofsky. Karpov will use the failure to usurp Govershin and take control of the KGB...

'A DECIDEDLY CONTEMPO THRILLER … ITS EDGE IS A FINE AURA OF REALISM. MICHAEL CAINE … GIVES A THOROUGH PERFORMANCE IN A PART THAT DOESN'T REALLY STRETCH HIS ABILITIES.' *VARIETY*

'CAINE IS A TRUE MASTER OF THE SCREEN, COMMUNICATING SO MUCH WITH SO LITTLE MATERIAL, BUT HERE HE IS GIVEN … TOO LITTLE.' *SUNDAY TIMES*

Frederick Forsyth became a best-selling novelist in the 1970s and 1980s with a succession of thrillers like *The Day of the Jackal* and *The Odessa File*, books with a veneer of verisimilitude. Several were transformed into successful films. When *The Fourth Protocol* was published in 1984, the author set up a production company with his old friend Caine to transform the story into a movie. Both invested money in the project. Forsyth was determined to write the adaptation himself, preparing seven drafts of the screenplay.

Director John Mackenzie was approached, having previously directed Caine in *The Honorary Consul* (1983). In an exclusive interview for this book, Mackenzie recalled the development process: 'With the best will in the world, Freddie Forsyth can write a certain type of novel, but he's not a screenwriter. The script was awful! This was a guy who was putting a million of his own money into the damn thing. I said I'll only do it if I can rewrite the script. The producer, Timothy Burrill, eventually persuaded him to let me rewrite it. Forsyth instantly regretted it, of course, but the thing had to get going.' Mackenzie brought in a writer called Richard Burridge. 'The film was practically underway. It was all last minute. We had a lot of problems, but I just carried on

BELOW: The future James Bond encounters the former Harry Palmer – Pierce Brosnan and Caine in a promotional image from *The Fourth Protocol* (1987).

and made the film. We tried to make something more than had been in the original script.'

The $7 million production began shooting in February 1986. Finland was used to represent scenes in Russia, with the bulk of shooting carried out on location in the UK and at Elstree Studios. Caine acknowledged similarities between his role in *The Fourth Protocol* and another British spy he had played previously, Harry Palmer, during an interview with the *New York Times* in 1987. But he also maintained the characters had their differences: 'To me, Harry was a gifted amateur, which is what the British were 15 or 20 years ago. Preston is a top professional, which I think the British have become lately.'

He also discussed the two roles with the *Daily Mail*. 'Someone asked me the other day

what the difference was. I said Harry Palmer was Woody Allen and John Preston is Clint Eastwood – and I am one of the few actors who can play both.'

Mackenzie found it difficult getting any intensity of performance from Caine. 'He'd done much more exciting parts of this type before. It was a dull part, there was nothing there. He sort of walked through it, it didn't stretch him.' Mackenzie attributes this to flaws in the script: 'We did try and give him a sort of background, some depth, a dead wife and things. But that central character was not such a great character.'

The director campaigned for Burridge to receive proper credit. Ultimately the screenplay was attributed solely to Forsyth, with other credits going to Burridge for additional material and to George Axelrod for 'screen story' adaptation.

The film opened in the UK in March 1987. It received a mixed reaction from critics, who felt the plot got in the way of characterisation, and grossed just over $1 million. *The Fourth Protocol* was more successful in the US, where it grossed more than $12 million.

The Fourth Protocol never catches fire, with nearly half the film over before the main threat is revealed. In the meantime British intelligence has been pursuing what proves to be an utterly irrelevant subplot. Attempts to inject some life into the central characters fail, with Preston just an older, slower version of Harry Palmer. Caine gives a professional but thoroughly uninvolving performance, outshone by Pierce Brosnan's compelling work as Petrofsky. At the time this film was made, Brosnan was being considered to replace Roger Moore as James Bond. Here you can see a sneak preview of the ruthless streak he now displays as 007. *The Fourth Protocol* is better than some thrillers Caine made during the mid-1980s, but it still feels like a big-budget TV movie.

LEFT: Caine as John Preston in *The Fourth Protocol* (1987).

FUNERAL IN BERLIN (1966)

Cast: Michael Caine (Harry Palmer),
Paul Hubschmid (Johnnie Vulkan),
Oscar Homolka (Stok), Eva Renzi (Samantha
Steel), Guy Doleman (Ross), Hugh Burden
(Hallam), Heinz Schubert (Levine), Wolfgang
Volz (Werner), Thomas Holtzmann (Reinhardt),
Gunter Meisner (Kreutzman).
Crew: Guy Hamilton (director), Charles Kasher
(producer), Evan Jones (writer), Konrad Elfers
(music), Otto Heller (cinematography), John
Bloom (editor), Ken Adam (production designer).

British agent Harry Palmer is sent to Berlin.
A local operative, Johnnie Vulkan, claims
that Colonel Stok of the KGB wants to defect.
Palmer meets Stok, who is in charge of the
Berlin Wall, and the colonel says he will defect
but wants the operation run by Kreutzman, who
has supervised some of the most daring escapes
across the wall. Harry is picked up by Samantha
Steel, an Israeli secret agent. Vulkan arranges for
Harry to meet with Kreutzman, who agrees to
run the defection. The price is 60,000 American
dollars and a set of genuine British identity
papers. The defection proves to be a trap for
Kreutzman, but the identity papers are another
matter. The Israelis want them to retrieve two
million dollars of Jewish money looted by
a Nazi called Paul Louis Broum during
the war. Palmer learns that his old friend
Vulkan used to be Broum, a German guard
at a concentration camp. Harry tricks Vulkan
into the open, where the former Nazi is gunned
down by the Israelis…

Right: A spanner in the works – British agent Harry Palmer (Caine) is under attack from the traitorous Johnnie Vulkan (Paul Hubschmid) in *Funeral in Berlin* (1966).

ABOVE: Caine returns in his second appearance as down at heel British agent Harry Palmer for *Funeral in Berlin* (1966).

'*FUNERAL IN BERLIN* PILES IT ON
THICK AND FAST WITH A PLOT
WHICH HAS SO MANY TWISTS
THAT EVEN SHERLOCK HOLMES
MIGHT HAVE BEEN BAFFLED.'
MONTHLY FILM BULLETIN

'IT IS DIFFICULT TO IMAGINE THE
FIRST FILM WITHOUT MR CAINE ...
IN THE CASE OF THE SECOND IT IS
IMPOSSIBLE: THE ACTOR MAKES
THE FILM.' ***SUNDAY TIMES***

The film of *The Ipcress File* (1965) proved a success in Britain and the US. By the time it reached cinemas, author Len Deighton had already written two further novels featuring his nameless British spy – christened Harry Palmer for the big screen. Producer Harry Saltzman wasted no time exercising his option on another of the Deighton novels, selecting the third book of the series, *Funeral in Berlin*. Saltzman hoped the Palmer films might grow to rival the James Bond films, which he co-produced with Cubby Broccoli.

Evan Jones was chosen to adapt the complex plot of the novel into a screenplay. Guy Hamilton came on board as director, replacing the more mercurial Sidney J Furie. For Saltzman and Broccoli, Hamilton had excelled on the third 007 extravaganza *Goldfinger* (1964). Many of the team that had worked on *The Ipcress File* returned for the new Palmer movie, including production designer Ken Adam, cinematographer Otto Heller and producer Charles Kasher. Saltzman had Caine under contract so his participation was assured, but his asking price had jumped to £100,000 for this picture. Joining him again was Guy Doleman as Harry's superior, Colonel Ross.

The bulk of location work was filmed in West Berlin, with the crew constructing a replica of Checkpoint Charlie, the famous crossing point between east and west. Studio work took place at Pinewood back in Britain. Shooting near the Berlin Wall was problematic, with border guards on the eastern side deliberately disrupting filming by shining a mirror at the camera lenses. Caine told *Esquire* magazine that the city was different from any place he'd been: 'Here there's no such thing as anybody being pleased to see you ... I don't want to be unfair to anybody, so let's just say we're dancing to different tunes. It's not my scene.' Caine filled some of his time off by practising a Southern American accent for his next film, *Hurry Sundown* (1967). Director Otto Preminger had sent the Londoner tapes to help him master the distinctive speech patterns.

Funeral in Berlin received mediocre reviews in Britain when it opened in late 1966. Despite this, the new film made enough money for Saltzman to green-light a third Harry Palmer picture. *Funeral in Berlin* reached the US in 1967 where reviews were more favourable.

Funeral in Berlin is a drab, downbeat film with a complex plot that requires considerable concentration without offering much in return. Almost all the characters are unsympathetic, either utterly amoral or murderous zealots, making it hard to care what happens to them. In the midst of this, Caine repeats the assurance of his previous performance as Harry Palmer, but adds few new shadings to the part. He only comes alive on screen playing opposite his old nemesis Ross or his new enemy Stok. Oscar Homolka shines as the KGB colonel, stealing all his scenes with ease. Director Guy Hamilton replaces the eye-catching techniques of Sidney J Furie with more mundane imagery, reducing this film to a conventional espionage tale. That's adequate on its own terms, but a disappointment after *The Ipcress File* (1965).

G

GAMBIT (1966)

Cast: Shirley MacLaine (Nicole), Michael Caine (Harry), Herbert Lom (Shahbandar), Roger C Carmel (Ram), Arnold Moss (Abdul), John Abbott (Emile), Richard Angarola (Colonel Salim), Maurice Marsac (hotel clerk).
Crew: Ronald Neame (director), Leo L Fuchs (producer), Jack Davies and Alvin Sargent (writers), Maurice Jarre (music), Clifford Stine (cinematography), Alma Macrorie (editor), Alexander Golitzen and George C Webb (art direction).

Eurasian dancer Nicole is hired by British thief Harry to help him steal a priceless marble bust from the penthouse of the world's richest man, Shahbandar. Nicole bears a striking resemblance to the princess depicted in the bust, and to Shahbandar's late wife. Harry is assisted by French sculptor Emile but almost nothing goes according to plan. While Harry prepares to steal the bust, Nicole discovers Shahbandar has laid a trap for thieves. Nicole helps Harry get the statue but accidentally triggers the alarm system. She flees but Harry stays behind long enough to see that the real bust is kept in a secret safe.

News flashes around the world about the priceless statue's theft. Nicole is captured by the police and Shahbandar sends her to Harry with a message – return the bust or suffer the consequences. But Harry never stole the real bust. He concealed it within Shahbandar's penthouse. The fake bust was made for Shahbandar by Emile two years earlier. All Harry wanted was the publicity. Now he can make a fortune selling another replica of the bust made by Emile. Nicole is so disappointed by this duplicity, Harry smashes the replica to win her heart. After they have gone, Emile opens a cupboard to reveal three more replicas…

ABOVE: Shirley MacLaine hand-picked Caine to be her co-star for the heist comedy *Gambit* (1966).

'SHIRLEY MACLAINE AND MICHAEL CAINE STAR IN A FIRST-RATE SUSPENSE COMEDY, CLEVERLY SCRIPTED, EXPERTLY DIRECTED AND HANDSOMELY MOUNTED.' *VARIETY*

'THE FILM HAS AN ORIGINALITY OF ITS OWN IN THE WAY THAT REALITY KEEPS ASSERTING ITSELF TO SHATTER HARRY'S ILLUSIONS ABOUT HIS PERFECTLY PLANNED CRIME.' *MONTHLY FILM BULLETIN*

By the mid-1960s American actress Shirley MacLaine was a powerful player in Hollywood, able to select her own directors and leading men. She expressed an interest in having Sidney J Furie direct *Gambit* and watched a screening of his most recent film, *The Ipcress File* (1965). Furie proved to be unavailable, but MacLaine's eye was caught by the actor playing British spy Harry Palmer. She choose Caine to be her partner in crime for the caper movie. The screenplay by Jack Davies and Alvin Sargent was based on a Sidney Carroll story.

Gambit gave Caine his first experience of working on a Hollywood film, with the picture shot at Universal Studios. Having been paid just £7000 for his role in *The Ipcress File*, *Gambit* pushed the actor's price up to £50,000. Caine gave an interview to the *Sunday Express* during filming in February 1966, saying how much he liked Hollywood: 'A lot of people knock this place, I know, but I don't get it. There's plenty to eat and the sun is shining and there are lots of birds. What more can you want? Oh, I miss things about London, of course. The theatre, for instance. But how much time can you spend in the theatre? What about the time you spend walking around trying to keep warm?'

During production Caine dated Hollywood star Natalie Wood and Frank Sinatra's daughter Nancy. The actor played up his *Alfie* persona: 'They seem convinced that we English are just a bunch of Limey fags and I'm determined to change the image.'

Gambit was a hit with critics and audiences when it was released late in 1966. MacLaine, Caine and the film were all nominated for Golden Globes. Caine lost out to Alan Arkin in *The Russians Are Coming! The Russians Are Coming!* (1966). *Gambit* was also nominated for three technical awards – costumes, art direction and sound – at the Oscars.

In January 2002 *Variety* reported that brothers Joel and Ethan Coen were getting a seven-figure deal to script a remake of *Gambit*. The makers of *Fargo* (1996) and *Blood Simple* (1984) were commissioned by producer Michael Lobell to write the script as a potential star vehicle for British actor Hugh Grant. In November 2002 *Variety* reported that director Burr Steers was attached to the project and would be rewriting the Coens' script. Steers had won critical acclaim for his work on the feature *Igby Goes Down* (2002). 'It [*Gambit*] is a wickedly funny piece that is ready to go,' Steers said. 'I'll do a rewrite, but I'm working from a script by the Coens that makes you laugh out loud. It's a great mix of updated screwball comedy and sophisticated slapstick. The trick will be to find a cast with the chemistry that Michael Caine and Shirley MacLaine had in the original.'

Gambit is a lightweight crime caper that delights from start to finish. A clever opening sets out the masterplan for the theft. Then comes a twist where reality intrudes on Harry's fantasy of a perfect crime, generating humour and suspense. The relationship between the two leads develops into a true partnership, with MacLaine and Caine sparking off each other well. Ronald Neame directs with verve and panache, despite the obviously studio-bound setting. *Gambit* is not a particularly renowned entry in Caine's filmography, but it's one of the most enjoyable.

GET CARTER (1971)

Cast: Michael Caine (Jack Carter), Ian Hendry (Eric), Britt Ekland (Anna), John Osborne (Kinnear), Tony Beckley (Peter), George Sewell (Con), Geraldine Moffat (Glenda), Dorothy White (Edna), Petra Markham (Doreen), Alun Armstrong (Keith), Bryan Mosley (Brumby), Glynn Edwards (Albert), Bernard Hepton (Thorpe), Terence Rigby (Gerald Fletcher), John Bindon (Sid Fletcher), Godfrey Quigley (Eddie). Crew: Mike Hodges (director/writer), Michael

Klinger (producer), Roy Budd (music), Wolfgang Suschitzky (cinematography), John Trumper (editor), Assheton Gorton (production designer).

Professional killer Jack Carter works for two London gangsters, the Fletcher brothers. Jack is having an affair with Gerald Fletcher's wife, Anna. Jack travels to Newcastle to investigate his brother's death. Frank drowned after getting drunk and driving a car into a river, but Carter believes it was murder. He tries to get answers from Margaret, who sometimes slept with Frank. Jack is concerned about Frank's teenage daughter Doreen. Looking for a bookie called Albert Swift, Carter meets an old enemy – Eric Paice. This leads Jack to Kinnear, a Newcastle crime boss. Carter also encounters a rival gangland figure, Cliff Brumby.

The Fletchers send two men from London to bring Jack back but he escapes them. Kinnear's girlfriend Glenda takes Carter to meet Brumby, who offers £5000 if Jack will kill Kinnear. Carter discovers that his niece Doreen was used in a porn film made for Kinnear and arranged by Eric. The movie also featured Margaret, Glenda and Albert Swift. After seeing it, Brumby wanted to have sex with Doreen. Jack takes revenge on all those involved, leaving Eric until last. But Kinnear arranges for another assassin to get Carter. Just after he has killed Paice, Jack is shot dead.

'AT ANY TIME THIS WOULD BE A REVOLTING, BESTIAL, HORRIBLY VIOLENT PIECE OF CINEMA. IT IS ALL THE WORSE FOR BEING GIVEN A QUASI-REALISTIC SETTING AND BECAUSE CAINE (WHO SHOULD REALLY KNOW BETTER THAN TO STOOP TO THIS SORT OF THING) IS A HORRIBLY EFFECTIVE SMILING KILLER.' *EVENING NEWS*

'SO CALCULATEDLY COOL AND SOULLESS AND NASTILY EROTIC THAT IT SEEMS TO BELONG TO A NEW ERA OF VIRTUOSO VICIOUSNESS.' *THE NEW YORKER*

Ted Lewis' novel *Jack's Return Home* was still awaiting publication when it was optioned as a potential film by producer Michael Klinger, who then interested Caine in playing the lead. The actor saw the film as a way of portraying British criminals more realistically. 'I was a co-producer,' Caine told the *San Bernadino County Sun* in 2002. 'One of the reasons I wanted to make that picture was my background. In English movies, gangsters were either stupid or funny. I wanted to show that they're neither. Gangsters are not stupid, and they're certainly not very funny.'

Mike Hodges was given the job of adapting the book into a film. It was his first cinema feature, having started in TV on documentary series before helming dramas for the small screen. Hodges shared his documentary background with his cinematographer, Wolfgang Suschitzky. This proved useful in keeping the look and style of the film realistic. Hodges completed *Get Carter* in eight months, just 36 weeks elapsing from the day he received the unpublished novel until editing on the film was finished. 'That was the white heat this film was made in,' Hodges says on the commentary track of *Get Carter*'s DVD release. 'The shoot was only 38, 40 days. That wouldn't happen nowadays.' The movie had a budget of just $750,000.

The bulk of the film was shot in Newcastle, with Hodges rewriting his script to incorporate new locations as they were found. The director had never worked with a cinema star like Caine before and admits he had trouble adjusting. But Hodges found the actor was not worried about his public image being damaged by the character of Carter: 'Caine was prepared to be absolutely ugly and horrible. This picture was a career gamble, in my opinion.'

To satisfy American distributors MGM, Hodges cast Britt Ekland as Carter's lover Anna. This gave the director freedom to fill the other roles with British character actors. The key role of gangland boss Cyril Kinnear went to John Osborne, writer of the landmark play *Look Back in Anger* (1956); Caine and Osborne had become friends in the 1950s when both were struggling actors in London.

One person who did not like the film's star was Ian Hendry, cast as Eric Paice. 'He was very jealous of Caine,' Hodges recalls. Hendry had been a TV star in the early 1960s before drinking hurt his career. The night before shooting a scene where their characters meet for the first time at a race course, the director brought the two men together for a rehearsal. But Hendry was drunk and became abusive towards Caine. Hodges says that this disaster unwittingly succeeded in giving their performances an extra edge.

Caine talked about the picture in a 1997 interview with the *Guardian*. 'There was an

BELOW: Jack Carter offers cash to Eddie (Godfrey Quigley), one of his dead brother's friends, in *Get Carter* (1971). Watching the exchange is Keith (Alun Armstrong).

BELOW:
Cold-blooded killer
Jack Carter wields
his dead brother's
shotgun in *Get
Carter* (1971),
although he never
fires it during
the film.

extraordinary morality in *Get Carter* … one of the reasons Carter is prepared to kill everyone is that someone's put a person with his surname into a pornographic film. And that's an incredible moral judgment!' Caine was proud that the film chose to show the reality of violence. 'What you get these days, to a great extent, is a pornography of violence which is much more dangerous than a pornography of sex. I'd rather see people screwing each other than killing one another.'

'*Get Carter* is a Jacobean tragedy,' Hodges told *Pitch Weekly* in 2000. 'It's a heavy body count, and at its very heart is corruption. It's the sense of violence. There's not a lot of blood, and the violence is swift. You don't wallow in it. It's atmosphere.'

Roy Budd's distinctive score added to that atmosphere. In his DVD commentary, Hodges says he was delighted by the music Budd provided to accompany the titles: 'Imbedded in the theme was this melancholic little sound.' The director asked Budd to take the handful of notes and use it as a refrain throughout the film. 'It was so haunting.'

When the film was presented to the BBFC in November 1970, the censors required cuts to the scene where Carter stabs Albert to death. 'The knife was more evident,' Hodges told *Premiere* magazine in 2001. 'I quite wisely took it out, because the less you see of the knife, the more effective the scene is.' He had actor Glynn Edwards wear a white top to emphasise the blood, and replaced Albert's dying breath with a ship's mournful foghorn.

Get Carter was scorned by many reviewers when it was released across Britain in March 1971, rated X. The grim mood, seedy subject matter and downbeat ending all came in for criticism, but it was the film's depiction of violence that shocked and dismayed many. In America *Get Carter* was rated R and got buried as the second feature on a double-bill with

Dirty Dingus McGee (1970), a comedy Western starring Frank Sinatra.

Get Carter's archetypal story has provided fertile ground for other filmmakers. In 1972, the movie was remade with a cast of black Americans as *Hit Man*. Acclaimed US director Steven Soderbergh freely acknowledges the influence *Get Carter* had on his own revenge thriller *The Limey* (1999), featuring a former flatmate of Caine's, Terence Stamp. A year later Sylvester Stallone starred in a second remake, *Get Carter* (2000), with Caine making a cameo appearance as the Brumby character. For further details see the next entry in this book.

Hodges' film did not get released on VHS until 1993, its re-emergence coinciding with a new enthusiasm for British pop culture. A few months after *Get Carter* reached video rental stores, a new magazine called *Loaded* was launched. The magazine published a comic strip serialisation of the film, introducing the film to a new generation. Caine became a British icon and the picture's potent mix of brutal realism and eminently quotable dialogue marked it out as a classic British film. The movie's critical reassessment had begun. 'I used to think *Get Carter* was underrated,' Caine told *GQ* in 1997. 'But now it's been rated, now it's very rated.'

In June 1999 *Get Carter* was reissued in British cinemas to help publicise a video re-release. Three months later the BFI's poll of the Top 100 British movies of the 20th century placed *Get Carter* as the highest of seven Caine films on the list, voted 16th overall. A year later a DVD version was issued, with a commentary track by Hodges and Suschitzky, augmented by comments from Caine. The actor rarely provides commentaries for DVDs, a sign of how highly he rates this picture.

Caine discussed *Get Carter* during an interview with *Venice* magazine in 2002, saying he based the performance on a professional

killer he knew. Years after the film was released, the killer gave Caine his own verdict on it: 'He said, "I didn't think that *Get Carter* was good, Michael. No family life. Why do you people in the cinema always ignore this? I've got a wife, a mortgage, one of my kids is in hospital. All you guys go around fucking all the women, flashing all their money. I'm not gonna make any money, fucking convicted killer. In *Get Carter* you just showed the fancy side."'

Get Carter is a stunning piece of cinema. More than 30 years after its release, the movie retains the power to shock and surprise, both from the bleakness of its content and how fresh it still looks. The swinging sixties are well and truly over in this picture, the once industrious North reduced to a festering slag heap of corruption, pornography and violence. Caine gives a masterful performance as Carter, his movements precise and deadly. The moment when he watches his niece (who may be his own daughter) being abused in a porn film is Caine at his best, the tears and horror resolving themselves into murderous implacability. Compared to the clutch of corblimey Cockney crime capers that blighted British cinema in the 1990s, *Get Carter* just keeps getting better with age.

GET CARTER (2000)

Cast: Sylvester Stallone (Jack Carter), Miranda Richardson (Gloria), Rachael Leigh Cook (Doreen), Rhona Mitra (Geraldine), Johnny Strong (Eddie), John C McGinley (Con McCarty), Alan Cumming (Jeremy Kinnear), Michael Caine (Cliff Brumby), John Cassini (Thorpey), Mickey Rourke (Cyrus Paice), Mark Boone Jr (Jim Davis), Garwin Sanford (Les Fletcher).
Crew: Stephen Kay (director), Mark Canton, Elie Samaha and Neil Canton (producers), David McKenna (writer), Tyler Bates (music), Mauro Fiore (cinematography), Jerry Greenberg (editor), Charles J H Wood (production designer).

Jack Carter is a bone-breaker for Las Vegas mobster Les Fletcher. Jack goes home to Seattle for his brother Richie's funeral, against Fletcher's orders, and decides to investigate Richie's death in a drunk driving accident. Richie worked at a bar owned by Cliff Brumby.

Learning Richie had a mistress called Geraldine, Jack traces her to an old enemy, Cyrus Paice, who runs porn websites. Paice leads Carter to an internet millionaire, Jeremy Kinnear. Kinnear denies knowing about Richie's death.

Brumby tries to get Jack to leave town. Jack sees a security tape from Brumby's bar that shows Geraldine giving Richie a computer disc. Carter locates the disc, which shows Richie's teenage daughter Doreen being drugged and used in a sex show with Geraldine and one of Brumby's men, Eddie. Paice kills Geraldine with a heroin overdose. Jack murders Eddie and Paice in revenge. He threatens to kill Kinnear, who was involved with Paice. Kinnear says Paice was working for someone else. As Jack prepares to leave Seattle, he find Brumby trying to retrieve the computer disc. Carter murders Brumby.

'A USELESS REMAKE OF THE MIKE HODGES 1971 BRITISH GANGLAND CULT CLASSIC … THIS LATEST SYLVESTER STALLONE "COMEBACK" PICTURE LACKS EXCITEMENT, CREDIBILITY, SUSPENSE, CHARACTER INSIGHT OR ANYTHING ELSE THAT MIGHT CONCEIVABLY ENGAGE VIEWERS.' *VARIETY*

'IN SHORT, IT ISN'T A PATCH ON MIKE HODGES' VERSION; HOWEVER, APPROACHED AS A WORK IN ITS OWN RIGHT, IT'S NOT AS BAD AS MANY WOULD HAVE YOU BELIEVE.' *EMPIRE*

By the late 1990s Mike Hodges' film *Get Carter* (1971) was recognised as a modern classic. An American company acquired the rights to the original source material, Ted Lewis' novel *Jack's Return Home*, and commissioned a new version as a vehicle for ageing action star Sylvester Stallone. David McKenna wrote the adaptation, transferring the events from Newcastle to Seattle.

Stephen Kay was brought in as director, having only helmed two small independent movies. The new version of *Get Carter* was a step up to the big time with a $40 million budget and an international star as the lead. 'I was completely daunted by the notion of remaking a movie I really dug,' Kay says on the film's DVD commentary track. He demanded Caine's involvement. 'I don't think you make this movie if you don't have Michael Caine in it. When he said he would do it, there was no way they were going to drag me out of this movie. It was great to have him, and he's just a champ.'

But Caine took some convincing when first approached, as he told the *Daily Telegraph* early in 2000. 'The producer called and said, "It'll be fun." My agent said, "Michael's not in it for the fun, he's in it for money. Make an offer." If someone says to me, "Do it for fun," I always say, "No, give me the money. I'll have fun afterwards."'

The production began in October 1999, filming in Vancouver and with location work in Seattle and Las Vegas. Caine told an interviewer that the shoot *had* been fun. But preview audiences disliked the ending and Caine was called back for re-shoots. 'When I was Carter in the first film, I killed the character I play in the remake,' Caine told the *Evening Standard* in 2001. 'Sly Stallone didn't kill me and I went round telling journalists he would be a gentler Carter than I was. A few months later I got called back for a day's shooting. I turned up and Sly blew my brains out.'

In August 2000 Kay predicted the remake would not be well received in Britain. 'We're going to get crushed in London,' he told *Entertainment Weekly*. 'It doesn't matter what we bring – they're going to kill us. It's tantamount to a British filmmaker remaking Martin Scorsese's *Mean Streets*

(1973).' Released in the US during October 2000 with an R rating, the picture was derided by critics. It grossed less than $15 million.

In Britain, Mike Hodges told *Empire* that nobody had contacted him about the remake. 'I gather Carter's got a goatee beard and it's a redemptive film and at the end of it he survives,' the director said. 'So it's patently a completely different film. It seems to me like they've just kept the title.' The remake never reached British cinemas. It had to wait two years before being released directly to video and DVD.

In 2001 Caine told *Empire* he had never seen the remake. 'I thought maybe it would work. Sly's a friend of mine, which is why I did it. I didn't know anything about the movie. I mean, I take responsibility for the ones where my name's over the title. Otherwise…'

A year later, Caine's memories of the film had soured further. 'The moment I arrived on set, I didn't like it,' he told an interviewer for the Australian edition of *Empire*. 'I only worked for two days but they weren't two of the happiest days of my life. I just felt, what the hell am I doing here?'

Even if you've never seen the 1971 original, this film is unlikely to satisfy. A triumph of style over substance, the new *Get Carter* tries to create a hybrid of violent action and moody melodrama. Instead the film creates a right old mess, wasting a strong supporting cast and nearly two hours in the life of anybody who watches it. The new version abandons the original's powerful nihilism for a half-baked tale of redemption and forgiveness. Stallone never shows a fraction of his predecessor's depth or implacability. Caine only appears in four scenes. If you want a good Stallone movie, look elsewhere. If you want to watch an updated *Get Carter*, try *The Limey* (1999) – it's a lot better than this tripe.

HALF MOON STREET (1986)

Cast: Sigourney Weaver (Lauren Slaughter), Michael Caine (Lord Bulbeck), Patrick Kavanagh (General Sir George Newhouse), Faith Kent (Lady Newhouse), Ram John Holder (Lindsay Walker), Keith Buckley (Hugo Van Arkady), Ann Hanson (Mrs Van Arkady), Patrick Newman (Julian Shuttle), Niall O'Brien (Captain Twilley), Nadim Sawalha (Karim Hatami), Vincent Lindon (Sonny).

Crew: Bob Swaim (director/co-writer), Geoffrey Reeve (producer), Edward Behr (co-writer), Richard Harvey (music), Peter Hannan (cinematography), Richard Marden (editor), Anthony Curtis (production designer).

Dr Lauren Slaughter is an American academic working at the Institute for Middle Eastern Strategic Studies in London. The job is prestigious but the poor pay barely covers the rent for her rundown bedsit.

Dr Slaughter struggles to overcome entrenched establishment attitudes and, when anonymously sent a videotape about high-class prostitutes, she decides to become an escort – but on her own terms. Among her clients are a rich Palestinian called Karim and Britain's leading expert on the Middle East, Lord Bulbeck. Karim arranges for Dr Slaughter to take over his flat in Half Moon Street. She becomes romantically involved with Lord Bulbeck, who is busy arranging a secret peace summit near London and agrees to have dinner at her flat, despite security concerns. Dr Slaughter is attacked in her flat by a would-be assassin. She kills him but is then held hostage by Karim. The Palestinian is using her as bait to ensnare and murder Lord Bulbeck. Dr Slaughter is rescued by British security forces, who shoot Karim dead.

Two people from different worlds…

Can their love survive Half Moon Street?

AN RKO PICTURES/EDWARD R. PRESSMAN FILM CORP. PRESENTATION
A GEOFF REEVE PRODUCTION • A BOB SWAIM FILM

Sigourney Weaver
Michael Caine
Half Moon Street

'IT'S AN HONOURABLE FAILURE WHICH BOASTS AN INTERESTING SUBJECT AND AN INTELLIGENT PERFORMANCE FROM WEAVER. CAINE COULD HAVE DONE WITHOUT HIS GLUE-ON MOUSTACHE.' ***DAILY TELEGRAPH***

'*HALF MOON STREET* IS A HALF-BAKED EXCUSE FOR A FILM THAT IS REDEEMED NOT A WHIT BY HAVING SIGOURNEY WEAVER AND MICHAEL

CAINE IN THE STARRING ROLES.'
VARIETY

Half Moon Street was adapted from *Dr Slaughter*, a novel by Paul Theroux. In 1987, producer Geoff Reeve told *What's On* magazine about the film's genesis: 'I am a voracious book reader. I read *Dr Slaughter* and was really grabbed by its sardonic, almost brittle, approach to a story, which is fundamentally about a girl taking on the British establishment. There was an outsider's look at London, whether or not one liked the perception of the place. I gambled a huge amount of money to buy the rights because I thought it was a hot property.'

Reeve said he had wanted an outsider as director. He picked Bob Swaim after seeing the director's previous picture, *La Balance* (1982), a tough thriller that was a box-office hit and a critical success in France. Swaim and Edward Behr adapted the story for the big screen. 'My attitude is very simple,' Swaim told *Films and Filming* in 1986. 'A book is a book and a film is a film. The two creatures are very different. I create the whole story just as much as if I was working from an idea overheard in a bar.' The screenplay went through six drafts.

For the lead role of *Dr Slaughter* rising star Sigourney Weaver was chosen, having just finished the science fiction sequel *Aliens* (1986). Caine was cast as Lord Bulbeck, although he was nearly 20 years younger than Bulbeck

ABOVE:
Lord Bulbeck cooks a traditional English fry-up for American call girl Lauren Slaughter (Sigourney Weaver) in *Half Moon Street* (1986).

in Theroux's novel. *Half Moon Street* began shooting on locations around London and on set at Elstree Studios in the summer of 1985. But Reeve was not happy with the results. 'For the first time in my life I felt my own power reducing,' the producer told *What's On*. 'Heavyweight US agents came in and the script changed. It did become something of a studio picture, rather than be shot on locations. I felt positively excluded from any decision making. It was a lesson … an unhappy one as far as I'm concerned.'

Caine told the *Sunday Express* he had enjoyed working on the movie: 'It's the ideal sort of film for me. A short shooting schedule in a nice place with nice people. A film takes a lot of time out of your life so you'd better be sure you're going to be happy with the people and the place. *Half Moon Street* is great on both counts. I can't see myself going to the Antarctic with a load of people I hate just to get an Oscar nomination.' Caine obviously got on well with Reeve – this film was the first of five they have made together.

The movie opened in the US in September 1986. It was unpopular with critics and the public, grossing just over a million dollars. Response to the film was just as poor in the UK several months later, although some reviewers praised Weaver's performance. It was released on video in 1987 but has since been deleted. A DVD version was issued in North America in June 2003.

'Muddled' is the politest way to describe this movie. It tries to be a romance, a thriller, a political intrigue and an anti-establishment blow for feminism – and fails in all four. Things happen, more things happen, and finally a deus ex machina rescues Dr Slaughter just before the film stops. There is little emotional development in any of the characters, while seemingly important subplots are introduced and then

forgotten. The vignettes of Weaver as sex worker are laughably unerotic. Attempts to make a point about gender politics are delivered with sledgehammer subtlety. Caine strolls through a film that offers him nothing more challenging than sporting a moustache. It's hard to give a damn about this film or anyone in it.

THE HAND (1981)

Cast: Michael Caine (Jon Lansdale), Andrea Marcovicci (Anne Lansdale), Annie McEnroe (Stella Roche), Bruce McGill (Brian Ferguson), Viveca Lindfors (doctress), Rosemary Murphy (Karen Wagner), Mara Hobel (Lizzie Lansdale). Crew: Oliver Stone (director/writer), Edward R Pressman (producer), James Horner (music), King Baggot (cinematography), Richard Marks (editor), John Michael Riva (production designer).

Jon Lansdale is a cartoonist, writing and drawing the newspaper adventure strip *Mandro*. Dissatisfied with their life in the Vermont countryside, his wife Anne wants a trial separation and intends to take their young daughter Lizzie to New York with her. The couple are arguing about the move when Jon's right hand is severed in a car crash. The hand is lost and Jon is left handicapped, unable to draw for a living. He begins to have blackouts and sees visions of the severed hand. Jon accepts an offer to teach at a college in California, but Anne and Lizzie stay behind on the East Coast until Christmas. Jon makes friends with another teacher, Brian, and has an affair with a pupil called Stella.

Brian and Stella make plans to go away for two weeks to Los Angeles. Brian tells Jon the trip will be non-stop sex, unaware that Jon himself is sleeping with Stella. But she disappears before the pair can leave. Anne and Lizzie visit Jon in California. Brian accosts

Jon and accuses him of sleeping with Stella, whereupon he is murdered. Anne tells Jon she is leaving him for good and taking Lizzie with her. Jon is furious, and Anne is attacked and nearly strangled to death. The police are called and discover the corpses of Stella and Brian concealed in Jon's car. He is declared criminally insane and locked away.

> 'STONE TAKES A CONSIDERABLE RISK IN MAKING HIS HERO A BASTARD. CAINE GIVES A CREEPY FLARING-NOSTRIL-AND-BARED-FANG PERFORMANCE.'
> *NEW YORK* **MAGAZINE**

> 'MICHAEL CAINE … SPENDS MOST OF HIS TIME SWEATING AND GRIMACING INTO THE CAMERA LENS. IT'S NOT A PRETTY SIGHT.' ***VARIETY***

Oliver Stone won an Oscar for best adapted screenplay in April 1979 for *Midnight Run* (1979). The filmmaker had already directed one feature, a surrealistic horror movie called *Seizure* (1974). He wanted his next project to be an adaptation of a Vietnam memoir called *Born on the Fourth of July*. Stone spent a year writing the script and working with various directors. At one point Al Pacino was attached, but finance for the project fell through. So Stone returned to the horror genre for his next feature.

'Part of the reason I did *The Hand*,' Stone told *Playboy* in 1988, 'was that it was obvious studios weren't going to do the more dramatic material. I thought at least they'll do a horror movie. That's why I compromised, and I made a serious mistake. I wanted to work as a director. I really should have been directing *Platoon* or *Born on the Fourth of July*. [Stone eventually got to film those scripts in 1986 and 1989 respectively.] But there was no way they were

going to make those, let alone let me direct them.'

Instead Stone adapted Mark Brandel's novel *The Lizard's Tail* into *The Hand*, though the material relied on motifs from various Grand Guignol warhorses. The gifted artist losing a hand was taken from *The Hands of Orlac* (filmed in 1924, 1935 and 1960), while the marauding hand itself was lifted from *The Beast with Five Fingers* (1946) and numerous others.

Close to the end of shooting in 1980, the production was temporarily shut down by an actors' strike in Hollywood. Caine recalled working with Stone in an interview for *Venice* magazine in 2002: 'He was a very well-known screenwriter at that point. He decided he was going to direct this screenplay himself. I've always had a thing where I'll work with a first-time director sometimes. I did it with Ken Russell and I did it with Oliver. [In fact both Stone and Russell had directed a feature before working with Caine.] Ken Russell worked out all right with *Billion Dollar Brian* (1967), but *The Hand* didn't work so well. You've got to

be willing to give people a shot in this business. Oliver, of course, has gone on to become one of the great American directors.'

Caine said that he knew Stone had potential. 'I just didn't get it in my turn. He talked to me about *Platoon* quite a lot because I was an ex-infantryman myself, and so was he. There's always a little bit of a bond between ex-infantrymen. We also talked quite a bit about the JFK assassination, and how there was no way Oswald could have been the lone gunman.' For his part, Stone told *Playboy* that he had spent half his time on *The Hand* arguing with Caine. And at the 2000 *Empire* Awards he joked about having made the actor so depressed that Caine required medication to get over the experience.

The R-rated film was released to US cinemas in April 1981. Critics were not kind to *The Hand* and it grossed just under $2.5 million. The movie is a rare example of a Caine film that never received a cinema release in the UK. It turned up on video several years later, rated 18 by the BBFC. It is one of only two Oliver Stone films as yet un-issued on DVD.

The Hand tries to be both a psychological thriller and a slice of schlock horror. The movie never definitively states whether it is Caine's character or his disembodied hand killing people. Such ambiguity is an admirable goal, but Stone fails to achieve it. The special effects hand by Carlo Rambaldi (who next created *ET* for Spielberg) is clumsily rendered, while all the gushing red blood just screams tomato sauce. Stone's attempts at adding psychological depth are only puddle-deep. Caine plays his part with conviction but cannot save the film. He wisely stayed away from horror hereafter. The best fun to be had with this film is laughing at the risible effects and Caine's extraordinary hairstyle. The madder his character gets, the bigger his hair becomes. By the end of *The Hand*, the actor is almost sporting a white man's Afro.

HANNAH AND HER SISTERS (1986)

Cast: Barbara Hershey (Lee), Carrie Fisher (April), Michael Caine (Elliot), Mia Farrow (Hannah), Dianne Wiest (Holly), Maureen O'Sullivan (Norma), Lloyd Nolan (Evan), Max Von Sydow (Frederick), Woody Allen (Mickey). Crew: Woody Allen (director/writer), Robert Greenhut (producer), Carlo Di Palma (cinematography), Susan E Morse (editor), Stuart Wurtzel (production designer).

New York couple Elliot and Hannah host a Thanksgiving dinner for their extended family and friends. Elliot is infatuated with Lee, one of Hannah's sisters. Hannah lends money to her other sister Holly, a failed actress. Hannah's first husband is a hypochondriac TV comedy producer, Mickey, who visits a doctor about hearing loss and gets sent for further tests. Elliot woos Lee, claiming his marriage to Hannah is almost over. Tests prove that Mickey does not have a brain tumour. He is overjoyed, then depressed by the knowledge that he will still die some day. He quits his job and begins searching for a meaning to life. Elliot and Lee have a passionate affair, while Holly abandons acting to become a writer. At the next Thanksgiving dinner Lee tells Elliot the affair is over; she is seeing someone new. Elliot and Hannah are reconciled. Holly bumps into Mickey, with whom she once had a disastrous date. He is a much happier person, having contemplated suicide. Mickey concluded that life is too precious to waste, even if it has no meaning. A year later, at the Thanksgiving dinner, Holly tells her new husband Mickey that she is pregnant...

'THE ACTING IN *HANNAH* IS UNIFORMLY EXCELLENT, AND MICHAEL CAINE FITS INTO THE ALLEN REPERTORY COMPANY WITH

EVIDENT RELISH.' *SUNDAY TIMES*

'IT ISN'T THAT MR CAINE'S PERFORMANCE IS ALL THAT DIFFERENT FROM OTHER ROLES HE'S HAD … IT'S JUST THAT *HANNAH AND HER SISTERS* MAKES BETTER US OF HIS WISE, MELLOW, COMICALLY SELF-AWARE TALENTS THAN ANY FILM HE'S BEEN IN SINCE JOHN HUSTON'S *THE MAN WHO WOULD BE KING*.' *NEW YORK TIMES*

Woody Allen was inspired to write *Hannah and Her Sisters* after reading Leo Tolstoy's *Anna Karenina*. Allen told *Cinema Papers* that he thought it would be fun to adapt the book's storytelling techniques to a contemporary comedy. The writer-director cast many of his frequent collaborators in the film, but added several newcomers to his ensemble – including Caine. 'I've always been a great fan of his,' Allen explained. 'He's one of the few people around who can play serious *and* comedy. I wanted a normal man … just a regular man who could play both serious and comic, where you could see him suffer a little and he could also get some laughs … Michael seems to have a bigger scope than most actors: he just *can* play those things.'

'I took the role to get comedy experience,' Caine said in an interview with *Arena* magazine

BELOW: Caine won his first Oscar for playing the adulterous Elliot in *Hannah and Her Sisters* (1986), here hugging his on-screen wife Hannah (Mia Farrow).

in 1988, 'so that people would think of me being able to play comedy. Woody choosing me to do *Hannah* made me respectable as a comedy actor. Woody casts for what he needs. He didn't have anyone for my part so he asked me. I was only on set four weeks.' The $7 million movie was shot on location in New York during 1985, with an opera sequence filmed in Turin.

At the time Allen was in a long-term relationship with actress Mia Farrow, who played Caine's wife in the film. 'That was a wonderful experience, doing that film,' Caine told *Venice* magazine in 2002. 'I've known Mia since she was 16 or 17, so acting with her was easy. It was a bit like working with a family because our apartment in the film was her apartment in real life. It was all very sort of intimate, doing scenes in her bed with her lover directing us.' Caine added that Allen rarely gave him any direction on set: 'Woody just lets you go your own way, and you wind up with a performance.'

Caine recalled the shoot in his acting masterclass. 'Woody Allen just puts it all on film right from the start, so that the rehearsal and the take become indistinguishable. He just keeps shooting and shooting it.' Caine said some scenes in Farrow's apartment required 12 hours to light, such was the complexity involved. 'Woody rehearses everything down to the tiniest detail; his camera becomes a microscope. His pictures may look as if they are ad-libbed, but they are brought to that point by solid rehearsal, rehearsal, rehearsal.'

Allen significantly altered *Hannah and Her Sisters* after initial filming was complete. 'The whole of the second Thanksgiving party ... was an afterthought,' he told *Cinema Papers*. In the original script, there were only two parties: one at the beginning, one at the end. But after seeing a rough cut of the film, Allen decided he needed another sequence to provide character and plot development. 'I went out and shot the entire sequence ... some old scenes and some brand new scenes.'

Hannah and Her Sisters was released in the US in February 1986. Warmly praised by the critics, the film also became one of Allen's biggest box-office hits, grossing more than $40 million. It reached the UK in July 1986, taking $4 million. Across the Atlantic Allen's film was highly placed on many critics' Top 10 lists for the year, prompting talk of Oscar nominations. It won the best musical or comedy award at the Golden Globes, with Caine's performance among four other nominations received. At the BAFTAs Allen won prizes for his direction and script, while Caine was among six other nominations for the film.

When the Oscar nominations were announced in February 1987, Caine was one of those nominated as best supporting actor. Three times before he had attended the ceremony as a nominee for best actor, but had left empty-handed. 'I thought, "Sod it, I'm not turning up again,"' Caine recalled during his NFT interview in 1998. The actor was on location in the Bahamas shooting a small but lucrative role in *Jaws the Revenge* (1987) when the Oscar ceremony was held in March. Caine won, beating Willem Dafoe, Tom Berenger, Denholm Elliott and Dennis Hopper. The award came as a complete surprise to Caine. 'The film had been released in February, before the previous year's Oscars were given. Woody Allen was anti-Oscar, and there was no campaign,' the actor remarked in 2003. *Hannah and Her Sisters* also won awards for Dianne Wiest as best supporting actress and for Allen's original screenplay.

Caine considers the film a turning point in his career. 'I was beginning to change from leading man to character leading man,' he told *Variety* in 2000, 'like a teenager going through his awkward moment.' Certainly, his career reached a significant peak in 1986. The next ten years saw Caine struggling to find great roles and further opportunities to work with acclaimed directors.

What a wonderful film this is – funny and thoughtful, with the perfect balance of humour and pathos. *Hannah and Her Sisters* succeeds in juggling half a dozen major storylines and just as many subplots. This is one of Allen's warmest films, with a rare happy ending. Caine gives a fine performance, fitting in seamlessly with actors familiar from so many Allen pictures. The whole ensemble is a joy to watch. The only regret is that Caine hasn't worked with Allen again.

HARRY AND WALTER GO TO NEW YORK (1976)

Cast: James Caan (Harry Dighby), Elliott Gould (Walter Hill), Michael Caine (Adam Worth), Diane Keaton (Lissa Chestnut), Charles Durning (Rufus T Crisp), Lesley Ann Warren (Gloria Fontaine), Val Avery (Chatsworth), Jack Gilford (Mischa), Carol Kane (Florence), Kathryn Grody (Barbara), David Proval (Ben).
Crew: Mark Rydell (director), Don Devlin and Harry Gittes (producers), John Byrum and Robert Kaufman (writers), David Shire (music), Laszlo Kovacs (cinematography), Fredric Steinkamp, David Bretherton and Don Guidice (editors), Harry Horner (production designer).

Harry and Walter, bumbling entertainers on the American vaudeville circuit in 1892, are arrested for petty theft and jailed in Massachusetts. Adam Worth, meanwhile, is a millionaire celebrity who indulges in safecracking just for the thrills. Worth is arrested for cracking the safe of a bank in Lowell, Massachusetts, the manager of which – Rufus T Crisp – brags that his *new* bank is invulnerable. Worth is sent to prison in Massachusetts, but even there he is treated like royalty. Harry and Walter become his servants.

Having got hold of the blueprints for Crisp's new bank, the safecracker is visited by reporter Lissa Chestnut and a photographer from the *Advocate*, a people's paper published in New York. She invites Harry and Walter to visit her office when they are released. The bumbling pair use the *Advocate*'s camera to take a photo of the blueprints but in the process set fire to the plans, infuriating Worth.

Harry and Walter escape and travel to New York. They join the *Advocate*'s staff in order to retrieve the photo of the blueprints. But Worth reappears, having been released from prison. He threatens Lissa, her co-workers and Walter until Harry hands over the photo. Both sides race to rob Crisp's bank in Massachusetts first. Harry, Walter and friends succeed, using Worth's own plan. Back in New York Harry and Walter are welcomed to the criminal elite, with Worth leading the plaudits.

'IT'S NOT THE FAULT OF MICHAEL CAINE THAT *HARRY AND WALTER GO TO NEW YORK* IS A FOUR-STAR FLOP. CAINE AND MISS KEATON DO THEIR BEST TO SALVAGE SOMETHING FROM THE CHAOS, BUT THEY ARE CLOBBERED BY THE CRUDE FOOLING OF CAAN AND GOULD.'
DAILY MIRROR

'THIS FILM FAILS TO WORK AS A LIGHT COMEDY, AS A PERIOD PIECE, AS A JIGSAW PUZZLE … MAINLY, IT JUST SITS THERE AND DIES.'
NEW YORK POST

Harry and Walter Go to New York (*Harry and Walter* hereafter) began as a story by Don Devlin and John Byrum. This was adapted into a screenplay by Byrum and Robert Kaufman for

Mark Rydell to direct. Rydell had achieved some success as an actor, while his directing credits included work for both TV and the cinema. *Harry and Walter* was a lavishly mounted production, predominantly shot at Burbank Studios in California. An old penitentiary in Ohio was used for the prison scenes.

Caine was cast in the role of Adam Worth, gentleman safecracker and celebrity thief. He was interviewed on set by *Viva* magazine in 1975, explaining his criteria for choosing the project: 'How interesting is the part? Who will I be working with? Are they going to spend enough money on the production to get quality?' After a decade of success in cinema, Caine said he had no intention of returning to theatre acting. 'I associate the stage with misery, struggle, hardship, and no money. But motion pictures

have meant riches and delirious happiness. I keep reading about movie actors, particularly British actors, who say they need to "return to the well" – to legitimate theatre – to purify their art. But I definitely don't need any more of that.'

In January 1976 Caine told the *Evening Standard* about making *Harry and Walter*. 'The role I had in this film was entirely different for me. I play an American who has had an Oxford education and speaks with a posh Oxford accent. He aspires to being an English gentleman. I had to revert to my *Zulu* accent. James Caan and Elliott Gould are also in the film. We were just like three mates. I've known them a long time.'

Harry and Walter was lambasted by American reviewers and ignored by audiences when released in 1976. It reached the UK in August that year and bombed again, with critics being particularly savage about Caan and Gould. The film was issued on DVD for the US market in 2002.

This film is apparently only 111 minutes long, but it feels more like a three-hour epic by the time it finally finishes. For something billed as a period comedy, *Harry and Walter Go to New York* is painfully unfunny. A lot of money was spent making this movie look good, but the cash would have been better invested in a decent script. Rydell's direction drains all life from the screen, aided and abetted by a succession of one-note characterisations. Caan and Gould try to evoke the spirit of Laurel and Hardy, but only achieve tiresome clowning and laboured slapstick. Caine gives a measured, dignified performance in the midst of the general hysteria. Avoid.

THE HOLCROFT COVENANT (1985)

Cast: Michael Caine (Noel Holcroft), Anthony Andrews (Johann Tennyson), Victoria Tennant (Helden Tennyson), Lilli Palmer (Althene Holcroft), Mario Adorf (Jürgen Mass), Michael Lonsdale (Manfredi), Bernard Hepton (Leighton), Richard Munch (Oberst), Carl Rigg (Beaumont), Andre Penvern (Leger).
Crew: John Frankenheimer (director), Edie Landau and Ely Landau (producers), George Axelrod, Edward Anhalt and John Hopkins (writers), Stanislas (music), Gerry Fisher (cinematography), Ralph Sheldon (editor), Peter Mullins (production designer).

In 1945 three Nazi generals make a suicide pact, a covenant concerning a fortune stored in a Swiss bank account. Forty years later, New York-based architect Noel Holcroft is invited to Geneva to learn about the covenant. One of the dead Nazis was his father, and the three eldest sons of the dead generals are to take charge of $4.5 billion, with Holcroft as chairman. The money is to be used to right wrongs done by the Nazis.

In London Holcroft encounters an anti-Nazi group led by a man called Oberst. The architect also meets siblings Johann and Helden Tennyson. Johann is another heir to the covenant. Holcroft and Helden travel to Berlin, where they find the third heir, Jürgen Mass. Holcroft and Helden become lovers. Johann murders Oberst and Holcroft's mother, revealing himself to be a neo-Nazi.

The three heirs and Helden gather in Geneva to activate the covenant. Aware of Johann's treachery, Holcroft discovers that Helden is in league with her brother. After signing the covenant, Holcroft calls a press conference and tells the world's media about Johann's plan to create global anarchy and launch a new world order. Johann pulls a revolver. In the struggle both Mass and Johann are killed. Afterwards, Holcroft gives Helden a choice – kill herself or kill him…

> 'ROBERT LUDLUM'S BOOKS MAY BE CONFUSING, BUT THE FILMS BASED UPON THEM ARE WELL NIGH INDECIPHERABLE. CAINE GIVES FAR MORE THAN THE ROLE OF THE PUZZLED HEIR DESERVES.'
> **SUNDAY TELEGRAPH**

> 'MICHAEL CAINE IS THE ONLY DIGNIFIED ELEMENT IN THIS NAZI-REVIVAL HOKUM THRILLER, WHICH MAKES EVEN THE ORIGINAL ROBERT LUDLUM NOVEL LOOK LIKE A MASTERPIECE.' **MAIL ON SUNDAY**

Robert Ludlum's complex thriller *The Holcroft Covenant* was first published in 1978 and

became an international bestseller. Producers
Edie and Ely Landau acquired the film rights to
several Ludlum novels, but were determined to
retain control of this particular project by raising
the finance for it themselves. An initial
adaptation was written by Edward Anhalt
and John Hopkins. When director John
Frankenheimer was brought on board, he
recruited screenwriter George Axelrod. The pair
had worked together on the acclaimed political
thriller *The Manchurian Candidate* (1962).

American actor James Caan had already

been cast as Holcroft when Frankenheimer joined the project. 'He really was miscast,' the director told *Films and Filming* during shooting. 'Three things happened at the same time. Firstly he was miscast. Secondly he was emotionally upset at the time. Thirdly he was fighting with the producers for months and I didn't know that. The three things really fused together and you had a situation where it just could not work.' Caan pulled out just as the picture was entering production. The director was forced to start shooting without a leading man, otherwise the film would have collapsed altogether.

'We were terribly lucky to get Michael Caine for the role,' Frankenheimer says on the film's DVD commentary. 'I sent the script to him and he agreed to do it. We were so fortunate. He's not only a brilliant actor, he can just inspire a crew. He's a joy to work with.' Caine had just finished the comedy *Water* in June 1984 and was going on holiday. Instead he had only a weekend off before starting work on *The Holcroft Covenant*. 'He really saved this picture,' Frankenheimer says. 'Michael came in and acted as if he'd been cast for years. He just owned the part.'

The Holcroft Covenant was filmed on location in Germany and around London, with studio work at Twickenham. For Caine, the project fulfilled a long-held ambition to work with Frankenheimer. 'I get on very well with John, we have a rapport going,' the actor told *Films and Filming* during production. 'I think it is because he's also worked with a lot of troublesome actors and I am the least troublesome of actors to work with on a movie set. I just do it and get in a car and go home.' Caine was proud he had been thought sufficiently marketable in the US for the role. 'Normally another American actor would have replaced James Caan, but to all intents and purposes I *am* another American actor!'

The film was released in Britain with a 15 rating in September 1985, but reviews were poor. Critics complained about muddled plotting and a lack of credibility in the story, but reserved praise for Caine's efforts. The picture grossed less than $400,000 in the US.

Caine recalled the production during an interview for *Venice* magazine in 2002, just a few months after Frankenheimer had died. 'Oh, I loved John. I thought he was a great guy, very easy to work with. The film we did didn't turn out too well, although it was done under very extraordinary circumstances, so it really wasn't our fault.'

The Holcroft Covenant is a jumbled failure, trying to turn a 500-page suspense novel into a coherent two-hour film. The dialogue is confined to either endless exposition or cryptic comments, leaving the viewer simultaneously bored and confused. Attempts at injecting life into the one-dimensional characters are, sadly, few and far between. This story might have been better as a mini-series, but the raw material still stretches credulity far past breaking point. Caine does his best with a thankless role in a film that simply doesn't work.

THE HONORARY CONSUL (1983)
(US title: *BEYOND THE LIMIT*

Cast: Michael Caine (Charley Fortnum), Richard Gere (Dr Plarr), Bob Hoskins (Colonel Perez), Elpidia Carrilo (Clara), Joaquim De Almeida (Leon), A Martinez (Aquino), Stephanie Cotsirilos (Marta), Domingo Ambriz (Diego), Eric Valdez (Pablo), Nicolas Jasso (Miguel), Geoffrey Maguire (British Ambassador), Leonard Maguire (Dr Humphries).
Crew: John Mackenzie (director), Norma Heyman (producer), Christopher Hampton

RIGHT: British diplomat Charley Fortnum comforts his wife Clara (Elpidia Carrilo) after her lover is killed in *The Honorary Consul* (1983).

FAR RIGHT: Charley Fortnum contemplates his future in *The Honorary Consul* (1983).

(writer), Stanley Myers (music), Phil Meheux (cinematography), Stuart Baird (editor), Allan Cameron (production designer).

Dr Eduardo Plarr moves to a city in Northern Argentina, close to the Paraguayan border, and encounters an alcoholic called Charlie Fortnum, Britain's honorary consul to the region. Fortnum takes Plarr to a local brothel where a beautiful girl catches the doctor's eye. Plarr's father went missing in Paraguay two years earlier and the doctor asks for help in finding him from the local police chief, Perez. Plarr is approached by Leon,

an old friend from Paraguay, who claims that a man called Aquino has news of Plarr's father. The doctor returns to the brothel but the beautiful girl is gone.

Fortnum asks Plarr to examine his wife, Clara, and the doctor is surprised to discover that she is the girl from the brothel. Plarr and Clara have an affair and she becomes pregnant with his child. Aquino and Leon tell Plarr his father is a prisoner in Paraguay. The pair enlist the doctor's aid in abducting the visiting American ambassador. But Leon's men snatch Fortnum by mistake. Perez reveals that Plarr's father

was shot dead trying to escape a year ago.

Plarr visits Leon and the other revolutionaries in the tin shack where they are holding Fortnum hostage. Leon admits lying to secure the doctor's help. The kidnappers won't let Plarr leave. Leon says the doctor is jealous of Fortnum's ability to love. Fortnum overhears Plarr bragging that the unborn baby is his. The security forces surround the shack and kill one of the revolutionaries. When Plarr goes outside, he is shot too. The kidnappers are all killed. Perez has Plarr executed. Afterwards, Fortnum and Clara are reconciled. The consul says they will call the baby Eduardo, if it's a boy.

'STRONG TALENTS ON BOTH SIDES OF THE CAMERA HAVEN'T MANAGED TO BREATHE LIFE INTO THIS INTRICATE TALE OF EMOTIONAL AND POLITICAL BETRAYAL, AND RESULT IS A STEADY DOSE OF TEDIUM.' *VARIETY*

'UNFORTUNATELY RICHARD GERE … IS TOO MUCH A FILM STAR – IE, SOMEONE BIGGER THAN THE PARTS HE PLAYS – AND CANNOT CONVEY THE MAN WITHIN. MICHAEL CAINE, ON THE OTHER HAND, AS THE CONSUL, HAS NEVER BEEN BETTER.' *SUNDAY TIMES*

Adapting the novels of Graham Greene has long proven a challenge for filmmakers. *The Honorary Consul* was first published in 1973, but nearly a decade elapsed before a cinema adaptation began shooting. Producer Norma Heyman acquired the film rights and hired playwright Christopher Hampton to adapt the novel.

British director John Mackenzie joined the project, having attracted critical acclaim with his London gangster drama *The Long Good Friday*

(1980), starring Bob Hoskins. In an exclusive interview for this book, Mackenzie recalled the problems he faced: 'It's a fiendishly difficult thing to adapt, Graham Greene's work. The stories are often quite melodramatic. It's the background and characters and philosophic content that raise them to the level they're at. *The Honorary Consul* was certainly one of those.'

When Mackenzie joined the film, Heyman had interest from both Caine and American actor Richard Gere. The director confesses to early doubts about Caine's suitability for the role of Fortnum. 'I didn't associate Michael Caine with this class of guy, your public school educated minor diplomat with a drink problem. A lot of people think of Michael Caine as a corblimey guy who can do corblimey parts with a bit of humour in them. But when we got involved in doing it, I got excited by him. My prejudices changed. He found qualities in the part that certainly superseded any of my other worries. He has this depth to draw on, he can make the characters interesting and different in each film.'

Mackenzie spent two weeks in Argentina researching the background to the film. He decided it was the perfect place to shoot the movie and also convinced Heyman of this. But the day after the pair left Argentina, the South American country invaded the Falkland Islands, precipitating a war with Britain. As a result location filming was shifted to Mexico, with studio shooting at Shepperton near London.

Just as the production began, a film called *An Officer and a Gentleman* became a box-office hit in America. 'It made Richard Gere a sex symbol and a superstar,' Mackenzie recalled. 'When you've got someone like that in your film it can be very difficult.' *The Honorary Consul* was financed by Paramount, which began taking more interest in Mackenzie's picture. 'We had these ridiculous arguments with these ignorant people, who were looking after their assets.

They said, "You can't make him talk in any voice but his own." There were lots of calls through the night on telephones from LA.'

The film was released in the US in September 1983, where Paramount insisted it be renamed *Beyond the Limit* because American audiences would not know what a consul was – honorary or otherwise. 'We had lots of fights about that,' Mackenzie recalled. 'But in the end you can't do anything about it. You hand in the film and they change the title. I said no way can you change the title for Britain, we are not that ignorant.' The R-rated movie got mediocre reviews, with Gere pilloried for his accent. *Beyond the Limit* grossed just under $6 million in the US.

In Britain the original title was retained, but critical reaction was just as mixed when the 18-rated film was released in December 1983. Caine was nominated as best actor at the BAFTAs for his work on *The Honorary Consul*, but instead won the award for his performance in *Educating Rita* (1983). Soon afterwards the actor was approached by Greene in a London restaurant. 'Graham told me he didn't like *The Honorary Consul*,' Caine recalled for *Hello* in 2002. 'I mean, he really gave me an ear-bashing on that film. But he insisted he liked me in it. I don't know whether he *really* did or he just felt sorry for me.'

The Honorary Consul makes for an interesting contrast with *The Quiet American* (2002). Both are based on novels by Graham Greene, both were adapted by Christopher Hampton and both feature Caine as an ageing British expatriate with a young lover being wooed by another man. But *The Quiet American* is definitely the stronger film of the pair. *The Honorary Consul* makes a decent stab at adapting one of Greene's less cinema-friendly novels, but fails to convince. Although the film is suffused with the atmosphere of a seedy South

American border town, the script takes far too long to reach the moral dilemma at the heart of the story. Gere is a major handicap, thanks to his erratic accent and an inability to create empathy as Dr Plarr. Caine is outstanding as Fortnum, giving a masterly performance.

HURRY SUNDOWN (1967)

Cast: Michael Caine (Henry Warren), Jane Fonda (Julie Ann Warren), John Phillip Law (Rad McDowell), Diahann Carroll (Vivien Thurlow), Robert Hooks (Reeve Scott), Faye Dunaway (Lou McDowell), Burgess Meredith (Judge Purcell), Robert Reed (Lars Finchley), George Kennedy (Sheriff Coombs), Frank Converse (Clem De Lavery), Loring Smith (Thomas Elwell).
Crew: Otto Preminger (director/producer), Thomas C Ryan and Horton Foote (writers), Hugo Montenegro (music), Milton Krasner and Loyal Griggs (cinematography), Louis R Loeffler and James D Wells (editors), Gene Callahan (production designer).

Georgia farmer Rad McDowell returns home after serving in the Second World War. A new development has bought up all the surrounding land, except for the farms owned by Rad and his black neighbours, Rose Scott and her son Reeve. Rad refuses to sell his land, endangering a deal brokered by his ambitious cousin, Henry Warren. Rad is unhappy that his eldest son, Charles, is close to Henry. Henry sends his wife Julie to persuade Rose, who was her nanny years earlier. But Rose refuses and dies of a heart attack. Reeve and Rad form an alliance to improve their land by blasting irrigation channels.

Henry's troubled son Colie seriously injures himself while Henry tries to stop the blasting. Henry blames Reeve for the injury and tries to have the black farmer evicted, enlisting Julie's

help. The case goes to court, where a bigoted judge sides with Henry. But Rad provides documents that prove Reeve owns the disputed land. Julie discovers that Henry lied about the cause of Colie's injury and decides to divorce him. Determined to get revenge, he plants explosives above Rad's farm. But Charles is accidentally killed in the blast. Henry runs away, distraught. The local black community helps Rad reclaim his flooded land.

'MELODRAMA ON A GRAND SCALE … PERFORMANCES ARE SWAMPED BY A SCRIPT LIKE THIS. MICHAEL CAINE, DESPITE A FAIR SHOT AT A SOUTHERN DRAWL, IS WAY OUT OF HIS DEPTH.'

MONTHLY FILM BULLETIN

'OTTO PREMINGER HAS CREATED AN OUTSTANDING, TASTEFUL BUT HARD-HITTING, AND HANDSOMELY-PRODUCED FILM ABOUT RACIAL CONFLICT IN GEORGIA CIRCA 1945 … MICHAEL CAINE LEADS THE STARS, AND DELIVERS AN EXCELLENT PERFORMANCE…' **VARIETY**

Hurry Sundown was originally a thousand-page novel by K B Gilden, first published in two volumes in 1964. Director/producer Otto Preminger acquired the film rights and commissioned screenwriters Thomas C Ryan and Horton Foote to adapt the sprawling epic.

ABOVE: Co-stars Jane Fonda and Caine share a joke with director Otto Preminger during the filming of *Hurry Sundown* (1967). The tempestuous filmmaker drove other cast members to tears.

FAR LEFT: Ruthless tycoon Henry Warren rescues his son Colie (John Mark) from an explosion in *Hurry Sundown* (1967).

Preminger made a surprising choice for the leading role, casting London-born Caine as Southern bigot Henry Warren. The filmmaker approached him while Caine was in Hollywood shooting *Gambit* (1966) with Shirley MacLaine.

Mastering a Southern accent proved challenging for Caine. Preminger sent him voice tapes to practise with while the actor was working on *Funeral in Berlin* (1966). As soon as Caine finished the second Harry Palmer picture, he was flown to Louisiana to start work on *Hurry Sundown*. British journalist David Lewin visited the set and interviewed the leading man. Caine said he was not afraid that playing a racist would harm his public image: 'What I do is show the sadness of the man … The sadness of a man who destroys others and destroys himself. Nazis and racialists are yesterday's news. Everyone knows about them. I just feel sad for them.'

The production used both black and white actors. This caused problems during filming in Louisiana, where the civil rights movement was making headlines. The cast and crew had to be guarded by policemen and state troopers to protect them from the racist Ku Klux Klan organisation. One hotel initially refused to let black and white actors use the same swimming pool, until Preminger threatened to move everyone to another establishment. In the dining room black actors were insulted by other guests. Crew members were threatened with guns and production vehicles had their tyres slashed. 'We live in the compound of the hotel,' Caine told Lewin. 'It is like a stockade with armed guards on patrol.'

Austrian-born director Preminger was infamous for his fiery temper, but the leading man did not have problems. 'Otto was nice to me on *Hurry Sundown* but I didn't like how nasty he was to everyone else,' Caine told *Time Out* magazine in 1992. 'He was particularly nasty

to Faye Dunaway and I pulled him up on it. My attitude was if he says anything to me I'll fucking deck him.' Dunaway was making her movie debut on this picture.

Hurry Sundown opened in America in February 1967, attracting positive reviews. Critics were full of praise for Caine's Southern accent. In Britain reaction to the movie was less favourable, with Caine taking a drubbing from UK critics. Reviewers seemed unable or unwilling to see the actor as anything other than his Cockney public persona. A similar situation arose more than 30 years later when Caine adopted a New England accent for his role as Dr Larch in *The Cider House Rules* (1999).

They don't make them like this any more. *Hurry Sundown* is a sprawling, melodramatic epic about racism in which everything is writ large. The bad people are very bad and the good are very good, verging on the saintly. The contrast is so stark, it leaves little room for subtlety. A painfully slow first hour puts all the pieces in place before events build to a series of unconvincing climaxes. Caine's Southern accent isn't bad, it just sounds odd coming from him. Despite this, he gives a solid performance in an unsympathetic part. *Hurry Sundown* is best viewed for its curiosity value. How many films are there in which Jane Fonda simulates fellatio on a saxophone in order to arouse Michael Caine?

THE IPCRESS FILE (1965)

Cast: Michael Caine (Harry Palmer), Nigel Green (Dalby), Guy Doleman (Ross), Sue Lloyd (Jean), Gordon Jackson (Carswell), Aubrey Richards (Radcliffe), Frank Gatliff (Bluejay), Thomas Baptiste (Barney), Oliver MacGreevy

(Housemartin), Freda Bamford (Alice),
Pauline Winter (charlady), Anthony
Blackshaw (Edwards).
Crew: Sidney J Furie (director), Harry Saltzman
(producer), Bill Canaway and James Doran
(writers), John Barry (music), Otto Heller
(cinematography), Peter Hunt (editor),
Ken Adam (production designer).

British scientists are being abducted, with one,
Radcliffe, being taken from a London train.
Harry Palmer, meanwhile, is transferred to a
counter-espionage unit run by Major Dalby.
The prime suspects for the kidnappings are
a man called Grantby, codenamed Bluejay,
and his assistant, codenamed Housemartin.
The police arrest Housemartin near a warehouse,
but he is mysteriously murdered while in
custody. Palmer has the warehouse raided, but
it has already been vacated. Harry finds a tape
marked IPCRESS. Palmer is quizzed about the
case by his former boss, Colonel Ross from
the Ministry of Defence.

ABOVE: Harry Palmer protects fellow agent Jean Courtney (Sue Lloyd) in *The Ipcress File* (1965).

FAR RIGHT: Caine in the career-defining role of Harry Palmer in *The Ipcress File* (1965).

Dalby and Harry arrange to buy Radcliffe back from Grantby. At the exchange Palmer kills a US agent lurking in the shadows. Another US agent begins following Harry and threatens to kill him. The meaning of the word IPCRESS is discovered – it refers to brainwashing. An agent who borrows Palmer's car is murdered, having been mistaken for Harry. Palmer returns to his flat and finds the second US agent dead inside. The Ipcress file is stolen from Harry's desk. Palmer is abducted by Grantby and brainwashed, but manages to escape. Harry realises that either Dalby or Ross is working with Grantby. He confronts both men. Dalby is revealed as the traitor, ordering Palmer to murder Ross. But Harry kills Dalby in self-defence. Ross admits using Palmer as bait to catch Dalby.

'MICHAEL CAINE'S PERFORMANCE INSTALLS HIM AS THE FIRST MOD CONMAN OF THE NEW BRITISH CRIME WAVE.' *SUNDAY TELEGRAPH*

'MICHAEL CAINE WHO PLAYS HARRY PALMER IS THE NEW STYLE SECRET AGENT: EVERYTHING THAT JAMES BOND IS NOT AND ALL THE BETTER FOR IT.' *EVENING STANDARD*

Len Deighton's first novel, *The Ipcress File*, was published in 1962. The low-key espionage thriller, a stark contrast to the James Bond novels written by Ian Fleming, was told in the first person by an unnamed secret agent. The film rights were acquired by Charles D Kasher, who collaborated on the project with producer Harry Saltzman. Saltzman had produced the early Bond films in partnership with Albert Broccoli, but *The Ipcress File* required a different approach.

Christopher Plummer was offered the role of Harry Palmer, but turned it down in order to star in *The Sound of Music*. In a 1969 interview with *Films and Filming*, Caine recalled how he was offered the part: 'Saltzman saw *Zulu* and afterwards, I mean that same evening, he went to dinner at a restaurant … and I just happened to be there. He gave me the job just like that. Looking back, people imagine that my break came with *Zulu*. But quite honestly that's just what *didn't* happen, it was a year later … *The Ipcress File* made me a star.'

Canadian-born Sidney J Furie was hired to direct the movie. 'The whole idea was to do the opposite of Bond,' he explains on the film's DVD commentary. The project almost collapsed just before shooting was to begin, when its financing was withdrawn. Saltzman told Furie to start anyway, pledging to fund the production from his own pocket. 'He threatened Universal and Rank with a lawsuit and forced them to go ahead,' Furie says.

The Ipcress File was shot over three months on locations around London and at Pinewood Studios. Production designer Ken Adam transformed the rooms in a single house near Victoria Station into a series of sets, with Palmer's flat on the top floor. Saltzman and Furie clashed repeatedly during filming. 'The producer didn't like all the funny [camera] angles and what I was doing. Harry wanted me fired,' Furie says. Editor Peter Hunt was brought in

by Saltzman to assess what had been shot, wanting confirmation that Furie should be dismissed. Hunt refused to confirm Saltzman's suspicions and Furie stayed on the picture.

The director says he had no faith in the script: 'There were many scripts but we were never happy with them. The script was being rewritten every day. We could only shoot what had been written.' Furie was so upset by the script that he set fire to a copy during filming and then burst into tears. But he says Caine was able to get the best from the material. 'The dialogue on paper was nothing. Michael would give it this inflection – he made it work.' Furie adds that Caine was one of the greatest actors he ever worked with.

Problems continued during filming with studio bosses questioning the wisdom of having Palmer wear glasses and cook meals, as Caine recalled in a 2002 interview with *Venice* magazine: 'Up until that point, all heroes in action films had been perfect … With the glasses, we gave him an imperfection, to make him more like an ordinary person. Also, we had him cook a meal. One of the producers said, "No, no, you can't do that! Everyone will think he's gay!"' Caine pointed out that Harry was cooking for a woman in order to get her into bed, and the scene stayed. In the film it's Deighton's hands that are seen doing most of the cooking. The author's culinary newspaper column can also be seen pinned to Palmer's kitchen wall.

Caine talked about Harry Palmer in a 1965 interview with the *Evening News*. 'He's a very human fellow. We've gone for real people, and how they get out of real trouble. The things you remember about the Bond films are the Aston Martin, and the other gimmicky effects. In ours, if someone gets shot – they die. We work on the principle that the way to make a good thriller is to make it so realistic that everyone identifies with it.'

The Ipcress File reached British cinemas in

LEFT:
Palmer stalks the enemy operative codenamed Housemartin in *The Ipcress File* (1965).

March 1965, rated A. Most critics were full of praise for the anti-Bond film and it did brisk business at the box-office. *The Ipcress File* won BAFTAs for best British film, art direction and cinematography. Caine was nominated as best British actor and the screenplay also got a nomination. The picture reached US cinemas in August, where it impressed both reviewers and audiences. Caine told *Playboy* in 1967 that the film's success in the US had surprised him: 'I suppose I underestimated the intelligence of audiences, which people in show business do all the time. We made *The Ipcress File* very cheaply, expecting, if we were lucky, to break even or make a little profit. I thought it would be a rather specialised movie.'

In September 1999 the BFI took a poll of 1000 people within the industry to find the Top 100 British movies of the 20th century. *The Ipcress File* was one of seven Caine pictures on the list, being voted into 59th place. The US DVD release is superior to the UK one, with the film presented in widescreen and with a commentary track by Furie and Hunt. The UK disc is a budget price, full-screen version that utterly fails to convey the film's unusual and eye-catching cinematography.

Caine believes his film star status starts with *The Ipcress File* and you can see why. It's a great picture and a wonderful showcase for his burgeoning talent as a screen actor. He displays remarkable assurance in his first leading role, giving life and humanity to what could have been a very one-dimensional character. Furie's determination to shoot every scene from an unusual angle may irk some viewers, but it has kept this film feeling fresh nearly 40 years later, unlike subsequent Harry Palmer pictures. Mention must be made of John Barry's evocative score and the sparse sets by Ken Adam – both men giving the film a decidedly different flavour from the Bond features on which they also worked. *The Ipcress File* is among the best movies Caine made in the 1960s. But seek out the widescreen version so you can savour the full effect.

THE ISLAND (1980)

Cast: Michael Caine (Maynard), David Warner (Nau), Angela Punch McGregor (Beth), Frank Middlemass (Windsor), Don Henderson (Rollo), Dudley Sutton (Dr Brazil), Colin Jeavons (Hizzoner), Zakes Mokae (Wescott), Brad Sullivan (Stark), Jeffrey Frank (Justin). Crew: Michael Ritchie (director) Richard D Zanuck and David Brown (producers), Peter Benchley (writer), Ennio Morricone (music), Henri Decaë (cinematography), Richard A Harris (editor), Dale Hennesy (production designer).

Two thousand people and 600 boats have gone missing in three years near the Caribbean. Journalist Blair Maynard visits Miami to investigate the mystery, taking along his son Justin; the pair have not got on well since Justin's parents got divorced. All the boats having disappeared near an island called Navidad, Maynard and Justin go there and hire a fishing boat from an expatriate Brit called Windsor. Father and son are abducted by pirates and taken captive on an uncharted island. Maynard is kept alive as breeding stock, while Justin is brainwashed into believing his real father is Nau, leader of the pirates.

Maynard is overjoyed when he sees Windsor approaching the island in a boat. But Windsor is in league with the pirates. He says they have been on the island for 300 years, maintaining little contact with modern society. To him the pirates are a living anthropological specimen. Windsor tells Nau that a sailing ship is passing nearby. The pirates attack the ship,

which was smuggling cocaine. Maynard escapes the pirates but Justin refuses to go with him. A coastguard vessel approaches the island, searching for the drug smugglers. The pirates seize the ship and kill the crew. Maynard swims out to the vessel and kills nearly all the pirates. Nau orders Justin to murder Maynard, but the boy refuses. Maynard kills Nau and is reconciled with Justin as a coastguard helicopter arrives.

> '*THE ISLAND* IS A LETHARGIC VENTURE BY THE *JAWS* PRODUCTION TEAM INTO THE DUBIOUS TERRAIN OF CANNIBALISTIC DEGENERACY.'
> **THE OBSERVER**

> 'ONCE THE MYSTERY IS BANALLY RESOLVED … THE FILM DEGENERATES INTO A VIOLENT CHASE MELODRAMA. MICHAEL RITCHIE'S WITTY DIRECTION IS ABANDONED IN THE VIOLENCE.'
> **VARIETY**

Peter Benchley wrote the best-selling shark attack novel *Jaws*. It subsequently became a smash hit movie in 1975, directed by Steven Spielberg and produced by Richard D Zanuck and David Brown. Benchley followed that success with *The Deep*, which was also adapted into a successful film. When his novel *The Island* was published in 1979, Zanuck and Brown were quick to secure the film rights. Benchley wrote the screenplay himself, having co-written the previous two adaptations. Director Michael Ritchie was brought on board the $22 million project, having helmed notable films like *Downhill Racer* (1969) and political satire *The Candidate* (1972).

Caine was cast as journalist Blair Maynard. In an interview with *Film Comment* during shooting in August 1979, the actor said Benchley had always had him in mind for the character: 'I wanted this role very much. Universal didn't want me, they wanted to see if they could get an American actor.' Caine said the director and both producers wanted him to play Maynard and had got their way. Another attraction may have been the warm filming locations in Miami and Antigua. Caine had recently moved to America and said he hoped to get a better standard of script: 'I don't want to do any more schlock.' Unfortunately, his next three films were to be *Dressed to Kill* (1980), *The Hand* (1981) and *Victory* (1981).

Caine described *The Island* as a difficult film, because the subject matter could easily cause audience laughter in the wrong places.

'It's a modern pirate story, and when the pirates appear, the situation becomes very delicate. It's my job to control what the audience thinks about the pirates because I'm really the only representative of the audience who's there – in the film, I mean. And once you lose them, once they … decide things look foolish, it takes 20 minutes to get them back.'

The R-rated film reached US cinemas in June 1980, with the makers hoping for a summer box-office hit. William Goldman's book *Adventures in the Screen Trade* quotes producer David Brown about the differences between *Jaws* (1975) and *The Island*: 'We didn't know whether *Jaws* would work, but we didn't have any doubts about *The Island*. It had to be a smash.'

BELOW: Caine poses with writer Peter Benchley during shooting of *The Island* (1980). *Jaws* scribe Benchley had Caine in mind for the lead when creating the modern pirate story.

Everything worked. The screenplay worked. Every actor we sent it to said yes. I didn't know until a few days after we opened...' Brown encountered a studio executive in a bookstore: 'He said, "David, they don't want to see the picture."'

The Island grossed $15 million in the US but got pasted by critics. Caine's performance earned him a nomination as worst actor at the Razzie Awards, split between this film and *Dressed to Kill* (1980). *The Island* subsequently limped into British cinemas, where it was rated X.

You have to wonder how the producers of *The Island* could possibly think this film was a surefire hit. Sure, the novels of Peter Benchley had provided box-office gold in the past but *The Island* is simply awful, both banal and tedious. What little suspense the initial mystery generates is thrown away the moment the pirates start talking. The risible dialogue and their farcical appearance plunge the picture into a hole from which it cannot escape. Caine does his best to maintain some dignity in the face of overwhelming odds, but the film sinks beneath the weight of its own ludicrousness. Avoid.

THE ITALIAN JOB (1969)

Cast: Michael Caine (Charlie Croker), Noël Coward (Mr Bridger), Benny Hill (Professor Simon Peach), Raf Vallone (Altabani), Tony Beckley (Freddie), Rossano Brazzi (Beckerman), Maggie Blye (Lorna), Irene Handl (Miss Peach), John Le Mesurier (governor), Fred Emney (Birkinshaw), John Clive (garage manager). Crew: Peter Collinson (director), Michael Deeley (producer), Troy Kennedy Martin (writer), Quincy Jones (music), Douglas Slocombe (cinematography), John Trumper (editor), Disley Jones (production designer).

A criminal mastermind called Beckerman is murdered by the Mafia as he tries to leave Italy. In London Charlie Croker departs prison after two years inside, expecting to see Beckerman. Instead he is met by the dead man's widow, who hands over the plans for her late husband's greatest scheme.

Beckerman devised a way to steal $4 million from a security van travelling from Turin airport to the Fiat car factory in the city. The Italian metropolis has a sophisticated computer-controlled traffic system. Jam the computer and the resultant chaos creates an opportunity to steal the contents of the security van. Beckerman has mapped the only way out of the city during such a traffic jam. Within two hours the thieves could be over the Alps and in Switzerland.

Charlie realises he needs help to enact such a plan and enlists the aid of Mr Bridger, a British crime boss who runs his business from inside prison. The robbery goes like clockwork, despite attracting the interest of the Mafia, spiriting $4 million of gold out of Turin in three Minis. But disaster strikes as the coach containing the thieves and their loot travels up the winding road into the Alps. The bus skids out of control and is left balanced over a precipice...

'A THINLY SCRIPTED, ROUTINE THRILLER OF PERFECT CRIME AND INEVITABLE RETRIBUTION, LIFTED OFF THE GROUND ... BY SOME SUPERB STUNT DRIVING.' *MONTHLY FILM BULLETIN, 1969*

'A PERFECT BLEND OF CHEERY XENOPHOBIA, CHIRPY COCKNEY ANTICS AND DRY WIT.' *TOTAL FILM, 1999*

In 1967 Troy Kennedy Martin was a successful British television writer trying to get into movies. That breakthrough came with the idea

LEFT: Grin and bear it – Charlie Croker and Lorna (Maggie Blye) are threatened by intruders in *The Italian Job* (1969).

of a robbery set amidst a traffic jam, which had originally been conceived by his brother Ian. 'My brother came up with it, but his idea was set in London around Regent Street,' Kennedy Martin told *Esquire* magazine in 2001. 'We decided a financial agreement and I took it on. I decided to move the location to Turin, because it has a computer-operated traffic light system. From the very beginning, I had set my sights on Michael Caine as the hero and wrote a draft treatment accordingly.'

Having got Caine interested, the writer pitched his completed treatment to Robert Evans, head of production at Paramount. Evans wanted

BELOW:
Charlie Croker provokes the ire of Mr Bridger (Noel Coward) in *The Italian Job* (1969). Not considered a great success when first released, this film has become a cult classic.

Robert Redford to play Charlie Croker but was persuaded to stick with Caine. Michael Deeley was appointed by Paramount as producer and was keen to hire *Bullitt* director Peter Yates for the film, having seen the car chase in that picture. But Paramount opted for the less experienced Peter Collinson. Kennedy Martin began writing his first draft screenplay.

The Italian Job was a $3 million movie made during the second half of 1968. The production spent three months filming in Italy. Shooting in Turin was made considerably easier by help from Gianna Agnelli, who owned Fiat – the city's major employer. He ensured that the film received maximum co-operation from the local authorities. Conversely, the production got little help from British car company BMC, which made the Mini. Even though the film was a 100-

minute advertisement for the vehicle, BMC gave the picture almost no support. The company offered six Minis at trade price. The production had to buy more than two-dozen further Minis at retail prices.

All the stunt driving was performed by a French team. 'L'Equipe Remy Julienne were the best-known and the best choice in Europe,' Deeley says on the film's DVD commentary. 'They were able to do amazing work.' In the 1990s the long chase at the end of *The Italian Job* was named one of the greatest car chases in cinema history by *Total Film* magazine. But Deeley says this sequence only came alive with the addition of Quincy Jones' score in post-production. 'It was vital, particularly the last 15, 20 minutes of the movie. It just didn't hold together until Quincy put the music on. Like a

ABOVE: Charlie Croker, head of the Self Preservation Society in *The Italian Job* (1969).

tailoring job, it tied the whole thing in.'

Studio work was split between Twickenham and Isleworth, with further location shooting in England and Ireland, the latter for scenes featuring Caine's co-star, Noël Coward. The legendary actor/playwright was persuaded out of semi-retirement to play crime boss Mr Bridger and most of his scenes were shot at Kilmainham, a disused prison outside Dublin. Caine was full of praise for Coward when interviewed by *Films and Filming* before *The Italian Job*'s release in 1969: 'He's so warm … I think it's his best screen performance.' Caine was also impressed by the director: 'Peter Collinson will go out and shoot things that other people won't. He's an extremely determined young man and took this film into both hands and really went out and did it.'

The film gave Caine a chance to lure his brother in front of the camera. Stanley Caine had already made brief appearances in *Billion Dollar Brain* (1967) and *Play Dirty* (1969). 'I was trying to get him into acting and he didn't really take any interest in it,' Caine told the Australian edition of *Empire* in 2002. 'It wasn't for him, which was very disappointing for me as I was so enthusiastic about it.'

One of the biggest problems facing the filmmakers was how to end *The Italian Job*. Kennedy Martin wrote half a dozen different endings, but Deeley wasn't happy with any of them. 'They all ended up as dialogues in Switzerland,' the producer says in his commentary. 'I didn't feel, after all the excitement with the cars and the chase and the whole business, we should end up with dialogue. We were really stuck because all the endings were boring – they bored me.' Deeley flew to Hollywood to meet with Robert Evans about the problem. During the flight the producer developed an idea for the ultimate cliffhanger, creating the finale for the film: 'I thought it was a potential lead-in to a sequel if this picture was

successful.' Evans quickly agreed and Deeley flew back with Paramount's approval. The new ending was unpopular with the screenwriter, director and Caine himself. Collinson refused to shoot it, leaving the job to his second unit team.

The Italian Job reached British cinemas in 1969, rated U. Critics gave it a mediocre reception, with some dismissing it as just another crime caper with a good car chase thrown in. Reaction was just as muted in America, when the movie was rated G. In 2001 Caine told *Empire* magazine that his biggest disappointment was the US publicity campaign. He believed the film was doomed when he saw Paramount's poster of a machine-gun wielding gangster witha semi-naked woman: 'So I got on the next plane and came back.' Despite its failure to ignite the American box-office, *The Italian Job* won the Golden Globe for best English language foreign film.

Like *Get Carter* (1971), *The Italian Job* underwent a long-term rehabilitation in the eyes of the public and critics. Countless repeats on television and a video release in 1988 introduced the film to a new audience. The brash style, swinging sixties flavour and spectacular car chase helped create a cult following. Troy Kennedy Martin's satire of British antipathy to Europe was downplayed in the comedy caper, but the red, white and blue livery of the Minis underlined the subtext. By the mid-1990s, Cool Britannia hype was making Caine a British icon with *The Italian Job* a key part of his appeal. The film has been spoofed numerous times in advertising and music videos.

The Italian Job's reappraisal was completed in September 1999 when the picture was re-released to British cinemas for its 30th anniversary. The film grossed just over $250,000 but this was just a stalking horse for a subsequent VHS re-release. A BFI poll to find the Top 100 British movies of the 20th century ranked *The Italian Job* in the fourth highest place of seven Caine pictures on the list, voting it 36th over all.

Matthew Field's book *The Making of The Italian Job* was published in 2001 as a precursor to the movie's DVD debut. The volume contains almost everything you could want to know about the film. The movie made its DVD debut the following year. The disc includes a deleted scene, documentaries about the movie and a commentary track.

A new version of *The Italian Job* was filmed at the end of 2002 and released in US cinemas in May 2003. The picture opens in Italy but the bulk of the action takes place in America with the climatic traffic jam chase set in Los Angeles. American actor Mark Wahlberg plays Charlie Croker with Donald Sutherland as the older crime boss. There was talk of Caine having a cameo in the movie, but he expressed public doubts about this after his experience on the 2000 remake of *Get Carter*. A fan club devoted to the 1969 film expressed anger at the remake. Deeley told the *Sunday Telegraph* that shifting the setting to Los Angeles was ignoring the original's anti-European subtext: 'It seems like a complete waste of money to me.' But the remake was a box office success in the US. As this book was going to press *The Italian Job* (2003) was expected to gross nearly $100 million.

In 2003 Caine's most famous piece of dialogue from *The Italian Job* was voted the greatest one-liner in cinema history in a poll run by a mobile phone company. 'You were only supposed to blow the bloody doors off!' won out over quotes from *Gone With the Wind*, *Withnail and I*, *Taxi Driver* and *Apocalypse Now*.

The Italian Job is like a postcard from the late 1960s – swinging London, vibrant primary colours, great British inventions like the Mini – a snapshot of what you imagine life must have been like on the King's Road. Everyone's on the make, anything is possible and all it takes is a dozen London wideboys to sting Europe for millions. This movie is a fantasy from start to finish, but it's a warm, cosy fantasy full of memorable dialogue and automobile antics. The pace never drags, thanks to deft direction, dazzling design and a succession of clever cameos by British comedy actors. The characters may be one-dimensional, but you still want them to find a way out of the cliffhanger ending. Caine is perfectly cast as Charlie Croker, the ultimate lad icon. This movie is lightweight, xenophobic and dated in many respects, but it's still

BELOW: The US poster for *The Italian Job* (1969). Caine blames the film's box office failure in America on this image, which he believes failed to convey the essence of the movie.

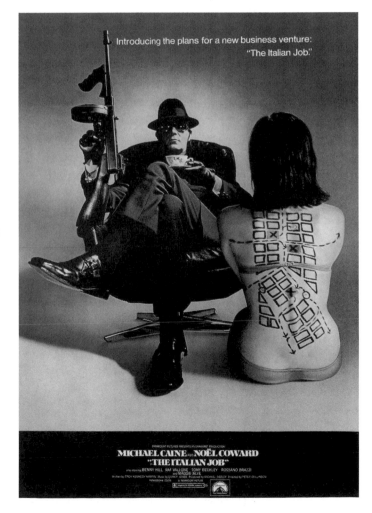

J

JAWS THE REVENGE (1987)

*Cast: Lorraine Gary (Ellen Brody),
Lance Guest (Michael), Mario Van Peebles
(Jake), Karen Young (Carla), Michael Caine
(Hoagie), Judith Barsi (Thea), Lynn Whitfield
(Louisa), Mitchell Anderson (Sean), Jay Mello
(young Sean), Cedric Scott (Clarence),
Charles Bowleg (William), Melvin Van Peebles
(Mr Witherspoon).*
*Crew: Joseph Sargent (director/producer),
Michael de Guzman (writer), Michael Small
(music), John McPherson (cinematography),
Michael Brown (editor), John J Lloyd
(production designer).*

A Great White shark kills Amity police deputy
Sean Brody just before Christmas. His mother
Ellen also lost her husband to such a shark and
becomes convinced the shark is hunting her
family. Ellen goes to the Bahamas to visit her
surviving son Michael, his wife Carla and their
daughter Thea. Michael is a marine biologist
doing research with his friend Jake. Ellen
becomes close to a pilot called Hoagie. Jake and
Michael encounter a Great White shark at sea.
Jake persuades Michael to help him study it.
The shark almost eats Thea. Ellen takes a boat
out to sea, determined to confront the shark.
Michael and Jake find her, with help from
Hoagie. Jake gets the shark to swallow a device
that will give it electric shocks. Ellen rams
the boat into the shark and it explodes.

'*JAWS THE REVENGE* IS MILD AND
PREDICTABLE, THE VERY THINGS AN
ADVENTURE MOVIE SHOULD NEVER
BE.' *NEW YORK TIMES*

'THE MOMENT-OF-ATTACK
SEQUENCES, FULL OF JAGGED CUTS
AND A GREAT DEAL OF NOISE, MORE
CLOSELY RESEMBLE THE VIEW FROM
INSIDE A WASHING MACHINE.'
VARIETY

Peter Benchley's novel *Jaws* became a hugely
successful film in 1975, grossing more than $250
million in the US. It spawned three sequels, but
each one was less successful than the last. The
third picture in the franchise, *Jaws 3-D* (1983),
had abandoned the original cast and setting for
a shark attack movie augmented with 3-D
effects. In 1987 Joseph Sargent became director
and producer for the next sequel, provisionally
named *Jaws 4*. Sargent's previous experience
came from 30 years in TV. Writer Michael de
Guzman was asked to develop a new story
based on Benchley's characters.

The $23 million film ignored the events of
Jaws 3-D, instead focusing on survivors of the
Brody family from the first two movies in the
franchise. Lorraine Gary reprised her role as
Ellen, while adult actors took the roles of her
grown-up sons. Caine was hired to play Hoagie,
Ellen's love interest. News reports claimed he
was paid between £1 million and £1.5 million for
this supporting role, filmed over a few weeks in
the Bahamas. In 1987 Caine told the *Sun* that his
teenage daughter Natasha had persuaded him to
make the picture. 'But I must admit there were
three other attractions – the location in the
Bahamas, the script and the money. This *Jaws*
film gets back to the basic terror of the first
Jaws films.'

Shooting began on location in New England
during February 1987, with Martha's Vineyard
used to depict the Long Island resort community
of Amity, as in *Jaws*. After a week the production
moved to Nassau in the Bahamas for two months
of location work. On 30 March Caine won his

first Oscar for *Hannah and Her Sisters*, but missed the ceremony because of filming commitments on *Jaws the Revenge*. 'I only had a tiny part in it,' Caine told *Hello* magazine in 2000. 'I thought that I would be able to be in Los Angeles for the Oscars but the filming over-ran by one day so I couldn't get there. It's a terrible regret for me that I couldn't be there to receive the Oscar in person. Instead I was spending that day on a picture which I'm told, because I have never seen it, turned out not to be very good.'

In April the cast and crew shifted to Universal Studios in California to finish shooting, with the production wrapping at the end of May. *Jaws the Revenge* opened in American cinemas just three months later, was savaged by critics and grossed just over $20 million. Caine was nominated as worst

supporting actor at the Razzie Awards for his performance.

The original US ending had Mario Van Peebles' character Jake killed by the shark, but this sequence was re-shot for foreign audiences. New footage had the Great White exploding and Jake surviving. In the UK the BBFC required 37 seconds of cuts before granting a PG rating. *Jaws the Revenge* bombed with British reviewers and audiences in August 1987, grossing less than $2 million. The film was released on VHS in 1988, reclassified as a 15 in the UK. For a 2000 re-release this rating was lowered to a 12. The movie made its DVD debut during 2001.

Over the years Caine has put forward various reasons for his participation in *Jaws the Revenge*. In November 1987 he told the *Sunday Express* that his large salary had enabled him to appear in the low-budget British movie *The Whistle*

ABOVE:
Loveable rogue Hoagie helps Ellen Brody (Lorraine Gary) stay afloat in *Jaws the Revenge* (1987). The movie sank without trace.

Blower (1987). In his 1992 autobiography Caine said *Jaws the Revenge* paid for a terrific house to be built, even if the film was terrible. In 2002 Caine told a gathering of Screen Actors Guild members in Los Angeles that he took roles like Hoagie because he was afraid of poverty and unemployment.

The subject of *Jaws the Revenge* still irks Caine, as he showed during an interview in the January 2003 Australian edition of *Empire*: 'What pisses you off is when, as happened this morning, a person says, "Why did you makes *Jaws 4*?" That's great! Of all the questions you could possible ask me, you decide to ask me about a film I was in for 10 minutes, 20 bloody years ago. That's when the interview gets very short. If you're going to talk about a duff film, at least talk about a picture in which I played the lead and was responsible for the bloody thing.'

Tiresome and pointless, *Jaws the Revenge* lacks all the qualities that made Steven Spielberg's 1975 film such a success. This dull retread has no suspense, no surprises and almost nothing to recommend it. Logic flies out the window and never comes back with this story.

A Great White shark that stalks one particular family? From New England to the Bahamas? How the hell does it find them? Did Ellen Brody leave her forwarding address underwater? The first *Jaws* film was fortunate in that its mechanical shark frequently malfunctioned, forcing Spielberg to merely hint at the terror beneath the waves. *Jaws the Revenge*'s shark must have worked fine because it pops up again and again and again, each appearance more laughable than the last. The film unwisely uses a few sepia-tinted flashbacks to the 1975 original, reminding you how much better that movie was. Caine strolls through in a minor supporting role, adding nothing to this sinking ship. Don't waste your time.

THE JIGSAW MAN (1984)

Cast: Michael Caine (Sir Philip Kimberley and Sergei Kuzminsky), Laurence Olivier (Admiral Scaith), Susan George (Penny Kimberley), Robert Powell (Jamie Fraser), Charles Gray (Sir James Chorley), Morteza Kazerouni (Boris Medvachian), Michael Medwin (Milroy), Eric Sevareid (himself), Sabine Sun (Dr Zilenka), David Kelley (Cameron), Patrick Dawson (Ginger), Vladek Sheybal (General Zorin). Crew: Terence Young (director), Benjamin Fisz (producer), Jo Eisinger (writer), John Cameron (music), Freddie Francis (cinematography), Derek Trigg (editor), Michael Stringer (production designer).

A British defector, Sir Philip Kimberly, has become a drunken embarrassment to the Russians. They have his face altered by plastic surgery and send him back to England to retrieve a dossier containing the names of Soviet agents in the UK. But Kimberley escapes his KGB minders by pretending to defect in London. The fugitive also outwits the British intelligence services, to the frustration of Admiral Scaith and his associate, Sir James Chorley. Kimberley, masquerading as a Russian called Kuzminsky, offers to sell the dossier to Scaith for £1 million. The defector seeks help from his adult daughter Penny. The Russians and Chorley try to kill Kimberley and, to protect his daughter, the defector eventually surrenders to Scaith. Chorley is revealed as a Russian mole. Kimberley offers Scaith the chance to go into business together, selling the dossier to the highest bidder…

'ALTHOUGH THE MAIN LINE OF THE STORY IS CLEAR ENOUGH, TRUNCATED SUBPLOTS … OCCASIONALLY CONFUSE MATTERS IN A WAY THAT SUGGESTS THAT MR YOUNG WAS TRYING TO PRESERVE

BELOW:
Fugitive defector Philip Kimberly seeks help from his daughter Penelope (Susan George) in *The Jigsaw Man* (1983).

ABOVE: Kimberly forges an uneasy alliance with Gerald Scaith (Laurence Olivier) in *The Jigsaw Man* (1983), but whose side is he really on?

TOO MUCH OF HIS SOURCE MATERIAL.' *NEW YORK TIMES*

'PROBABLY THE MOST GARRULOUS AND DODDERING SPY MOVIE EVER MADE … MORE FLABBY EXPOSITION THAN A MONTH IN THE HOUSE OF LORDS…' *VOICE* **MAGAZINE**

In November 1976 Michael Caine told a London newspaper, the *Evening Standard*, that he would soon be playing British defector Kim Philby in a major new film about the spy. The report claimed that *Get Carter* director Mike Hodges would helm the movie. Philby had already announced from Moscow how unimpressed he was by the casting of Caine. 'Marvellous, innit?' the actor responded. 'So much for equality. I'm playing him from 22 to 56. That's always murderous. The script is excellent. It goes in for the details of the man. In fact, it's more sympathetic towards him than I am myself. I'm rather anti-Communist.'

That film never went any further, but in the same year Dorothea Bennett had a novel published called *The Jigsaw Man*. This espionage thriller featured a Philby-like defector, Sir Philip Kimberley. Six years later director Terence Young (Bennett's husband) hired Caine to play the lead in a film of *The Jigsaw Man*, adapted by screenwriter Jo Eisinger. The other major role went to Laurence Olivier, thus reuniting the two men who had both been Oscar-nominated for their work on the acclaimed two-hander *Sleuth* (1972). Getting the pair back together helped guarantee the new film's financing.

Caine flew into Britain on Concorde early in 1982 to start work on *The Jigsaw Man*. 'It will be the first film I've made in London in six years,' he told the *Sunday Express*, 'and I'm really looking forward to it.' Caine believed his $900,000 fee was double what he could have expected as an actor resident in the UK, because he was now considered an international name. The $9 million production began shooting on location in England and Helsinki, with studio work at Shepperton. But Caine's good feelings about the movie quickly faded as financial troubles threatened it.

In June 1982 the *Sunday Express* reported that the movie had shut down because of cash difficulties. Olivier had already walked off the set on his lawyer's advice after receiving no pay, but Caine had continued working. 'They told me if I didn't there was no chance that they would be able to raise the money to finish the film,' he told the paper. 'So Mr Nice Guy kept on working. But two weeks ago everything came to a stop. It's a good story. It's just a shame all this happened.' Caine stayed in London for a fortnight in the hope that new funding could be raised to finish production. The actor only had six days' work left when the picture shut down.

A month later Caine discovered that his Concorde ticket was only one-way. He bought his own ticket back to Hollywood, still owed $900,000 and six weeks' living expenses. 'It had never occurred to me to look at the ticket before,' Caine told the *Sunday Times*. 'I'd have guessed if they couldn't afford to buy me a return ticket they couldn't afford to make the picture. I still keep getting messages that it's going to be finished. I'm fairly philosophical about the whole thing. It's not as if this film were a masterpiece… It's just a good, straightforward thriller.'

Caine filmed his Oscar-nominated role in *Educating Rita* next, and then moved on to *The Honorary Consul* (both 1983). In the meantime *The Jigsaw Man*'s producer, Benjamin Fisz, secured $4 million of new financing and Young re-mounted the movie at Shepperton. Caine returned to complete his work and finally got paid. But pulling the fragments together required many months of editing. The completed film was given a 15 rating by the BBFC in August 1983, but was subsequently pilloried by critics.

This pedestrian espionage picture tries the viewer's patience with its glacial pacing, limp dialogue and endless exposition. Unsurprisingly, considering how the movie was made, continuity is all over the place, with even Caine's hair colour varying from shot to shot. The direction is flaccid and stale, and it's hard to believe that a great cinematographer like Freddie Francis shot this drab, lifeless footage. Sadly, the film isn't bad enough to attain kitsch value. Two moments do stand out. Laurence Olivier, no less, pre-empts a catchphrase from British TV sitcom *The Royle Family* by muttering 'My arse!' at Robert Powell. Later, there's a running gag about Charles Gray's character wearing a wig. The actor then appears in a wildly unconvincing bald cap, as if to prove he sports a wig the rest of the time. Caine strolls through this banal tale, attempting several different accents without much success. Rather than being less than the sum of its parts, *The Jigsaw Man* manages the rare feat of being worth less than any of its parts.

KIDNAPPED (1972)

Cast: Michael Caine (Alan Breck), Lawrence Douglas (David Balfour), Vivien Heilbron (Catriona Stewart), Trevor Howard (Lord Advocate), Jack Hawkins (Captain Hoseason), Donald Pleasence (Ebenezer Balfour), Gordon Jackson (Charles Stewart), Freddie Jones (Cluny), Jack Watson (James Stewart), Peter Jeffrey (Riach), Roger Booth (Duke of Cumberland), Geoffrey Whitehead (Lt Duncansby).
Crew: Delbert Mann (director), Frederick Brogger (producer), Jack Pulman (writer), Roy Budd (music), Paul Beeson

BELOW: Is that a loch or a lock? Caine struggles with his Scottish accent as Jacobite rebel Alan Breck in *Kidnapped* (1971).

(cinematography), Peter Boita (editor), [Alex] Vetchinsky (art direction).

Scotland, 1746. In the aftermath of the battle at Culloden, Jacobite rebels are fleeing the forces of King George. The Stuart claim to the British throne is in tatters. Soon afterwards, teenager David Balfour arrives at the House of Shaws, home of his uncle Ebenezer, who tries to arrange an accidental death for David. When that fails, Ebenezer has David kidnapped by a slave trader, Captain Hoseason. But Hoseason's ship runs over a boat carrying Alan Breck. The rebel leader was trying to reach a vessel bound for France. Hoseason's ship crashes against rocks, throwing Breck and David into the water.

The pair make it to shore and start walking to Edinburgh. David and Breck see innocent women and children murdered by government forces led by Mungo Campbell. They stop at the home of James Stewart, a former Jacobite. David is smitten by James' daughter, Catriona. Next morning Mungo Campbell and his men come for James. Mungo is murdered by an unseen assassin and James is wounded. David, Breck and Catriona flee.

Later they hear that James survived and is going to stand trial in Edinburgh for murdering Mungo Campbell. David goes to the Lord Advocate and tries to give evidence that James is innocent, but the Lord Advocate refuses to listen. Unless Breck is captured, James will be found guilty in his place and executed. David inherits the House of Shaws after Ebenezer dies. Catriona begs David not to give evidence, or she will lose him and her father. Breck admits he killed Mungo Campbell. The Jacobite rebel surrenders himself, saving James…

'PERHAPS THE FACT THAT EVERYONE EATS SO MUCH PORRIDGE RENDERS THE SCRIPT SO CONSTIPATED.'
GUARDIAN

'THAT THE BOOK HAS BEEN ADAPTED AND FILMED BEFORE IS NOT SURPRISING … BUT WHAT DOES SURPRISE ME IS THAT THE LATEST VERSION, DIRECTED BY DELBERT MANN, IS SO DISAPPOINTINGLY PEDESTRIAN … EVEN MICHAEL CAINE SEEMS UNEASY…'
FILMS AND FILMING

In 1971 American director Delbert Mann was hired to shoot a new version of the much-loved Robert Louis Stevenson novel *Kidnapped*. The tale had already been adapted for the cinema three times before, so the production sought a new approach. Screenwriter Jack Pulman drew on both *Kidnapped* and Stevenson's sequel *Catriona* (also known as *David Balfour*) for his plot. Mann told *Film Making* magazine that most literary scholars considered the books had to be read together to be fully acceptable as classic novels: 'Each depends on the other to give the reader full enjoyment.'

The movie was shot on location in Scotland over the summer of 1971, using the working title of *David and Catriona*. Stirling Castle stood in for Edinburgh Castle during the shoot, while the township of Kinross took the place of Edinburgh circa 1746. Studio work was lensed at Pinewood, near London.

Fresh from filming *Get Carter*, London-born Caine was cast in the unlikely role of Jacobite rebel Alan Breck. Mann said that using a famous actor was important for a healthy box-office: 'Stars do still have a pull on the public. Michael, for example, is one star who can get the public in on his name!' In the film's official pressbook, Caine said he wanted to play Breck because *Kidnapped* would be seen by a far wider audience than most of his previous films. 'It has a marvellous script by Jack Pulman, which is another reason why I accepted the part.

Of course, I've had to adapt my Scots accent to make it sound easy and natural. It won't fool the Scots, but I trust they'll forgive me. After all, it's my job to make Alan Breck easily understood by audiences all over the world.'

The funding for *Kidnapped* ran out during filming and producer Frederick Brogger struggled to keep the cameras rolling long enough to finish. Caine deferred his salary to help the film stay solvent. Nobody was fully paid for the picture, and Caine rarely discusses *Kidnapped*. William Hill's biography, *Arise Sir Michael Caine*, quoted the actor on the troubled production: 'I never got paid for it so I refuse to discuss it. I'm a professional, and if I don't get paid I don't talk about it. They made it when they didn't have the money to make it. I got a small percentage just so they would be able to release it, to get at least some money back on it. It was an absolute and utter disaster from beginning to end.'

The picture reached British cinemas in June 1972, renamed *Kidnapped* and rated U. Critics were underwhelmed, but reserved praise for Caine's acting, if not his accent. The film was not a box-office success in the UK or the US. The movie has never been available on DVD and is much sought after by Caine collectors.

Kidnapped is a plodding adaptation of Robert Louis Stevenson's interlinked novels that never gets out of second gear. Some nice scenery and a few skirling bagpipes cannot make up for the lack of excitement generated by this workmanlike effort. The central characters stroll around Scotland, searching for the end of the film. Part of the problem lies with source material that has never been made into a successful movie, despite numerous attempts. Caine does his best as Highland adventurer Alan Breck, but struggles to master a Scottish accent. At least his presence gives this drab, lifeless picture some much-needed novelty value.

LAST ORDERS (2001)

Cast: Michael Caine (Jack), Tom Courtenay (Vic), David Hemmings (Lenny), Bob Hoskins (Ray), Helen Mirren (Amy), Ray Winstone (Vince), J J Field (young Jack), Cameron Fitch (young Vic), Nolan Hemmings (young Lenny), Anatol Yusef (young Ray), Kelly Reilly (young Amy), Stephen McCole (young Vince), George Innes (Bernie).
Crew: Fred Schepisi (director/writer), Elisabeth Robinson (producer), Paul Grabowsky (music), Brian Tufano (cinematography), Kate Williams (editor), Tim Harvey (production designer).

Three old friends meet in a South London pub to remember their late friend Jack. The dead man's son, Vince, drives the trio to Margate Pier so they can scatter Jack's ashes. Meanwhile, Jack's widow Amy visits her retarded daughter June for the last time. During the day each person remembers incidents from their past, hidden truths and personal revelations about how they have shaped each other's lives…

'AMBITIOUS IN STRUCTURE AND CASTING, IT PACKS A LOT INTO ITS SCREEN TIME. QUALITY CRAFTSMANSHIP FOR A DISCERNING CROWD.' *EMPIRE*

'SCHEPISI'S INTELLIGENT AND THOUGHTFUL ADAPTATION ENSURES THAT THE FILM WORKS SMOOTHLY THROUGH A COMPLEX SERIES OF TIME SHIFTS, AND, THOUGH THERE'S PLENTY OF HUMOUR, THE FILM SUCCEEDS BEST ON AN EMOTIONAL LEVEL.' *VARIETY*

Graham Swift's novel *Last Orders* was first published in 1996 and won the prestigious Booker Prize that year, arguably the highest honour in British fiction. Soon afterwards, film producer Elisabeth Robinson showed the book to Australian writer/director Fred Schepisi. The pair persuaded Swift to let them adapt it into a film. Schepisi began writing the screenplay with Swift providing critiques on each successive draft. The project had the commitment of actors Caine, Tom Courtenay, Bob Hoskins and Ray Winstone, but it took another two years to raise sufficient finance to begin shooting.

In his DVD commentary, Schepisi remembers offering the key part of Jack to Caine: 'He said, "Oh damn, okay. Yes, I've got to do this. I knew I'd be playing my father one day."' Caine found himself acting the role of a man dying of cancer at St Thomas' Hospital – just as his own father had done. There was another strong resonance for the actor. In the film Jack's wife Amy visits her retarded daughter at a care home once a week for 50 years. Caine's own mother had given birth to an illegitimate son in the 1920s who suffered from epilepsy. At the time the illness was treated as a form of insanity and the boy spent half a century in an asylum, secretly visited by his mother every week. Caine only learned about his half-brother after their mother had died. 'It was a very personal reason for him doing this film,' Schepisi says in the commentary.

The $12 million production was shot over nine weeks from October to December 2000, during the wettest autumn for nearly 250 years. A pre-shoot had already taken place during summer in Kent for a sequence showing hop-picking. Filming took place at locations around London and Kent, with studio work at Pinewood and a disused warehouse in Peckham. Caine was only required for three weeks of the shoot before flying to the South of France to join the cast of

Quicksand (2002). *Last Orders* reunited him with old friend Bob Hoskins, with whom he had appeared in *The Honorary Consul* (1983), *Sweet Liberty, Mona Lisa* (both 1986) and *Blue Ice* (1992).

In 2002 Caine told the *Hollywood Reporter* he did low-budget projects like Schepisi's film when he liked them. 'I was in *Last Orders* with all my friends. I was only on the picture for 10 days, but I do that – it's not like the big movie star who doesn't come out unless it's a full budget and everything. Apart from being with my friends, a very good script and very good director, there was that thing of getting a British movie off the ground.'

The film received its world premiere at the Toronto Film Festival in September 2001, with a screening at the London Film Festival two months later. *Last Orders* opened in American cinemas in December, with many critics giving it strong notices and the picture grossing nearly $2.5 million from a limited release. The cast won the US National Board of Review's award for best ensemble performance. *Last Orders* was released to British cinemas in January 2002, gathering glowing reviews from critics and grossing $1.3 million. The film was a bigger hit in Australia, taking more than $1.7 million at the box-office. *Last Orders* was issued on DVD and VHS in 2002.

If you want action, adventure and high-octane thrills, go elsewhere. If you want a moving, funny and emotionally satisfying film about life, love and friendship, then *Last Orders* is the picture for you. Schepisi succeeds in adapting a heartfelt novel into a small gem of a movie, his script and direction effortlessly guiding you through a complex interweaving of narratives and flashbacks. Paul Grabowsky contributes a haunting, jazz-tinged score that never overwhelms or overstates, just like the rest of this classy feature. The cast is uniformly excellent, with Caine in fine form as a man facing his own mortality. If you can watch this film without shedding a tear, you must have a heart of stone. Never crass or sentimental, *Last Orders* is emotionally draining and life-affirming at the same time.

THE LAST VALLEY (1970)

Cast: Michael Caine (the Captain), Omar Sharif (Vogel), Florinda Bolkan (Erica), Nigel Davenport (Gruber), Per Oscarsson (Father Sebastian), Arthur O'Connell (Hoffman), Madeline Hinde (Inge), Yorgo Voyagis (Pirelli), Miguel Alejandro (Julio), Christian Roberts (Andreas), Brian Blessed (Korski), Ian Hogg (Graf), Michael Gothard (Hansen), George Innes (Vornez).
Crew: James Clavell (director/producer/writer), John Barry (music), John Wilcox (cinematography), John Bloom (editor), Peter Mullins (art direction).

BELOW: *The Last Valley* premiered in London's West End in 1971 and went on to achieve disappointing box office returns.

In the early 17th century, Europe is riven by the Thirty Years' War between Catholics and Protestants. A wandering teacher, Vogel, stumbles into a prosperous village untouched by the conflict. But a gang of marauding mercenaries also finds the hamlet in its secluded valley. Vogel persuades their leader, the Captain, not to loot the village. Instead the soldiers take up residence for the winter, protecting the valley and its inhabitants from other intruders, the Captain killing any dissenters among his own men in order to maintain order. Vogel acts as mediator between the villagers and the mercenaries, ensuring his own survival.

A soldier called Hansen tries to rape one of the villagers, Inge, but she is rescued by Vogel. Hansen rides out of the valley and brings back two dozen men, determined to seize control of the hidden oasis. But the intruders are ruthlessly despatched by the Captain, with help from his men and the villagers. When spring comes the mercenaries ride out to war again and most of them die in battle. The Captain makes it back to the valley before dying. Vogel leaves the valley, returning to the world of war and plague beyond the hills…

'ELEGANTLY SHOT, CONFIDENTLY ACTED, WITH A SUPERB CENTRAL PERFORMANCE, THIS HISTORICAL SPECTACULAR IS ALSO MODERN AND INTIMATE.' *MONTHLY FILM BULLETIN*

'A DISAPPOINTING 17TH CENTURY PERIOD MELODRAMA … TOO LITERAL IN HISTORICAL DETAIL TO SUGGEST ARTFULLY THE ALLEGORIES INTENDED AND, PARADOXICALLY, TOO ALLEGORICAL TO MAKE CLEAR THE ACTUAL REALITIES OF THE THIRTY YEARS WAR.' *VARIETY*

BELOW: The Captain leads his gang of murderous mercenary scum into *The Last Valley* (1970).

ABOVE: Caine won acclaim for his performance in James Clavell's historical epic *The Last Valley* (1970).

J B Pick's novel *The Last Valley* was first published in 1959. Ten years later James Clavell began adapting the historical epic for the big screen, as producer, director and screenwriter. Clavell was best known for writing blockbuster novels like *King Rat*, but he had also directed several films, including *To Sir, with Love* (1966). Caine got top billing for his role ahead of Omar Sharif, and a reported fee of $750,000. Caine studied German dialect records in preparation for playing the Captain.

The bulk of the $6 million movie was made at Trins in the Tirol, near Innsbruck. Filming took place over 14 weeks in 1969, with studio work at Shepperton near London. A battle sequence outside a castle was shot beside a lake near Windsor. The cast included George Innes, who had appeared with Caine in *The Italian Job* (1969). Interviewed exclusively for this book, Innes said *The Last Valley* was a massive endeavour: 'They built an entire village, using local people. It was quite amazing. It was a huge movie, but the problem was they had to cut it down. Clavell said, "They're going to make me cut this, they just won't show a film of this length." That's what really did it in. *The Last Valley* is a movie of great scope but it lost a lot in the cutting.'

It lost a little more when presented to the BBFC in November 1970, with cuts required before the film was granted an AA certificate. Reviews for the picture were decidedly mixed. Some critics praised its intelligence and Caine's performance, while others found the feature too talky and Caine's accent disconcerting. Despite that, Caine was voted best actor of 1970 by *Films and Filming* magazine. The film failed at the British box-office and did no better in America. The movie was issued as a budget-price DVD in the UK during 2001, and is also available in America.

Caine considers *The Last Valley* his most unjustly neglected film, as he told *GQ* magazine in 1997: 'It went completely nowhere. It's my elder daughter's favourite film – not only of mine, but of all time. I thought that was a wonderful film, with an unbelievable score by John Barry.'

The Last Valley is a film with a lot on its mind. Conflicts of religion, morality and philosophy are all debated in a small-scale setting, hinting at the greater war raging beyond the valley. The attention to historical detail and characterisation is compelling, but the film less so. The many subtexts threaten to overwhelm the text, with Clavell's movie making its points too strongly for the good of the story. You don't get the chance to make your own discoveries about what is driving the characters – instead they announce their motivations to all and sundry. Despite this, *The Last Valley* looks sumptuous and features a lush score by John Barry. Caine gives a fine, restrained performance as the Captain, his clipped Germanic accent utterly convincing from start to finish. If only Clavell's direction had been as accomplished.

LITTLE VOICE (1998)

Cast: Brenda Blethyn (Mari), Jane Horrocks (LV), Ewan McGregor (Billy), Philip Jackson (George), Annette Badland (Sadie), Michael Caine (Ray Say), Jim Broadbent (Mr Boo), Adam Fogerty, James Welsh (the bouncers), Karen Gregory (the stripper), Fred Feast (Arthur), Graham Turner (LV's dad).
Crew: Mark Herman (director/writer), Elizabeth Karlsen (producer), John Altman (music), Andy Collins (cinematography), Michael Ellis (editor), Don Taylor (production designer).

LV is an agoraphobic woman who lives with her overbearing mother, Mari, in a dilapidated house

ABOVE: Dodgy showbusiness agent Ray Say begins to get an inkling that his lover's daughter LV (Jane Horrocks) may possess a special talent in *Little Voice* (1998).

with faulty wiring in a faded seaside town. When shy telephone engineer Billy visits them to install a new line, he is smitten by LV. She says almost nothing, retreating to her bedroom and the solace of her late father's record collection to escape her raucous mother. Mari brings home her latest lover Ray Say, a talent agent from London whose acts have no talent. He hears LV singing and is stunned by her ability to mimic the likes of Judy Garland and Shirley Bassey. Billy asks LV out but she declines.

Ray brings local club owner Mr Boo to hear LV sing. They decide she must go on stage, aided and abetted by Mari. But LV's first appearance is a disaster – she will only sing in the dark. Ray convinces LV to try again by hinting that it is what her father would have wanted. The agent puts all his money and more into the show, creating a Las Vegas-style extravaganza with a big band but also running up large debts with loan sharks. LV does the show, singing to the ghost of her father, but refuses to repeat the performance. Ray is ruined. The wiring in LV and Mari's home gives out and the house burns down. Billy rescues LV from the flames. She finally confronts her mother about all the years of neglect and abuse. LV leaves, free at last.

BELOW: A candid off-set moment between Caine and his co-star Brenda Blethyn during the making of *Little Voice* (1998).

STARRING **MICHAEL CAINE**

> '*LITTLE VOICE* IS A SMALL PICTURE WITH BIG HEART. THE FILM HAS ALMOST EVERYTHING GOING FOR IT … INCLUDING BRENDA BLETHYN AND MICHAEL CAINE AT FULL TILT…'
> ***VARIETY***

> 'AN ALMOST PERFECT BLEND OF BITING WIT, HEART-WARMING COMEDY AND SUPERB ACTING … CAINE AND BLETHYN STEAL THE SHOW; THE FORMER'S WIDEBOY ACT GOES DOWN A STORM.' ***EMPIRE***

Jim Cartwright wrote his play *The Rise and Fall of Little Voice* as a vehicle for actress Jane Horrocks' ability to mimic many different singers of the 20th century. The Sam Mendes-directed play was a smash hit in London's West End in 1992 and film rights were soon snapped up, with America's Miramax studio helping fund the production. The company wanted the story transplanted to a US setting with an American actress in the title role – Gwyneth Paltrow was among those linked to the project.

But British filmmaker Mark Herman rejected such suggestions when he was brought on board to write and direct the adaptation. 'To hear a Judy Garland impression coming out of an apartment in Chicago isn't as quirky as hearing Garland come out of a little apartment in Scarborough,' he told *Entertainment Weekly* in 1998. 'It seemed immoral to do a version of *Little Voice* without Jane. This is Jane's movie.'

Pete Postlethwaite played sleazy talent agent Ray Say in the original play but was too busy filming Steven Spielberg's *Jurassic Park* sequel *The Lost World* to reprise his role. Herman was unsure when Caine was suggested to replace Postlethwaite. 'Michael is one of those actors I thought would come with all this baggage. Then I spoke to him on the phone and we realised we both had the same vision for his character. After seeing *Blood and Wine* (1996), in which he plays a pretty sleazy man, I knew he was dead right.'

In a public interview at the NFT in 1998, Caine recalled getting the script for *Little Voice*. 'I hadn't worked for about two years really, not on a movie-movie. [In fact Caine starred in a film called *Shadow Run* (1998) and two TV projects.] I'd just sat waiting for a good script. I got *Blood and Wine* … But this was the movie I was really waiting for, and it came.' Caine had been up for the role of the villain in *The Avengers* (1998) film, but was passed over for Sean Connery. The next day the script for *Little Voice* arrived. 'I read the first 20 pages … I just screamed at Shakira [his wife], "I got it! I got it! This is it."' Caine recalled the scene in which he persuades LV to perform: 'That was the best piece of writing I've had in a long time and the best scene I've done in a picture in years.' He offered to act the part with a Northern accent, but Herman felt that might distract the audience.

Production began in October 1997, with location shooting in Scarborough and studio work at Twickenham in London. 'I put on 25 pounds to play the role,' Caine told *Hello* in 1999. 'I grew my hair. I wanted to take him as far away from me as possible. He was awful. I didn't want anyone thinking he had anything to do with me!'

Little Voice had its premiere at the Toronto Film Festival in September 1998 before reaching US cinemas three months later. The picture received strong reviews and grossed nearly $5 million in a limited release. Greater success followed in January 1999 when the film reached British cinemas, grossing more than $14 million. UK critics were full of praise and the picture also attracted kudos during the awards season. Caine won his second Golden Globe film trophy, for best actor in a musical or comedy, while Brenda Blethyn and Jane Horrocks were both nominated. At the BAFTAs *Little Voice* earned six

nominations, including one for Caine as best actor, but took home no trophies. Caine won the London Critics' Circle film award as best supporting actor. At the Oscars Blethyn was the only nominee from the film.

Once a year British filmmakers hit the jackpot with a small film that is funny, thought-provoking and touching. *Little Voice* is such a movie. Mark Herman does a remarkable job in opening out the original stage play, making the theatrical origins far from obvious. *Little Voice* may have been created as a vehicle for Horrocks,

but her performance is negligible once you get past her karaoke skills. By comparison Blethyn's acting almost strips paint from the walls, such is its caustic nature. Caine matches her in outrageousness, but also succeeds in making his character's quiet moments just as compelling. If *Blood and Wine* (1996) reminded people he was still alive, this film got the Caine career revival rolling – and launched a lucrative relationship with Miramax. Despite a resolution that feels too neat, *Little Voice* is an enjoyable example of the small British movie.

ABOVE: Ray Say persuades LV (Jane Horrocks) to perform in public while her late father (Graham Turner) looks on from the picture on the wall. A classic scene from *Little Voice* (1998).

M

THE MAGUS (1968)

*Cast: Michael Caine (Nicholas Urfe),
Anthony Quinn (Maurice Conchis),
Candice Bergen (Lily), Anna Karina (Anne),
Paul Stassino (Meli), Julian Glover (Anton),
Takis Emmanuel (Kapetan), George Pastell
(Andreas, priest), Daniele Noel (Soula),
Jerome Willis ('false' German officer),
Ethel Farrugia (Maria).
Crew: Guy Green (director), John Kohn and
Jud Kinberg (producers), John Fowles (writer),
John Dankworth (music), Billy Williams
(cinematography), Max Benedict (editor),
Don Ashton (production designer).*

Nicholas Urfe leaves England to escape a failed romance with Anne, an air hostess. He becomes a teacher on the Greek island of Phraxos. Nicholas encounters a mysterious local, Maurice Conchis, who was thought to have died during the war and now puts the teacher through a series of tests, tricks and illusions. Anne visits Nicholas on the island and they make love, but he refuses to take their affair any further. Soon after he is sent a newspaper report about Anne having committing suicide.

Nicholas finds himself in a re-creation of an incident from the war, when the Germans occupied Phraxos. Conchis reveals he was made mayor of the island by the Nazis. When three Greek partisans from the mainland murdered four Germans on Phraxos, Conchis was given a stark choice – kill the partisans himself or see 80 local men murdered in cold blood. Conchis could not choose and the Germans killed everyone – except the mayor. Conchis staged his own death to escape the shame of what had happened. Just when Nicholas thinks he understands, Conchis forces him to experience yet another hallucination. Finally, Nicholas sees Anne, still alive. His journey of discovery is over…

'BOTH ACTING AND DIRECTION ARE COMPETENT ENOUGH IN AN UNINSPIRED, WORKMANLIKE WAY, BUT THIS DOESN'T PREVENT THE FILM FROM BEING FAINTLY LUDICROUS SOME OF THE TIME AND PAINFULLY UNEXCITING ALL OF THE TIME.' *MONTHLY FILM BULLETIN*

'AN ESOTERIC, TALKY, SLOWLY-DEVELOPING, SENSITIVELY-EXECUTED, AND SOMEWHAT DULL FILM. MICHAEL CAINE STARS, IN ONE OF HIS BETTER PERFORMANCES.' *VARIETY*

British writer John Fowles' chilling novel *The Collector* was made into a well-regarded film in 1965, collecting several Oscar nominations. Caine had known one of the producers, John Kohn, for several years. 'When I saw *The Collector*, I knew I wanted to do John Fowles' next novel,' the actor told *Films and Filming* in 1969. 'That was before he had even written it. John Kohn and Jud Kinberg had the option on it, and I said, "I'll do that no matter what it is" as part of my Fox contract.' Caine had signed a non-exclusive two-picture deal with Hollywood studio Twentieth Century-Fox. The first half was fulfilled by the poorly received *Deadfall* (1968); *The Magus* became the second picture in the deal. 'When I read the book I was absolutely fascinated by it,' Caine told *Films and Filming*. 'It's a very personal thing and I suppose *The Magus* can really be taken by each individual for what it means to them.'

Director Guy Green grabbed the opportunity to make the film when offered it by Kohn. 'One

FAR LEFT:
Nicholas Urfe
undergoes a
baffling test of will
during *The Magus*
(1968), an
infamously bad
adaptation of John
Fowles' celebrated
novel.

seldom gets offered anything that one is really fascinated in,' he told *Films and Filming*. 'Most films fit into the major categories like Westerns, spy stories, comedies … *The Magus* seems to be outside these customary limits; it is unusual, a different kind of picture.' Green worked with Fowles to adapt the novel into a workable screenplay. 'He was better for the job than anyone else, but being a first script it wasn't easy to shoot what he wrote. It isn't a routine straightforward plot, but one that is built up out of impressions; in fact, the kind of story that only the cinema can really tell.'

The production started shooting in Greece but political unrest forced the unit to shift to Spain. Scenes were also filmed on location in England. Fowles made a brief cameo appearance as a sailor in the picture's opening sequence. In his 1992 autobiography *What's It All About?*, Caine confessed that he could not understand the script and admitted he had never finished reading Fowles' novel. The actor also found it hard to cope with the entourage surrounding his co-star, Anthony Quinn.

The film was released late in 1968, rated X in the UK. Reviewers on both sides of the Atlantic slated *The Magus*, with Green and Fowles taking the brunt of the criticism for failing to translate the novel's magical essence to celluloid. Billy Williams, however, received a BAFTA nomination for his cinematography. *The Magus* was a box-office flop and has never been released on video or DVD. Caine talked about the film in an interview with *Time Out* in 2000: 'That was a contract picture for Fox so I had to do it. I didn't know what it was about. Nobody knew what it was about. Still, it was nice filming in Majorca…'

'This may not be the most misguided movie ever made, but it's in there pitching,' observed distinguished US critic Rex Reed, while Woody Allen, when asked what he would change if he could live his life over again, is reputed to have said he would do everything exactly the same – except he wouldn't see *The Magus*.

Some novels should never be converted into movies, simply because the internalised nature of the narrative defies easy adaptation into the predominantly externalised style of cinema. Green's direction is flat, lifeless and pretentious, while the attempts to inject fantasy sequences into a realistically shot film are laughable. The actors stumble through the production, with Caine plainly baffled by all that he beholds. Only once does *The Magus* come close to bringing alive the essence of Fowles' novel, in the flashback sequence when Conchis faces his terrible dilemma with the Nazis. The rest of the time this film is just terrible – strictly for cinematic masochists.

THE MAN WHO WOULD BE KING (1975)

Cast: Sean Connery (Daniel Dravot), Michael Caine (Peachy Carnehan), Christopher Plummer (Rudyard Kipling), Saeed Jaffrey (Billy Fish), Doghmi Larbi (Ootah), Jack May (District Commissioner), Karroom Ben Bouih (Kafu Selim), Mohammed Shamsi (Babu), Albert Moses (Ghulam), Paul Antrim (Mulvaney), Graham Acres (officer), Shakira Caine (Roxanne). Crew: John Huston (director/co-writer), John Foreman (producer), Gladys Hill (co-writer), Maurice Jarre (music), Oswald Morris (cinematography), Russell Lloyd (editor), Alexander Trauner (production designer).

Writer Rudyard Kipling is working his office at the *Northern Star* newspaper in India when he is approached by a crippled, disfigured beggar. Kipling eventually recognises the beggar as Peachy Carnehan, an ex-soldier whom he met three years before. Peachy stole Kipling's watch

FAR RIGHT:
Caine as the crippled, disfigured Peachy Carnehan, seen in the opening and closing sequences of *The Man Who Would Be King* (1975). The make-up took two hours to apply.

RIGHT: Peachy Carnehan tries to help his friend Daniel Dravot (Sean Connery), who gets delusions of grandeur after being mistaken for a god in *The Man Who Would Be King* (1975).

and then returned it after discovering they were both Masons. Peachy and his friend Daniel Dravot had Kipling witness a contract between them foreswearing alcohol and women until they completed a mission. The pair of rogues planned to become kings of a backward country called Kafiristan, north of Afghanistan. Kipling said it was impossible. A survey team had tried to map the country and never returned. The last white man to make it back was Alexander the Great, 2200 years earlier. Kipling gave Danny a Masonic symbol for luck.

Peachy and Danny went ahead with their plan, overcoming many dangers to reach Kafiristan. They met Billy Fish, a Ghurka warrior and sole survivor of the survey team who acted as interpreter with the people of Kafiristan.

Danny and Peachy trained the men of one village to be soldiers, then led them into battle successfully against their neighbours. An arrow hit Danny but did not kill him, merely lodging in the leather of his bandolier. The locals took this as evidence that Danny was the son of the god Sikander, their name for Alexander the Great. Danny and Peachy's army swept across the country, conquering all before it. The high priest of Kafiristan, Kafu Selim, summoned the Englishmen to the Holy City of Sikandergul. Selim did not believe Danny was a god but became convinced when he saw the Masonic symbol hung around Dravot's neck. Alexander the Great also bore the symbol of a Mason.

Danny ruled wisely but began to have delusions of grandeur. He decided to take a wife, a beautiful native woman called Roxanne, against the wishes of Selim. At the wedding ceremony Roxanne bit Danny's face, drawing blood. Everyone saw Danny was a man, not a god. He was thrown into a ravine and Peachy was crucified. But when Peachy did not die, the priests let him go. Kipling listens to the beggar relate all of this in amazement. Peachy departs, leaving behind the severed head of his friend Danny – still wearing the crown of the king of Kafiristan…

'THE FILM IS BEAUTIFULLY SERVED BY THE PERFORMANCES OF SEAN CONNERY AND MICHAEL CAINE, VERY FUNNY AS TWIN INCARNATIONS OF TYPICALLY ENDEARING KIPLING RANKER-ROGUES.' *MONTHLY FILM BULLETIN*

'WHETHER IT WAS THE INTENTION OF JOHN HUSTON OR NOT, THE TALE OF ACTION AND ADVENTURE IS A TOO-BROAD COMEDY, MOSTLY DUE TO THE POOR PERFORMANCE OF MICHAEL CAINE.' *VARIETY*

Rudyard Kipling's short story *The Man Who Would Be King* was first published in 1888. Nearly a century later, director John Huston got the chance to fulfil his long-held ambition to film the high adventure tale. The maker of such beloved movies as *The Maltese Falcon* (1941), *The Treasure of the Sierra Madre* (1947) and *The African Queen* (1952) had almost succeeded in launching the project in the 1950s, with Clark Gable and Humphrey Bogart in the leads. The combination of Paul Newman and Robert

LEFT:
Shakira Caine and her husband enjoy a joke during the making of *The Man Who Would Be King* (1975). Shakira was persuaded by John Huston to appear in the film as Roxanne.

Redford was also considered before Huston settled on Caine and Sean Connery.

The two leads had been friends for more than a decade, but this was the first chance for Caine and Connery to make a feature together. 'It was one of the most delightful films I've ever made in some of the most uncomfortable conditions,' Caine told *Venice* magazine in 2002. 'I'd never met John before that film. It could've been a dreadful experience if it had been done with two other men.'

The $8 million production was shot near Marrakesh in Morocco, with further filming on the Grande Montée at Chamonix in France and studio work at Pinewood. Caine rates Huston as the director who has most influenced him. 'I'd been shooting a couple of days and he stopped me in the middle of a take,' the actor told the *Sunday Times* in 1992. 'I said, "What's wrong?" He said, "You can speak faster, Michael. He's an honest man." And I thought that's right, and I got the whole character then and there.'

Huston insisted everyone came to see the rushes of what had already been shot during filming – even Caine, who had refused to attend such screenings since *Zulu* (1964). Huston rarely gave direction to his leads, as Caine recalled for *Venice*: 'I said to him one day, "You don't really tell us much, do you?" He said, "You're being paid a lot of money to do this, Michael. You should be able to get it right on your own." Sean and I were obviously giving him what he wanted, so he said nothing. Good directors always do that. Bad directors can't shut up.'

During shooting Huston changed his mind about who should play Roxanne, the Kafiristan woman that Daniel disastrously takes as his wife. The part had originally been given to actress Tessa Dahl, daughter of writer Roald Dahl and actress Patricia Neal. The director decided that Roxanne had to be played by a woman with dark skin. In 2002 Caine told the *San Bernadino*

County Sun how his Indian-born wife Shakira was chosen over dinner one night. 'John said, "We've got to find an Arab princess somewhere." And we were all eating away and we stopped eating and looked at Shakira [Caine's wife]. She didn't want to do it. She had never acted before. But I said, "Don't worry about that. I'll show you how."'

The film was released in December 1975, rated A in the UK and PG in America. Reviewers praised the picture, although influential US trade paper *Variety* singled out Caine's performance for criticism. *The Man Who Would Be King* was nominated for four Oscars, including screenplay adaptation and one for the costumes by Hollywood legend Edith Head. The film also received BAFTA nominations for its costumes and cinematography. *Entertainment Weekly* later singled out Caine's work in the film as one of 100 performances unjustly overlooked for an Oscar.

The Man Who Would Be King is a delightful film that only seems to improve with age. Full of spectacle and stirring music, this is a *Boy's Own* adventure of the highest standard. As in many Huston films, this is a story about the dreams and follies of men – women are kept very much on the margins. Nevertheless, the script is funny and wry, while Caine and Connery give some of the warmest performances in their careers. It's only a shame the duo haven't had a similar vehicle since.

THE MARSEILLES CONTRACT (1974)
(US title: *THE DESTRUCTORS*)

Cast: Michael Caine (John Deray), Anthony Quinn (Steve Ventura), James Mason (Jacques Brizard), Maurice Ronet (Briac), Alexandra Stewart (Rita Matthews), Maureen Kerwin (Lucienne Brizard), Catherine Rouvel (Brizard's

*mistress), Marcel Bozzuffi (Calmet), Patrick Floerscheim (Kovakian), André Oumansky (Marsac), Georges Beller (Minierini).
Crew: Robert Parrish (director), Judd Bernard (producer and writer), Roy Budd (music), Douglas Slocombe (cinematography), Willy Kemplen (editor), Willy Holt (production designer).*

In Marseilles an undercover agent for the American Drug Enforcement Agency (DEA) is murdered while trying to infiltrate the organisation of drug smuggler Jacques Brizard. The crime boss has political connections within France that protect him. The DEA boss in Paris, Steve Ventura, decides the only way to get Brizard is hire a professional assassin. French police inspector Briac arranges a meeting for Ventura with such a killer. The DEA man is surprised to find the hitman is an old friend, John Deray. Ventura gives Deray $50,000 to kill Brizard. The assassin infiltrates Brizard's family by romancing the drug dealer's beautiful daughter. Ventura learns Brizard is receiving a massive shipment of drugs soon. Brizard discovers Deray is an assassin and tries to have him eliminated. Deray and Ventura collaborate to bring down Brizard as he oversees the drugs shipment. Briac intervenes, planning to kill Brizard and steal the drugs. Briac and Deray die in a shootout but Brizard escapes. Ventura finds and silently murders Brizard...

'A THRILLER THAT THROWS MOST OF THE CURRENT CLICHÉS – CRASHING CARS, BOUNCING MOTORBIKES, VIGILANTE COPS – INTO ONE UNEASY STORY AND COMES UP WITH NOT VERY MUCH.' **SUNDAY TELEGRAPH**

'THE PLOT ... ALLOWS MR CAINE TO MAKE LOVE AND SHOOT A FEW PEOPLE. BUT JUDGING BY HIS ONE EXPRESSION, I'M NOT SURE WHICH HE PREFERRED.' **DAILY MIRROR**

In the winter of 1973 producer Judd Bernard approached Caine with an offer – five weeks in a warm climate shooting a thriller with Anthony Quinn and James Mason. 'It was just after my daughter [Natasha] was born, and to get her out of London in the winter into the south of France was wonderful,' Caine told *Time Out* in 1992. 'I never even read the script. I said: "I'll fucking do this! I'm out of here!"'

The Marseille Contract was a $2 million movie written by Bernard and directed by American Robert Parrish, who had won an Oscar for editing *Body and Soul* (1947) before moving behind the camera. Caine said *The Marseille Contract* was a bad film 'where I had the best bloody time in my life. We started off in Nice, went to Cannes, St Tropez and wound up in Paris.' The picture was shot almost entirely on location, with post-production at Pinewood in England. It reunited Caine with cinematographer Douglas Slocombe and stunt driver Remy Julienne, both of whom had worked with him on *The Italian Job* (1969).

In his 1988 book *Hollywood Doesn't Live Here Anymore*, Parrish recalled making the film. 'It was a pleasure working with James Mason, Michael Caine, and Anthony Quinn. We all tried, but sometimes you win and sometimes you lose.' The director also recalled how a studio representative insisted that a main character share his initials. The representative demanded that the actor playing that character be dressed in expensive monogrammed shirts and possess a nine-piece set of monogrammed luggage from Louis Vuitton. The representative, of course, acquired all of these when shooting concluded.

The BBFC required cuts before passing the film with an A certificate in August 1974. Critics were less than impressed by the results. In America the picture was cryptically renamed *The Destructors* and rated PG, but also failed to catch fire. The film is as yet unavailable on DVD.

The Marseilles Contract is cut-rate thriller material cast with first-rate actors. A slight script never engages you while the actors meander through the action, waiting for their pay packet to arrive. Slocombe's cinematography gives the picture a look far better than the production's limited budget or imagination deserves. There's a spectacular sequence, arranged by Julienne, with two speeding vehicles playfully duelling on a tight, twisting mountain road, a scene replicated in the James Bond film *GoldenEye* (1995). Otherwise, the film offers little of interest. Caine may play an assassin dressed like Jack Carter, but he spends much of his time grinning like a Cheshire cat. You will probably not share his enthusiasm.

MIDNIGHT IN ST PETERSBURG (1997)

Cast: Michael Caine (Harry Palmer), Jason Connery (Nick), Michelle Rene Thomas (Brandy), Michael Gambon (Alex), Michael Sarrazin (Craig), Tanya Jackson (Tatiana), Serge Houde (Dr Vestry), Anatoly Davidov (Yuri), Vlasta Vrana (Hans Schreiber), John Dunn-Hill (Louis), Lev Prygunov (Colonel Gradsky).
Crew: Doug Jackson (director), Edward Simons, Kent Walwin, Alexander Goloutva, John Dunning and André Link (producers), Peter Welbeck [pseudonym for Harry Alan Towers] (writer), Rick Wakeman (music), Peter Benison (cinematography), Vidal Beique (editor), Chris Tulloch (production designer).

Former British secret agent Harry Palmer runs a private investigation agency in Moscow, aided by Nick and several more former employees of

Alex, a deadly crime boss in St Petersburg. Nick is dating a ballerina, Tatiana, whose father Feodor is a curator at the Hermitage art gallery in St Petersburg. Harry is hired to recover a kilogram of enriched plutonium, enough to make three atomic bombs. Alex tries to kill Palmer with a letter bomb. Harry and Nick travel to St Petersburg, seeking the missing plutonium, and Tatiana is abducted. Alex threatens to kill her unless Feodor helps him. Harry asks for help from Yuri, a St Petersburg gangster and rival of Alex.

Nick becomes suspicious when Feodor does not report Tatiana's abduction to the police. He follows Feodor to an old film studio, but is captured by thugs and imprisoned with Tatiana. Palmer discovers that the plutonium is being traded in a deal at the film studio. Harry gets into the studio, with help from Yuri. Alex abducted Tatiana to make Feodor bring $5 million worth of paintings from the Hermitage. An American art dealer was buying the paintings and Alex was using the money to buy the plutonium. But Nick escapes and helps Palmer stop the deal. The paintings are returned to the Hermitage and the plutonium is safely recovered.

'MORE LIKE A TRAVELOGUE THAN A THRILLER, THE STORY'S DEBILITATING LACK OF MOMENTUM … IS ACCENTUATED BY RICK WAKEMAN'S ABYSMAL SCORE AND A SET OF CARDBOARD SUPPORTING CHARACTERS WHO DEPOSIT CLUES AND COMPLICATIONS WITH MONOTONOUS REGULARITY. NONETHELESS, CAINE'S DOGGED PROFESSIONALISM IS IMPRESSIVE.'
SIGHT AND SOUND

In 1994 Caine went to Russia to make a new Harry Palmer movie for maverick producer

Harry Alan Towers, who also wrote the film under his 'Peter Welbeck' pseudonym. That picture, *Bullet to Beijing*, finished shooting in October and director George Mihalka departed, but Caine agreed to stay on for an extra month to make another Harry Palmer movie. *Midnight in St Petersburg* was never intended for cinemas, instead being made to premiere on the Showtime cable network in America. 'I said okay, since the entire company, same people, same places were utilised,' Caine told *Variety*. 'But my main interest is in the feature.' There was talk of further Harry Palmer made-for-TV movies if *Midnight in St Petersburg* proved successful, but Caine was not interested in such projects.

Showtime planned to premiere *Midnight in St Petersburg* a few months after the theatrical release of *Bullet to Beijing*. 'It would be difficult to get Michael Caine to do an original [TV] movie,' Showtime's senior vice president of programme acquisitions and planning, Michael Duda, told the *Los Angeles Times*. 'He's a well-established star who comes with a certain price. By having a theatrical locomotive we could make it work.'

Caine told the *Los Angeles Times* about his reluctance to make *Midnight in St Petersburg*. 'I did the TV movie because it was the only way they could make the feature.' Towers was inspired to set up the deal after visiting Russia. He heard about the country's first licensed private security organisation, a firm largely staffed by ex-Red Army intelligence. This provided the basis for the agency Palmer establishes in *Midnight in St Petersburg*.

Journeyman director Doug Jackson was brought in to helm the TV movie. A leading female role went to Tanya Jackson, an actress with no previous film experience. To keep costs down, much of the picture was set in and around the film studio where it was being shot. Post-production on the movie was completed in 1995

but the expected broadcast was delayed by the failure of *Bullet to Beijing* to secure a theatrical release. *Midnight in St Petersburg* eventually made its American debut on cable TV in 1997, rated R by the MPAA. In Britain the TV movie went straight to video in April 1997, rated 15, but has since been deleted. The film has been released on DVD in North America but not in the UK.

Most of the criticisms applied to *Bullet to Beijing* apply twice over to this execrable effort, bankrupt both in imagination and execution. Caine looks like a man haunted by how low his career prospects have sunk. This direct-to-video dog is arguably the nadir of his film career in the 1990s, although *On Deadly Ground* (1994) and *Shadow Run* (1998) also lay claim to that honour. They have the advantage of being so bad that some ironic pleasure can be derived from seeing them. *Midnight in St Petersburg* is just wooden, lifeless and dull.

MISS CONGENIALITY (2000)

Cast: Sandra Bullock (Gracie Hart), Michael Caine (Victor Melling), Benjamin Bratt (Eric Matthews), Candice Bergen (Kathy Morningside), William Shatner (Stan Fields), Ernie Hudson (McDonald), John DiResta (Agent Clonsky), Heather Burns (Cheryl 'Rhode Island'), Melissa De Sousa (Karen 'New York'), Steve Monroe (Frank Tobin), Deirdre Quinn (Mary Jo 'Texas'), Wendy Raquel Robinson (Leslie 'California').
Crew: Donald Petrie (director), Sandra Bullock (producer), Marc Lawrence and Katie Ford and Caryn Lucas (writers), Ed Shearmur (music), Laszlo Kovacs (cinematography), Billy Weber (editor), Peter Larkin (production designer).

Gracie Hart is a mannish agent for the FBI. The FBI receives a letter from the Citizen, a domestic

terrorist, who threatens to attack the Miss United States beauty pageant in Texas, and Gracie is chosen to go undercover as a contestant. The FBI employs a pageant consultant called Victor Melling to make Gracie a credible candidate. She gets a makeover and emerges as a beautiful woman, to the surprise of her boss Eric Matthews. Forensic tests suggest the threatening letter was sent by a woman. Gracie believes the pageant organiser, Kathy Morningside, is involved. But the FBI arrests the real terrorist in Nevada and closes down the operation in Texas. Gracie decides to stay at the pageant, believing Kathy is planning a copycat bombing. Gracie realises that the bomb is hidden in the winner's tiara. She throws the tiara into the air just as Kathy detonates the bomb. Afterwards the other contestants give Gracie the title of Miss Congeniality…

'MISS CONGENIALITY IS YET ANOTHER MISCALCULATED VEHICLE FOR THE EVER-FEISTY SANDRA BULLOCK … CAINE HAS A FINE TIME AS THE MAKEOVER MASTER EVEN IF HE'S VASTLY OVERQUALIFIED FOR THE MODEST ASSIGNMENT.' **VARIETY**

'GOSSAMER-THIN ENTERTAINMENT OF THE SORT THAT WOULD MAKE FOR AN INOFFENSIVE FIRST-DATE MOVIE. THERE IS A COMPLETELY INCONSEQUENTIAL FEEL TO THE WHOLE EXERCISE.' **EMPIRE**

This screwball comedy was created in 1999 as a vehicle for producer/actress Sandra Bullock. Donald Petrie was brought on board as director, having previous helmed hits like *Mystic Pizza* (1988) and *Grumpy Old Men* (1993). Caine was hired to play gay beauty pageant consultant Victor Melling soon after receiving his Oscar

nomination as best supporting actor for *The Cider House Rules* (1999). 'I couldn't refuse working with Sandra Bullock,' he told *Variety*.

In the film's pressbook Caine discussed why he accepted the part: 'What I liked about the role was that it was funny, it was different and it was a comedy. In my most recent films, I played the man who destroyed the Marquis de Sade, an abortionist and a very violent gangster. After reading the script and finding it such a great comedy, it was such a relief. I said, "I'll do it. I'll do it. I'll do it." I was just dying to get a laugh on set.'

He started work on the $45 million movie in May 2000, soon after finishing his performance as the lead in *Shiner* (2000). The bulk of *Miss Congeniality* was shot in Austin, Texas, with brief location work in San Antonio and New York. Caine studied with a Texan pageant expert for his role as Victor and also sought tips from wife Shakira, who had come third in the 1967 Miss World contest. The picture reunited Caine with Candice Bergen, with whom he had co-starred more than 30 years earlier in *The Magus* (1968). The actor predicted significant success for *Miss Congeniality*. 'It's very funny. I think it will be a great vehicle for Sandra,' he told *Variety* just before the picture opened.

The film was released across America in December 2000. Reviews were mixed but *Miss Congeniality* became a Christmas hit at the box-office, grossing more than $105 million – the biggest hit of Caine's career at that time. This success was echoed around the world. In Britain the movie opened in March 2001 and grossed more than $15 million. It was released on video and DVD later in the year. The DVD includes two commentary tracks, deleted scenes and documentaries.

In 2002, some sources reported that work had already begun on a sequel in which Bullock's character would use her new-found

FAR LEFT: Victor Melling tries to teach Gracie Hart (Sandra Bullock) to walk more gracefully in the hit comedy *Miss Congeniality* (2000).

ABOVE: Bob Hoskins, Michael Caine and Cathy Tyson in the British gangster classic *Mona Lisa* (1986). Neil Jordan's bleak love story brought fine performances from all three actors.

beauty queen skills to become a model and hunt for a serial killer. Producers were reported to be hopeful of persuading Caine to reprise his role.

Miss Congeniality is a lightweight film that amuses you while it's happening, but doesn't stand up to any scrutiny. The movie wants to have its cake and eat it, scoring laughs from the baroque excesses of beauty pageants while still holding up the contestants as admirable for using their good looks to get ahead. The anorexic plot is just a vehicle for Bullock to exhibit her not inconsiderable comedic skills. Still, everyone hits their marks nicely, with Caine offering a delicate, understated performance as a disappointed gay man. *Miss Congeniality* is disposable fun – nothing more, nothing less.

MONA LISA (1986)

Cast: Bob Hoskins (George), Cathy Tyson (Simone), Michael Caine (Mortwell), Robbie Coltrane (Thomas), Clarke Peters (Anderson), Kate Hardie (Cathy), Zoë Nathenson (Jeannie), Sammi Davis (May), Rod Bedall (Torry), Joe Brown (Dudley), Pauline Melville (George's wife), Hossein Karimbeik (Raschid). Crew: Neil Jordan (director/co-writer), Patrick Cassavetti and Stephen Woolley (producers), David Leland (co-writer), Michael Kamen (music), Roger Pratt (cinematography), Lesley Walker (editor), Jamie Leonard (production designer).

George gets out of prison after serving seven years. He gets a job from his old boss, Mortwell, driving high-class prostitute Simone to her clients. She asks George to help her friend Cathy, a teenage prostitute. Both women were being pimped by a violent, brutal man called Anderson. George begins falling in love with Simone. He discovers that Anderson works for Mortwell. When George visits Mortwell at home, he finds Cathy being used by a client of Mortwell. George rescues Kathy but Mortwell sees them escape. George, Simone and Cathy go to Brighton. George realises that Simone and Cathy are lovers. Simone used him to get Cathy away. Mortwell and Anderson find the fugitives, but Simone murders her two hunters. She is ready to murder George too, despite everything he has done for her. George leaves, a sadder, less naïve man.

'A FILM TO SEE AGAIN, WITH THE CERTAINTY THAT EACH VIEWING WILL ADD SOMETHING NEW.' ***MONTHLY FILM BULLETIN***

'A PIC THAT SKILFULLY COMBINES COMEDY AND THRILLER, ROMANCE AND SLEAZE. MICHAEL CAINE IS … IN A GENEROUSLY SELF-EFFACING SUPPORTING ROLE AS A SINISTER, DANGEROUS VICE KING.' ***VARIETY***

BELOW: Mortwell sneers at George for falling in love with lesbian prostitute Simone (Cathy Tyson) in *Mona Lisa* (1986).

ABOVE: London gangster Mortwell lays down the law to naive George (Bob Hoskins) in *Mona Lisa* (1986).

Irish writer/director Neil Jordan originally began developing this story with Sean Connery in mind as the central character. Jordan invited screenwriter David Leland to write a screenplay based on the concept. The director then wrote six more drafts, inviting Leland to pass criticism on his work. Connery was approached for the role of George but the Scotsman was busy on another project and Jordan shifted his focus to Bob Hoskins. The London actor eventually agreed to star in the feature after completing work on Alan Alda's *Sweet Liberty* (1986). Jordan began writing new drafts with Hoskins in mind.

The film was originally to be financed by EMI but the multinational suddenly pulled out after a change in corporate strategy. Jordan began hastily searching for new funding and secured backing from Handmade Films, owned by former Beatle George Harrison. Handmade had released Hoskins' breakthrough movie *The Long Good Friday* (1980).

Mona Lisa was shot on location in London and Brighton at the end of 1985. Caine joined the picture for five days of filming, playing the murderous gangland boss Mortwell. His presence was crucial to ensure foreign distribution sales for the picture. Caine told the BBC programme *Film 86* what his role required: 'What you need is a leading actor, except it's too small for a leading actor to do it. My great friend is Bob Hoskins and I am a great admirer of Neil Jordan. So I said I'd do the part for them.'

In the film's publicity material, Caine said that playing a completely evil, unsympathetic character was another attraction: 'It's a great deal of fun for me to play someone who is an absolute, frightening creep. He's absolutely based on reality. I grew up in that milieu, you see. I've had a whale of a time … shouting and screaming at Bob, frightening the life out of everybody … I'm not a tough guy at all, but I really look it when I play it.'

Jordan recalled working with Caine for Robert Seller's 2003 book *Always Look on the Bright Side of Life*: 'We only had him for about a week, and he'd be quite impatient … you'd feel he'd want to get it in two or three takes. And then I'd get him to develop it and develop it and suddenly he wouldn't want to go … It was like a man who really wanted to act seriously and here was a part he could get his teeth into. It was wonderful working with him because he is such a good actor. It was wonderful actually getting him to express the dark-hearted stuff. Michael loved playing that part.'

The picture made its debut at the Cannes Film Festival in May 1986, where Hoskins won the best actor award and Jordan was nominated for the prestigious Golden Palm. The R-rated movie received a limited release in America a month later. Reviews were strong, particularly for Hoskins' performance, and the picture grossed nearly $6 million. It reached Britain in September to more praise, with reviewers noting Caine's short but telling performance. In 1987 Hoskins won a Golden Globe and a BAFTA for best actor and was nominated for an Oscar.

In a BFI poll to find the Top 100 British

movies of the 20th century, *Mona Lisa* was one of seven Caine pictures on the list, voted 67th. A DVD version was issued in 2001, with a commentary track and archive footage from 1986. In April 2003 Neil Jordan told the *San Francisco Examiner* that he had been approached by a producer interested in updating *Mona Lisa*. The director expressed incredulity at the idea: 'They asked me if I would remake it! Can you believe that?'

Mona Lisa is powerful picture that pushes a lot of buttons. It manages to present humour, pathos, skin-crawling distaste and excitement without ever being gratuitous or striking a wrong note. Jordan lets his story build gradually while maintaining a remorseless progression towards the inevitable, bloody denouement. Hoskins delivers a career-best performance as the naïve George, falling in love with a manipulative lesbian prostitute. Caine's role is small but exudes almost as much menace as he did in the whole of *Get Carter* – even while stroking a white rabbit. This is a compelling, intelligent film.

MR DESTINY (1990)

Cast: James Belushi (Larry Burrows), Linda Hamilton (Ellen Burrows), Michael Caine (Mike), Jon Lovitz (Clip Metzler), Hart Bockner (Niles Pender), Bill McCutcheon (Leon Hansen), Rene Russo (Cindy Jo), Jay O Sanders (Jackie Earle), Maury Chaykin (Guzelman), Pat Corley (Harry Burrows), Douglas Seale (Boswell), Courteney Cox (Jewel Jagger).
Crew: James Orr (director/co-writer/co-producer), Jim Cruickshank (co-writer/co-producer), David Newman (music), Alex Thomson (cinematography), Michael R Miller (editor), Michael Seymour (production designer).

Fifteen-year-old Larry Burrows strikes out and his team loses a championship baseball game. Twenty years later he still rues what happened, believing that his whole life would have been better if he'd just hit the ball. On his 35th birthday Larry gets fired from his job at a sports equipment corporation when he discovers that executive vice president Niles Pender is plotting behind the scenes to sell the company. Larry's car breaks down on the way home. He enters a bar where the barman, Mike, gives him a special elixir that rewrites history. Larry *did* hit the ball 20 years ago and became a hero. He is now president of the sports equipment corporation and married to the owner's daughter. But Larry soon finds himself hankering after his old life. He is framed for murder by Pender and flees, going back to the bar. After another drink of the elixir, Larry's old life is restored. He stops Pender selling the company and becomes executive vice president...

> 'MICHAEL CAINE, OF COURSE, IS FLAWLESS ... BUT THE MOVIE IS A SLOW MARCH THROUGH FOREGONE CONCLUSIONS.'
> **CHICAGO SUN-TIMES**

> 'THE DESTINY OF THIS PICTURE FROM WRITER-PRODUCERS JAMES ORR (WHO ALSO DIRECTS) AND JIM CRUICKSHANK IS NOT HARD TO FORECAST: EXPECT A FAIRLY QUICK EXIT FROM THEATERS.'
> **HOLLYWOOD REPORTER**

Filming on this small-scale comedy began on 17 March 1990 with location work in North Carolina. Caine received third billing in the credits but appeared in only a handful of scenes. He joined the production after completing his starring role in *A Shock to the System* (1990). Curiously, this picture goes unmentioned in Caine's autobiography and is also missing from several books about the actor's life and career.

The film's lead actress was Linda Hamilton, who had starred in *The Terminator* (1984) and the US TV series *Beauty and the Beast*. During an interview with *Starburst* magazine to promote her role in *Terminator 2: Judgment Day*, she made mention of *Mr Destiny*: 'It was another mediocre movie. I've had more than my share of those. I'd just gone off to do *Mr Destiny* in North Carolina and *T2* was offered.' *Mr Destiny* featured early, minor roles for Rene Russo and Courteney Cox, both of whom would become well-known actresses during the 1990s.

Mr Destiny was released to America cinemas in October 1990, grossing more than $15 million. The picture got mediocre reviews, with critics finding the central premise all too familiar. (Ironically, an inverted version of *Mr Destiny*'s plot was used a decade later for the film *The Family Man* (2000), starring Nicholas Cage.) In Britain the BBFC rated the film PG in December 1990, but it apparently went straight to video in 1991. It has since been deleted in the UK. A DVD version is available in the US.

This movie has 'straight to video' written all over it. B-movie regular James Belushi does his usual everyman routine in a tired, witless retread of Frank Capra's vastly superior *It's a Wonderful Life* (1946). That film showed how one man's life can touch the lives of an entire community. *Mr Destiny* shows that if Belushi had only hit one baseball, he could have been rich, adulterous and unhappy – all at the same time. Caine's role is of the blink-and-you'll-miss-it variety. This movie is strictly for Caine completists.

THE MUPPET CHRISTMAS CAROL (1992)

Cast: Michael Caine (Ebenezer Scrooge), Dave Goelz (The Great Gonzo, Robert Marley, Bunsen Honeydew and Betina Cratchit), Steve Whitmire (Rizzo the Rat, Bean Bunny, Kermit the Frog,

RIGHT: Ebenezer Scrooge looms over his long suffering clerk Bob Cratchit (Kermit the Frog) in *The Muppet Christmas Carol* (1992).

*Beaker and Belinda Cratchit), Jerry Nelson
(Tiny Tim Cratchit, Jacob Marley and Ma Bear),
Frank Oz (Miss Piggy, Fozzie Bear, Sam Eagle
and Animal), Steven Mackintosh (Fred),
Meredith Braun (Belle), Robin Weaver (Clara).
Crew: Brian Henson (director/co-producer),
Martin G Baker (co-producer), Jerry Juhl
(writer), Miles Goodman (music), John Fenner
(cinematography), Michael Jablow (editor),
Val Strazovec (production designer).*

Ebenezer Scrooge is a tight-fisted moneylender.
On Christmas Eve he is visited by the spectres
of his dead partners, Jacob and Robert Marley.
They are trapped in purgatory, bound by the
chains of greed and avarice which they embraced
in life. The Marley brothers tell their former
partner that three spirits will haunt him during
the night. Scrooge is indeed visited by ghosts of
Christmas past, present and future. The old man
realises that he abandoned love in his pursuit of
money. He is unwanted and unloved, with
nobody to mourn his passing. Scrooge becomes
a new man, vowing to be generous and to honour
the spirit of Christmas…

'CAINE RESISTS THE TEMPTATION
TO HAM UP HIS LEAD ROLE, AND
THE MUPPETS ARE FAR MORE
SPONTANEOUS THAN SOME OF
HIS RECENT REAL LIFE CO-STARS.'
CITY LIMITS

'NOT AS ENCHANTING OR AMUSING
AS THE PREVIOUS ENTRIES IN THE
MUPPET SERIES … MICHAEL CAINE
IS PERFECTLY CAST AS THE NASTY
SCROOGE, THOUGH HIS ROLE IS TOO
DOMINANT.' *VARIETY*

The Muppet Christmas Carol was the first major
project undertaken following the death of the

Muppets' creator, Jim Henson. His son Brian
stepped forward to direct the picture, his first
feature film. Screenwriter Jerry Juhl adapted the
story by Charles Dickens, turning the author into
an on-screen narrator and commentator. In an
interview on the DVD release, Henson confesses
to early trepidation about the project: 'I didn't
know how we could do a Muppet version of
A Christmas Carol that would stand out from all
the others. It was Jerry Juhl's idea to cast Gonzo
as Charles Dickens and have him telling the
story. That's when we knew we had a film.'

The filmmakers decided that Scrooge had to
be played by a human actor and offered the part
to Caine. The part required him to sing two of
the songs written by Paul Williams for the
picture – a first for the actor. The production
was filmed entirely at Shepperton Studios.
The movie reunited Caine with Frank Oz,
his director on *Dirty Rotten Scoundrels* (1988).

'People think I'll be a silly old Scrooge,'
Caine told *Empire* magazine in 1992, 'because
it's a silly old Muppets film. You have to play
Scrooge absolutely seriously, otherwise it's not
funny. So what you've got is my performance as
Scrooge, had I been at the National Theatre.
It's a very stretching, difficult role funnily
enough, because you have to sing and you
have to act with puppets.'

In publicity material for the film,
Caine described what inspired his performance:
'My basic role models for Scrooge were not
Victorian, they were very modern and came
from watching CNN and seeing the trials and
tribulations of all the Wall Street cheats and
embezzlers. I thought they represented a very
good picture of meanness and greed! My
Scrooge looks particularly irredeemable
and is more psychotic than most.'

The Muppet Christmas Carol was released in
December 1992. Critics gave it mediocre notices
but the picture still grossed $27 million in the US

and more than $4 million in Britain. A video release followed in 1993 and the movie made its DVD debut in 2002.

The Muppet Christmas Carol strikes an uneasy balance as it blends the Dickens story with musical numbers, pithy asides and clowning puppets. The result is a halfway house that chops and changes its mood too often. The saccharine songs quickly wear out their welcome, but the running commentary on events by Gonzo and Rizzo the Rat provides welcome comic relief for adult viewers too familiar with the film's source material. Caine wisely plays it straight as Scrooge, leaving the humour to the felt-faced creations around him. The less said about his singing, the better. The Muppet Christmas Carol has its moments, but will try the patience of any adult who sees it more than once.

ABOVE:

Caine poses with his puppet co-stars for *The Muppet Christmas Carol* (1992).

N

NOISES OFF (1992)

Cast: Carol Burnett (Dotty Otley and Mrs Clackett), Michael Caine (Lloyd Fellowes), Denholm Elliott (Selsdon Mowbray and The Burglar), Julie Hagerty (Poppy Taylor), Marilu Henner (Belinda Blair and Flavia Brent), Mark Linn-Baker (Timm Allgood), Christopher Reeve (Frederick Dallas and Philip Brent), John Ritter (Garry Lejeune and Roger Tramplemain), Nicollette Sheridan (Brooke Ashton and Vicki). Crew: Peter Bogdanovich (director), Frank Marshall (producer), Marty Kaplan (writer), Tim Suhrstedt (cinematography), Lisa Day (editor), Norman Newberry (production designer).

British sex farce *Nothing On* is having its opening night on Broadway. Director Lloyd Fellowes flees the theatre, convinced the show will be a disaster. He remembers all the problems that plagued the show during six months on tour – from the dress rehearsal in Iowa to a disastrous matinée in Miami and the final horror of a crazed performance in Cleveland. The cast is filled with temperamental actors who hate themselves and each other and have endless romantic intrigues. To Lloyd's amazement, the show is a hit…

RIGHT: What else can go wrong? Dotty Otley (Carol Burnett), Lloyd Fellowes (Caine), Belinda Blair (Marilu Henner), Selsdon Mowbray (Denholm Elliott), Brooke Ashton (Nicollette Sheridan) and Poppy Taylor (Julie Hagerty) can only watch as their play unravels in *Noises Off* (1992).

LEFT:
Caine displayed
his gift for comedy
as harassed stage
director Lloyd
Fellowes in
Noises Off (1992).

ABOVE:

Director Peter Bogdanovich's adaptation of *Noises Off* (1992) flopped, despite an accomplished cast including (from Left) Caine, Carol Burnett, Marilu Henner and Denholm Elliott.

'*NOISES OFF* IS NOT SO MUCH A BAD FILM AS ONE WHICH SHOULD PROBABLY NEVER HAVE BEEN MADE AT ALL … IT SIMPLY DOESN'T FEEL LIKE CINEMA.' *THE GUARDIAN*

'IF EVER A PLAY WAS DESIGNED NOT TO BE FILMED, THAT PLAY IS *NOISES OFF* … IT POSITIVELY REEKS OF GREASEPAINT.' *SUNDAY EXPRESS*

Michael Frayn's stage farce *Noises Off* had been a smash hit, running for five years in London's West End and almost as long on Broadway. The film rights were acquired by Steven Spielberg's Amblin Entertainment but the stage-bound story defied an easy conversion to celluloid. Director Peter Bogdanovich had been Oscar-nominated twice over for his work on *The Last Picture Show* (1971), but had grown up in the theatre. He persuaded producer Frank Marshall to let him make a movie version of *Noises Off*. 'Nobody could figure out how to do it as a movie,' Marshall said in an interview with the *Sunday Times* in 1992, 'but Peter thought he knew how.'

'With a play everybody usually starts to discuss how to change things, but I wanted to do the opposite,' Bogdanovich told the *Sunday Times*, 'to preserve as much as possible, especially everything that had worked

in the theatre.' He discovered that extra
sequences had been added to Frayn's original
script over the years. Bogdanovich hired the
London show's assistant director to help
compile the definitive version of the play.

The film's director and producer hand-
picked the main cast, with Caine chosen as long-
suffering stage director Lloyd Fellowes. 'Michael
Caine was very much who we wanted for that
part,' Bogdanovich said. 'I've always wanted to
work with Michael, and now that I have, I want
to work with him again! He told me he didn't
think he'd ever had so much dialogue in a
picture in his life.'

Normally one minute of screen time is equal
to each page of a film's script. But Bogdanovich
wanted Noises Off to maintain its frantic pace
and therefore shot 225 pages of script at a rate
of only 25 seconds per page. The director also
rehearsed the cast for five weeks before shooting
began, a rare luxury for any film. The picture
was made predominantly on sets at Universal
Studios in Los Angeles during 1991. The
production reunited Caine with two old friends
– Christopher Reeve, his co-star from *Deathtrap*
(1982), and British actor Denholm Elliott. Caine
and Elliott had shared memorable scenes in *Alfie*
(1966) and starred in the gritty war drama *Too
Late the Hero* (1970).

Noises Off was released in America in March
1992. Despite strong reviews, the movie took
less than $2.5 million at the box-office, opening
against the smash-hit erotic thriller *Basic Instinct*
(1992). It reached British cinemas three months
later but only grossed just over $150,000. The
movie was rush-released onto video in
November 1992 and deleted six months later.
Never available on DVD, *Noises Off* is much
sought after by collectors and copies fetch
high prices on internet auction sites.

In his autobiography Caine describes the film
as an honourable failure: 'The play was brilliant

and we kept very close to it, and the actors could
not have been better … all the ingredients for
a wonderful film. The people who saw it loved
it, but we could not get the general public into
the cinemas.'

This version of *Noises Off* is often
hysterically funny, but despite the best efforts
of the filmmakers rather than because of them.
Frayn's source material is so strong that the farce
shines through all Bogdanovich's attempts to put
his own stamp on it. The film's pointless framing
sequence and feeble happy ending dull the play's
lustre and hold back the laughs for too long.
At least the director has the good sense not to
tamper with 90 per cent of the original and that's
enough to keep the laughs coming thick and fast.
Caine shows his usual gift for comedy but,
frankly, Bogdanovich would have been better
off just filming a performance of the play.

O

ON DEADLY GROUND (1994)

*Cast: Steven Seagal (Forrest Taft), Michael
Caine (Michael Jennings), Joan Chen (Masu),
John C McGinley (MacGruder), R Lee Ermey
(Stone), Shari Shattuck (Liles), Billy Bob
Thornton (Homer Carlton), Richard Hamilton
(Hugh Palmer), Chief Irvin Brink (Silook),
Apanguluk Charlie Kairaiuak (Tunrak).
Crew: Steven Seagal (director/co-producer),
Julius R Nasso and A Kitman Ho (co-producers),
Ed Horowitz and Robin U Russin (writers), Basil
Poledouris (music), Ric Waite (cinematography),
Robert A Ferretti and Don Brochu (editors),
William Ladd Skinner (production designer).*

A rig owned by Aegis Oil catches fire in Valdez,
Alaska. Ruthless company boss Michael

Jennings brings in trouble-shooter Forrest Taft to stop the blaze. Rig foreman Hugh Palmer blames Jennings for the disaster, claiming his boss forced him to use faulty safety equipment. Forrest discovers that the allegation is true. Jennings has to get the world's biggest oil rig, Aegis-1, online soon or else oil rights worth billions of dollars a week will revert to the native Eskimos. The company is deliberately using faulty equipment because waiting for replacements would mean missing the deadline. Jennings has Palmer murdered and tries to kill Forrest too. But Taft survives the blast and is nursed back to health by the Eskimos. Forrest takes vengeance on the oil company, sabotaging Aegis-1 just before it goes online and drowning Jennings in oil. The Eskimos reclaim their land.

'THIS IS A VANITY PRODUCTION PARADING AS A SOCIAL STATEMENT.'
VARIETY

'AN EMBARRASSED MICHAEL CAINE LOOKS TO BE HAVING SECOND THOUGHTS FROM HIS FIRST FRAME TO HIS LAST, WHEN HE BEGS, "GO AHEAD, SHOOT ME!" THE FILM PROBABLY FEELS THE SAME WAY.'
WASHINGTON POST

RIGHT:
Black-hearted oil tycoon Michael Jennings sends in his best trouble-shooter, Forrest Taft (Steven Seagal, right), watched by henchman MacGruder (John C McGinley) in *On Deadly Ground* (1994).

Martial arts expert Steven Seagal was just a minor action movie hero until *Under Siege* stormed the US box-office in 1992. Its success gave him the clout to make *On Deadly Ground*, an action movie with a pro-environmental message. Seagal was the star of the film, one of its three producers and also made his directing debut. Shooting began in early spring 1993 with five weeks on location in Alaska. The cast and crew endured blizzards and wild extremes of temperature. 'This is a picture I care deeply about,' Seagal said in the movie's publicity material. 'If it wasn't something special, I wouldn't have gone to the great effort and risk.'

He hired Caine to star as evil oil company boss Michael Jennings, continuing a Hollywood trend of hiring British actors to play villains for action features. Caine praised his boss in the studio-approved publicity material: 'A first-time director brings a whole new load of fresh ideas. Steven has a very strong vision of what this movie is and should be. He earned my trust. I wouldn't have come and just done a crash, bang martial arts film. There's more to *On Deadly Ground* than that. Although we have an exciting piece of entertainment, the film does carry an important message as well.' The actor explained his reasons for taking the role: 'In a film called *Mona Lisa* (1986) I played a really dark character with no nice side at all, and I had a great time. I thought it would be fun to do it again.'

Behind the scenes Caine was less than impressed. During a public interview at the NFT in 1998, the actor said his experiences while making *On Deadly Ground* helped drive him into semi-retirement: 'I ... sort of stopped worked because the joy had gone out of doing it. I finally wound up in Alaska with Steven Seagal, which took quite a lot of joy out of it. I remember ringing down to the desk in my hotel and saying, "Could you send someone up for the laundry?" And they said, "The laundrette's next door." And I was freezing my butt off, and I thought, "I don't need this," so I stopped.'

After Alaska the production moved to the state of Washington for more location filming before concluding back in Los Angeles. There followed a dispute between Seagal and Warner Bros over the final cut of *On Deadly Ground*. The picture concludes with the star delivering an environmental lecture that attacks big business and alleges political collusion in pollution. Rumours at the time suggested that in Seagal's original cut the lecture lasted up to 15 minutes, but the studio insisted this be edited down to four.

On Deadly Ground was released in America with an R rating in February 1994. Lambasted by critics, it grossed nearly $40 million – less than half what *Under Siege* had taken. Seagal won the Razzie award as worst director for this feature and has not directed a film since. *On Deadly Ground* reached British cinemas a month later, with the BBFC requiring 70 seconds of cuts before granting a 15 rating. It grossed more than $2 million.

On Deadly Ground has a car-crash quality, being so compulsively awful it is difficult to tear your eyes away. Seagal's pro-environment sentiments are laudable but his delivery of them is laughable. After an orgy of violence, the lecture at the finale carries no weight or credibility. Caine's performance is among the worst of his career, with an accent that veers from Cockney to California and back again. Just as variable is his hair colour, appearing jet black in some scenes and dark brown in others, as if Caine was combing his locks with Marmite. Comparisons to his performance in *Mona Lisa* are risible, to say the least. Whatever the size of his fee for this farrago, it was not enough to match the indignity *On Deadly Ground* heaped upon his career.

P

PEEPER (1975)

Cast: Michael Caine (Leslie C Tucker),
Natalie Wood (Ellen Prendergast), Kitty Winn
(Mianne Prendergast), Michael Constantine
(Anglich), Thayer David (Frank Prendergast),
Timothy Agoglia Carey (Sid), Liam Dunn
(Billy Pate), Don Calfa (Rosie).
Crew: Peter Hyams (director), Irwin Winkler
and Robert Chartoff (producers), W D Richter
(writer), Richard Clements (music), Earl Rath
(cinematography), James Mitchell (editor),
Albert Brenner (production designer).

Leslie C Tucker is a British private eye working
in Los Angeles in 1948. He is hired to a find
a woman called Anya by her father, Anglich.
Twenty-nine years earlier Anglich left his
daughter at a local orphanage. Now he has come
into some money, the father wants to share the
wealth with Anya. But she was adopted while
still a child. Tucker tracks Anya to the wealthy
Prendergast family of Beverly Hills. He deduces
that one of the two daughters, Ellen and Mianne,
is really Anya. Anglich sends Tucker a suitcase
of cash for Anya. Soon after Anglich's murdered
body is dumped in the private eye's office.
Tucker cuts through a complex web of lies,
blackmail and embezzlement to discover which
daughter is Anya. He gives her the money, but
falls in love with the other sister...

'*PEEPER* IS FLIMSY WHIMSY. PETER
HYAMS' LIMP SPOOF OF A 1940S
PRIVATE-EYE FILM ... SHOWS FAR
MORE CARE IN PHYSICAL DETAILS
THAN ARTISTIC ONES.' *VARIETY*

FAR RIGHT: Ellen
Prendergast (Natalie
Wood) gets up
close and personal
with Tucker in the
hard boiled parody
Peeper (1975).

RIGHT:
Caine starred as
unlikely private eye
Leslie C Tucker in
Peeper (1975).

'IT'S WORTH LOOKING OUT FOR,
IF ONLY TO SEE MICHAEL CAINE'S
KNOWING FUNNY PERFORMANCE
AS AN ENGLISH OPPORTUNIST
WHO FETCHES UP IN CALIFORNIA.'
DAILY MAIL

Keith Laumer's novel *Deadfall* (no relation to
the 1968 Caine film of the same name) was first
published in 1971, spoofing the hard-boiled
private eye genre popularised by writers like
Raymond Chandler and Mickey Spillane.
The film rights were acquired by producers
Irwin Winkler and Robert Chartoff, who hired
screenwriter W D Richter to adapt the novel.

Director Peter Hyams was chosen to helm the project, made with the working title *Fat Chance*.

Caine was hired to play private detective Leslie C Tucker. He was old friends with co-star Natalie Wood, as the pair had dated briefly in the 1960s when Caine was in Hollywood making *Gambit* (1966). *Fat Chance* was Wood's first film for five years. The former child actress had become a star in classic movies like *Rebel Without a Cause* (1955) and *West Side Story* (1961), but in the 1970s turned down roles in order to have a family. Caine cited the opportunity to work with her as a key factor in accepting the role.

The film was shot in Los Angeles early in 1974, with extensive location work aboard a cruise liner. The 1990 book *Candidly Caine* quotes Caine on the experience: 'It was fine to make; we all went down to Mexico on a ship, and we called at all the Caribbean ports. It was like a lot of films; you have the time of your like making it, but it didn't work at all.'

Twentieth Century-Fox was so underwhelmed by *Fat Chance*, it kept the picture on the shelf for more than a year. But in 1975 film noir movies became hot property at the box-office, thanks to the success of *Chinatown* and *Farewell, My Lovely*. *Fat Chance* was re-edited and released with a PG rating and a new title: *Peeper*. But critics found the results sadly wanting and the picture sank without trace at the box-office.

Caine mentioned it in a *Photoplay* interview in 1976. 'I made *Fat Chance* some time ago in Hollywood with Natalie Wood. It was made before both *Chinatown* and *Farewell, My Lovely*. But because it's just been shown, everyone thinks it was made as a cheap quickie following on from the success of the other two.' The film did no better in Britain, where it was released in the summer of 1976. *Peeper* was released on video in 1987 but was soon deleted. No DVD

version has been issued.

Peeper has a neat opening, with a Humphrey Bogart double speaking the credits aloud in a dark alleyway. Alas, that's all the wit and invention this film possesses. The other 86 minutes are a purgatory of half-hearted attempts at hard-boiled dialogue and pointlessly convoluted plotting. As noted, *Peeper* was made before *Chinatown* or *Farewell, My Lovely* but both films are still ten times better than this dull, undramatic collection of clichés. Caine tries his best but brings nothing fresh or compelling to the material. Thanks to its obscurity and a rare 1970s film appearance by Natalie Wood, *Peeper* has a slight curiosity value – but little more.

PLAY DIRTY (1968)

Cast: Michael Caine (Captain Douglas), Nigel Davenport (Cyril Leech), Nigel Green (Colonel Masters), Harry Andrews (Brigadier Blore), Patrick Jordan (Major Watkins), Daniel Pilon (Major Allwood), Martin Burland (Dead Officer), George McKeenan (corporal at quayside), Bridget Espeet (Ann), Bernard Archard (Colonel Homerton), Aly Ben Ayed (Sadok), Enrique Avila (Kalarides), Mohsen Ben Abdallah (Hassan), Mohamed Kouka (Assine), Stanley Caine (German officer). Crew: André de Toth (director), Harry Saltzman (producer), Lotte Colin and Melvyn Bragg (writers), Michel Legrand (music), Edward Scaife (cinematography), Jack Slade (editor), Tom Morahan, Elven Webb and Maurice Pelling (art direction).

Colonel Masters runs an unconventional team of guerrilla warriors in North Africa during World War II. Brigadier Blore wants to close the operation down, but Masters gets one last chance. His men are to destroy a German fuel dump 400 miles behind enemy

FAR RIGHT:
Caine as reluctant soldier Captain Douglas in the gritty war drama *Play Dirty* (1968). The production was beset by problems, with co-star Richard Harris walking off the set and original director René Clément being fired after a fortnight.

IF YOU WANT TO SURVIVE...
PLAY DIRTY

FORGET THE MEDALS,
THROW AWAY THE RULE BOOK,

HARRY SALTZMAN presents

MICHAEL CAINE "Play Dirty" ⊗

also starring NIGEL GREEN · HARRY ANDREWS and BERNARD ARCHARD · DENNIS BRENNAK · JEREMY CHILD · PATRICK JORDAN · DANIEL PILON · MIKE STEVENS

Co-starring NIGEL DAVENPORT · NIGEL GREEN · HARRY ANDREWS and ALY BEN AYED · VIVIAN PICKLES

with MOHSEN BEN ABDALLAH · ENRIQUE AVILA · TAKIS EMMANUEL · MOHAMED KOUKA · SCOTT MILLER

Produced by HARRY SALTZMAN · Directed by ANDRE DeTOTH · LOTTE COLIN and MELVYN BRAGG

TECHNICOLOR PANAVISION

Based on an original story by GEORGE MARTON · A LOWNDES Production

United Artists
Entertainment from
Transamerica Corporation

lines.
An engineer
on loan to
the Allies
from British
Petroleum,
Captain Douglas,
is put in charge of
the mission. He is
shocked to discover
that his team is made
up of murderers, junkies,
homosexuals and thieves.
The true leader of this
rabble is Cyril Leech, who is
offered £2000 to ensure
Douglas gets back alive.

The eight-man squad travels across
the desert, surviving sandstorms, landmines
and booby traps. When they reach the
fuel dump, it is just a decoy. The team heads for
the nearest port disguised as German soldiers,
planning to steal a boat. Douglas and Leech

discover that
the real dump is at the
port. They decide to blow it up as a
diversion. Meanwhile, the Allied advance has
broken through the German lines and wants to
secure all the enemy's fuel. Blore orders Masters
to betray the squad's location to the Germans.
Douglas and his men attack the fuel dump but
only Douglas and Leech escape. Next morning
the Allies overrun the port. When Douglas and
Leech try to surrender, they are gunned down
by British soldiers.

'IT DEVELOPS INTO A REASONABLY
TIGHTLY MADE AND SUSPENSEFUL
ACTION FILM … MICHAEL CAINE AND
NIGEL DAVENPORT … PLAY WITH
THEIR USUAL CASUAL AUTHORITY.'
MONTHLY FILM BULLETIN

'*PLAY DIRTY* PLODS ACROSS
THE SCREEN LIKE A CAMEL
IN A SANDSTORM.' **TIME**

Play Dirty started as a story by George Marton,
inspired by a real-life incident in which 12
Palestinians were sent to blow up German fuel
dumps during the Second World War but were
betrayed by the British. The story was adapted
into a screenplay by Lotte Colin and Melvyn
Bragg. Producer Harry Saltzman already had
Caine under contract and selected him to play
reluctant soldier Captain Douglas. American
actor Warren Beatty expressed interest in the
other leading role, the guerrilla warrior Cyril
Leech, but after Beatty pulled out Richard Harris
was hired to play Caine's antagonist. French
director René Clément was chosen to shoot the
gritty war drama, filmed on location in the south
of Spain. Earlier plans to film in Israel
were abandoned after insurance problems.

British actor Nigel Davenport was
approached by Saltzman for the supporting role

ABOVE: Captain
Douglas signals for
help in *Play Dirty*
(1968).

of Colonel Masters. In an exclusive interview for this book, Davenport recalled the troubled making of *Play Dirty* in early 1968: 'Richard Harris was becoming a pop star, having recorded 'MacArthur Park' [a Top 5 hit single in 1968] and also been in the film musical *Camelot*. Because Harris never showed up for days on end, we shot all the scenes that could be shot without him. He arrived looking like a sort of pop star, which was not really suitable for the subject. There were all sorts of to-ings and fro-ings. He finally left, at which point Harry Saltzman said to me, "Do you want to play the part?" I said, "Sure." He said, "Okay, we'll have dinner later on, but now I've got to go and fire the director!"'

In 1969 Caine told *Films and Filming* magazine about Clément's brief stay: 'We worked for two weeks, but I don't really know what film he was making. René, I don't think, was ever really sure. Then René left the picture. André de Toth … was the associate producer and had directed 133 movies or something like that number – so at least he knew about lenses – so everybody let him direct it. And so that was that. We got on with it.'

Davenport accordingly became Leech and Nigel Green was brought in to take over the role of Masters. It was a happy reunion for Caine, whose first major film appearances had been alongside Green in both *Zulu* (1964) and *The Ipcress File* (1965). Veteran director André de Toth was already on set, so Saltzman had him take over helming the picture. Almost all the material already filmed had to be reshot with the revised cast.

Davenport had never met Caine before starting work on *Play Dirty*. 'He was enormously supportive, an extremely generous man, very hospitable. We were working in very adverse conditions. For one of the sequences we were supposed to be in a sand-storm. We worked in a sand-storm for real. There was this howling wind, sand flying around and it was bloody uncomfortable. We started off with ten cameras covering it and there was only one camera fit to use by the end of the day. It took much longer to shoot than it should have done because of adverse weather and all sorts of problems.'

Caine told *Films and Filming* he would never make another film in Spain: 'The conditions are so bad. I've got it in my contract from now on. André de Toth made an extremely good job of a very difficult situation. The script was never right, and a lot of it was done at the last minute, but it's one of those things where I still think it's a valid picture. No one was ever satisfied with the ending.'

Davenport says that he and Caine discussed how best to conclude the film: 'Between the two of us, he and I dreamed up the actual ending, that we should get shot, because of that irony in the film. Harry Saltzman thought that was a terrible idea, he said we should get saved. I remember talking to Michael about it and we both thought the ending we had dreamed up was a better one than marching off into the sunset.'

Caine had served in the Korean War during the 1950s. 'One minute someone was there, then the next minute they weren't,' he told *Films and Filming*. 'I couldn't have those two men [Douglas and Leech] go through all that and then be treated like film stars at the end … coming back and getting medals.' Caine and Davenport got their way.

The film was released to mixed reviews, with the BBFC requiring cuts before granting it an AA rating. 'It wasn't particularly well received at the time,' Davenport said. 'I think the public were rather tired of war films. Since then I think it's achieved a certain sort of cult position. All the people who have seen it that I've met think it's terribly good. That was a great deal due to Michael.'

Play Dirty had to wait nearly 30 years for

a video release, reclassified as a 15 in the UK. The tape has since been deleted and the film has yet to make its DVD debut.

Play Dirty is arguably the *Get Carter* of Michael Caine's war films. Grim and gritty, the story is superficially similar to the likes of *The Dirty Dozen* (1967). But the movie's relentlessly downbeat tone and abrupt, bleak ending mark it out as more than just an action romp. The idea that war is hell is hardly new but here the point is made with enough humour and excitement to maintain your interest. The script requires Caine to play the more passive role, while Davenport steals the show as the murderous, mercenary Leech. It's no surprise that *Play Dirty* struggled to find an audience in the late 1960s, but this is a picture overdue for reassessment.

PULP (1972)

Cast: Michael Caine (Mickey King), Mickey Rooney (Preston Gilbert), Lionel Stander (Ben Dinuccio), Lizabeth Scott (Betty Cippola), Nadia Cassini (Liz), Dennis Price (the Englishman), Al Lettieri (Miller), Leopoldo Trieste (Marcovic), Amerigo Tot (Partisan), Roberto Sacchi (The Bogeyman), Giulio Donnini (Typing Pool Manager), Joe Zammit Cordina (the Beautiful Thing), Luciano Pigozzi (clairvoyant).
Crew: Mike Hodges (director/writer), Michael Klinger (producer), George Martin (music), Ousama Rawi (cinematography), John Glen (editor), Patrick Downing (production designer).

Mickey King is a pulp fiction author living in the Mediterranean. He is asked to ghost-write a famous person's autobiography by a man called Dinuccio, but not given the name of his subject. Instead King is sent on a five-day coach tour and told he will be contacted. The writer thinks that

an American called Miller is the contact. Instead King is met by a beautiful woman who takes him to meet the subject of the book. Preston Gilbert was a Hollywood star who appeared in dozens of films as a gangster before being deported to Europe. He dictates his memoirs to King in a week. Afterwards Gilbert organises a lunch for his friends and King at a restaurant. Gilbert is murdered by a man disguised as a priest, but King survives.

A clairvoyant gives the writer clues about why somebody wanted to kill the former film star. Gilbert was involved in a scandal years earlier about a teenage girl who died at a hunting lodge while being raped by hunters. The others believed that Gilbert was going to mention the incident in his autobiography. King goes to a beach where the girl's body is buried. The hitman reappears, gunning for the author. King runs him over with a truck, discovering that the assassin was Miller. The writer realises he has been shot in the leg. King is taken in and cared for by a powerful political family that was involved with the scandal. He is warned to stay silent or else he'll be charged with killing Miller…

'HODGES HAS NOT ONLY GOT HIS DISTANCE IN *PULP*, HE HAS ALSO FOUND A STYLE AND VOICE OF HIS OWN. ALWAYS AN ADEPT ACTOR, CAINE IS SPLENDID HERE.' *TIME*

'A REASONABLY ENTERTAINING PIECE OF ROCOCO RECALL … AT ITS BEST AS VISUAL CAMP. CAINE … DELIVERS HIS USUAL ATTRACTIVE TURN.' *VARIETY*

A trio of Michaels – Caine, Hodges and Klinger – had startled cinema patrons with the brutal realities of *Get Carter* (1971). A year after

ABOVE: Hack writer Mickey King dodges a bullet from gangster Ben Dinuccio (Lionel Stander) in *Pulp* (1972), Mike Hodges' little seen follow-up to *Get Carter* (1971).

as very surreal and rather bleak.'

The plot about a young girl found dead on a beach was based on a scandal that rocked Italian high society in the 1950s. Hodges' script was also prompted by the rise of neo-fascism in Italy in the early 1970s, while the film's off-beat style was inspired by John Huston's film *Beat the Devil* (1954). United Artists agreed to help finance the film and Hodges went to Italy on a research trip. But when the location manager tried to secure the locations chosen by Hodges, they found themselves dealing with the Mafia. The director had a house on Malta and suggested the Mediterranean island as a new home for the production. The film was shot entirely on location during the winter of 1971-72.

At the time Caine told journalists he did not enjoy working on Malta, complaining about the barren landscape and lack of trees. When asked what no visitor to the island should miss, the actor's reply was short and pithy: 'The plane home.' Twenty years later, Caine had a different recollection of the movie in his autobiography. '*Pulp* never made any real money, but I ... had a wonderful experience making it so I remember it with affection.'

Pulp was released in 1972, rated AA in Britain. Critics were bemused by the movie and it failed at the box-office. Reviews were stronger in America but the film never got a chance to capitalise on them, quickly disappearing from cinemas. Sixteen years later it was released on video in the US, but has since been deleted. The picture has never been released on VHS or DVD in Britain. 'It puzzles and saddens me why it's not on video or DVD,' Hodges informed the current author. 'Some films seem to just get lost in the shuffle. *Pulp* is one. On the other hand *Black Rainbow* [a much-praised but rarely seen Hodges film from 1990] is about to come out on DVD – so you never know! In a recent exchange of letters with J G Ballard, he

making that film, the three men reunited for *Pulp*. This was made from an original screenplay written by Hodges, with the working title *Memoirs of a Ghostwriter*. 'I wanted to do something light, as a bookend to *Carter*, to get away from the violence,' Hodges told interviewer Steven Paul Davies for the book *Get Carter and Beyond: The Cinema of Mike Hodges*. 'Mind you, my humour might be described voiced his love of *Pulp*. I've noticed that writers, in particular, like it.'

The word quirky could have been invented to describe *Pulp*. It shares plot similarities with *Get Carter* (1971), but it's hard to imagine two more different movies. The first 20 minutes is a flurry of running gags and visual humour, with Caine's world-weary voiceover a witty counterpoint to the on-screen action. After that, the movie settles into a slightly more conventional mode. The tone is uneven, but Hodges keeps driving the story forward fast enough to overcome this. There's a succession of sub-textual references to the conventions of pulp fiction and cinema that are worthy of a thesis, but it's the performances of Caine and Mickey Rooney that bring the film alive. *Pulp* is a cult movie in waiting.

QUICKSAND (2002)

Cast: Michael Keaton (Martin Raikes), Michael Caine (Jake Mallows), Judith Godreche (Lela Forin), Rade Serbedzija (Oleg Butraskaya), Matthew Marsh (Michael Cote), Xander Berkeley (Joey Patterson), Kathleen Wilhoite (Beth Ann), Rachel Perjani (Rachel), Elina Lowensohn (Vannessa), Clare Thomas (Emma), Hermione Norris (Sarah), William Beck (Nicoli).
Crew: John Mackenzie (director), Jim Reeve (producer), Timothy Prager (writer), Anthony Marinelli (music), Walter McGill (cinematography), Graham Walker (editor), Jon Bunker (production designer).
The Russian Mafia is smuggling drugs and sex slaves into the French port of Nice, aided by corrupt cops. But crime boss Oleg Butraskaya

decides to stop making payments to the local chief of police, Pillon. Oleg's henchman Nicoli murders two cops at the port. In retaliation, Pillon has Oleg's lover killed. In New York, Martin Raikes runs the compliance department of City and Trust Bank. His job is detecting attempts to launder illegally earned money. Raikes discovers a French film company called Groupe Lumière has transferred an abnormal payment of $6 million. The compliance officer flies to Nice to investigate.

Group Lumière's beautiful executive Lela Forin shows Raikes around a film studio where the company is making a film called *Quicksand*. The banker meets ageing action movie star Jake Mallows, who stars in the picture. When Raikes asks to see the company accounts, Nicoli tries unsuccessfully to buy him off. Next morning Oleg has Pillon assassinated and frames Raikes for the murder. The banker flees when he sees Nicoli among the police. Raikes finds Lela and saves her from a bomb planted by Nicoli. Lela admits that she sent the abnormal payment, hoping the police would investigate. The movie wasn't real, just a way of laundering illegal money. Raikes then discovers that Oleg's men are using the studio to film rapes for internet porn sites.

The banker tries to surrender to police inspector Cote, but the cop is working for the Russian Mafia. Oleg has Raikes' young daughter Emma abducted and brought to Nice. The gangster uses Jake to film a ransom demand for Raikes, offering to swap Emma for Lela. Raikes confronts Mallows and tells him the truth about the fake film. Oleg tricked the actor, using Jake's gambling debts to control him. Raikes, Mallows and Lela trick Oleg into surrendering Emma. The police arrive. Cote murders Oleg and Nicoli, unaware that his actions are being broadcast on the internet. Afterwards Jake and Lela launch their own film company and Raikes returns to

New York, his name cleared…

Desmond Lowden's novel *Boudapesti 3* was first published in 1979. Nearly 20 years later British film director John Mackenzie received a script based on the thriller. 'It was dreadful,' Mackenzie recalled during an exclusive interview for this book. 'I said no and didn't hear anything back. A year later producer Geoff Reeve sent me a revised version by Timothy Prager. I knew the writer rather well. I read it and it was like a different film, with wit and all sorts of things in it. So I said "I'll do it" and that's how it started.'

The $10 million project was funded from several different countries. Shooting began in December 2000 and ran for eight weeks, mostly on location in the South of France but with some sequences lensed in New York. American actor Michael Keaton was hired to play banker Martin Raikes while Caine was cast as ageing film star Jake Mallows. It was Caine's fifth collaboration with Reeve, following on from *Half Moon Street, The Whistle Blower* (both 1986), *Shadow Run* (1998) and *Shiner* (2000). A sequence from *Shadow Run* was used in *Quicksand* as footage from the film within a film.

'They were very good in it, Caine and Keaton,' Mackenzie recalled. 'They make quite a nice contrast with each other. Keaton's the lead. Michael plays a down-and-out star, on the skids to obscurity – all the things he actually isn't. He eats the part up, he's great. They are great together and I think it'll be quite an interesting movie.' Once Caine's part was concluded, he flew to Vietnam to begin work on *The Quiet American* (2002).

Quicksand's troubles began once shooting was completed, according to Mackenzie. 'The big problem was the producers fell out. The money came from ten different sources. I've never known a film with so many associate or executive producers. When the film was finished, they all fought amongst each other. They kept on wanting to have other versions. The film got sort of raped several times. Lots of vicious things happened. I said my name had to come off. Geoff Reeve, the guy who'd started the whole thing, was trying to satisfy all these people. His son, Jim Reeve, took over.'

In July 2002 *Variety* announced that *Quicksand* would receive its world premiere at the Taormina Film Festival in Sicily. Mackenzie was invited but refused to go. 'That was when I was saying my name wouldn't be on it. They had redubbed the film and recut it, rather badly. It may have been shown, I don't know. I doubt it. Eventually, after a year and a half, the film came back to me. I reinstated some of it, not all of it and we came to an agreement on it. But it's been a scarring experience. It was crucified by the amount and disparity of people who put money into it. They've sold it to Europe. I've not heard of any deal done in America or Britain. It'd be a pity if it just got dumped on video.'

Quicksand was released on DVD in Scandinavia late in 2002. The film was given an R rating for America by the MPAA in 2003, but no release date had been announced when this book went to press. Nor had the movie been to the BBFC for British classification.

Quicksand is a taut, efficient thriller. The concept of a good man being falsely accused of a crime is nothing new, but the tension is steadily increased through the film's 90 minutes. The only let-down is a trick used to dupe the Russian Mafia, who have presumably never seen *The Sting* (1973). Keaton acquits himself well and the international cast all give strong performances. Caine's role is little more than a cameo for much of the film, but he comes into his own as an ageing cinema icon in the finale. Considered on its own merits, this is a decent, if unremarkable, thriller.

THE QUIET AMERICAN (2002)

Cast: Michael Caine (Thomas Fowler), Brendan Fraser (Alden Pyle), Do Thi Hai Yen (Phuong), Rade Serbedzija (Inspector Vigot), Tzi Ma (Hinh), Robert Stanton (Joe Tunney), Holmes Osborne (Bill Granger), Quang Hai (General Thé), Ferdinand Hoang (Mr Muoi), Pham Thi Mai Hoa (Phuong's sister), Mathias Mlekuz (French captain).
Crew: Phillip Noyce (director), Staffan Ahrenberg and William Horberg (producers), Christopher Hampton and Robert Schenkkan (writers), Craig Armstrong (music), Christopher Doyle, Huu Tuan Nguyen and Dat Quang (cinematography), John Scott (editor), Roger Ford (production designer).

Thomas Fowler is a British journalist for the *Times* based in Saigon, Vietnam, during the early 1950s when the French Army was fighting a war against Communists. Fowler has a young Vietnamese mistress, Phuong. The reporter meets Alden Pyle, an American who says he is part of the medical team with an economic aid mission in Vietnam. The *Times* summons Fowler back to its London office, but the correspondent asks for more time, claiming he is working on a big story.

Pyle meets Phuong and falls in love with her. Fowler goes into the country and visits a town where the people have been massacred. Pyle turns up, claiming to be on a medical mission. He believes a third force must take over Vietnam from the French, to save the country from Communism. A new political party emerges, led by the self-appointed General Thé. Fowler writes to his Catholic wife in England, asking for a divorce, which she subsequently refuses. The reporter tries to interview Thé, asking if the general's men had any involvement with the massacre. Pyle is at the general's camp and protects the journalist. He lies to Phuong about the letter but she discovers the truth and leaves him for Pyle.

A terrorist bombing in central Saigon kills dozens of civilians, including women and children. Fowler sees Pyle in the aftermath, speaking fluent Vietnamese. The correspondent realises that

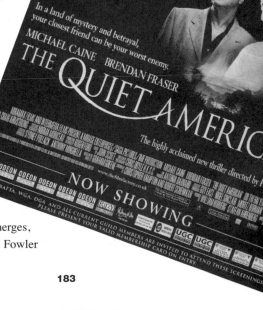

RIGHT: British journalist Thomas Fowler and his Vietnamese lover Phuong (Do Thi Hai Yen) travel through Saigon in *The Quiet American* (2002). Philip Noyce's film was a small-scale success despite its anti-intervention stance at a turbulent time in global politics.

Pyle works for the CIA. Fowler confronts the American about his part in the bombing, but Pyle is unrepentant. He admits arming Thé but says such massacres will guarantee more American funding and ultimately save lives. Fowler realises Pyle is behind both atrocities. The reporter betrays Pyle to the Communists, who murder the American. Fowler persuades Phuong to resume being his mistress. Fowler stays on as the *Times* correspondent as events escalate into the Vietnam War...

'THIS MAY IN FACT BE THE BEST PERFORMANCE OF MICHAEL CAINE'S CAREER.' *CHICAGO SUN-TIMES*

'A CAREER-CAPPING PERFORMANCE BY MICHAEL CAINE. ONE OF THE YEAR'S MOST THOUGHTFUL FILMS.' *TIME*

Graham Greene's novel *The Quiet American* was first published in 1955, inspired by his time spent as a newspaper correspondent in Vietnam. Director Joseph L Mankiewicz shot the first adaptation of the book in 1958, with Michael Redgrave and Audie Murphy. Greene was infuriated by the film, which downplayed the book's anti-CIA stance. He wrote a vitriolic article accusing Mankiewicz of using the movie as a weapon to murder an author.

Four decades later Australian director Phillip Noyce finally got the go-ahead for a new version of *The Quiet American*, after five years' preparation. Christopher Hampton and Robert Schenkkan wrote the adaptation, Hampton having previously scripted another Greene adaptation, *The Honorary Consul* (1983). The crucial part of British journalist Thomas Fowler went to Caine, on a roll following his Oscar win as best supporting actor for *The Cider*

House Rules (1999). 'When they offered the part to me,' the actor told the Australian edition of *Empire*, 'I thought it was Christmas. How many roles are there for men of my age with that emotional range?'

Caine finished filming *Quicksand* (2002) early in 2001 and began preparing for his new role. The actor would turn 68 during the production but was going to be playing a 55-year-old. 'I lost 25 pounds, dyed my hair and had four pounds of make-up on,' he told *The Age* newspaper in 2003, 'and I tried to suck my stomach in on the wide shots.' The actor removed carbohydrates from his diet and walked five miles a day to shed the weight.

Caine partly based his performance on Greene. 'I didn't know him very well,' he told a BBC cinema website, 'but I knew a great deal about him. One of my best friends is Bryan Forbes, who was one of Graham's best friends. So I knew a lot by proxy. I just copied something of the way he [Green] spoke, and his movements. They were very small.' The actor also spent time with a journalist in Vietnam, observing what the reporter did, and was advised on how to play an opium user by an addict.

Production of the $30 million picture began in Vietnam during February 2001 and continued for three months. Location shooting took place at Ho Chi Minh City, the ancient port town of Hoi An, in the northern province Ninh Binh and at the capital Hanoi. Studio work was lensed in Sydney, Australia. Caine told the *Hollywood Reporter* he was surprised at how welcoming the people of Vietnam had been and how beautiful the country was. 'I expected to see a war-torn land, and I saw no sign of war at all. It was fabulous for me ... to be in actual places where he [Greene] was. People pointed at windows saying, "That window in the Continental Hotel, that's the room where he wrote *The Quiet American*." This part was the maximum degree of difficulty because it's so subtle; I put my heart and soul into it. At the end of that picture, when we got back to England, I sat in the armchair looking at my wife, and I said, "I've got nothing left here."'

The film got its first screening as a rough-cut in New York on 10 September 2001. The next day terrorists attacked America, flying two jumbo jets into the twin towers of New York's World Trade Centre and killing thousands of people. Another plane was crashed into the Pentagon at Washington, DC. Overnight, a film with award-winning potential turned into the movie nobody wanted. American and British distribution rights had been acquired by Miramax for $5.5 million. Co-chairman Harvey Weinstein told the *New York Times* what happened next: 'I showed the film to some people and staff, and they said, "Are you out of your mind? You can't release this now, it's unpatriotic."'

Miramax considered dumping the movie and began shopping it around to other distributors. Meanwhile Noyce continued working on the film's post-production, with computer-generated imagery used to make modern Vietnamese cities resemble their 1950s counterparts. Weinstein reportedly ordered the toning down of a scene in which a character accused America of adventurism. The final cut of *The Quiet American* was delivered to Miramax in May 2002.

Word leaked out that the distributors planned to release the film in January 2003, too late for Oscar consideration and a month when only lesser movies are dumped in cinemas. Caine lobbied Weinstein for the film's release to be brought forward. He even threatened to do no promotional work for his starring role in another movie to which Miramax held US distribution rights, *The Actors* (2003). Caine's cause was supported by Noyce, Australian actress Nicole Kidman and two Oscar-winning executive producers attached to *The Quiet American*, Anthony Minghella and Sydney Pollack. But Weinstein was still reluctant to distribute a film critical of American intervention in foreign countries, especially with the US government preparing to go to war with Iraq.

Miramax eventually relented and agreed to give the picture its world premiere at the Toronto Film Festival in September 2002. Caine told the American Press Association that he gave Weinstein a promise: 'If it doesn't go well in Toronto, I'll bring a shovel and help you bury it.' Noyce used guerrilla tactics to create a buzz for *The Quiet American* before the festival, organising special screenings for key American film critics. The Toronto screening got a standing ovation and raves in the US media, with several reviewers calling Caine's performance a certainty for an Oscar nomination. Miramax gave the picture a two-week run in a handful of US cinemas so it qualified for consideration at the Oscars.

Caine campaigned relentlessly on behalf of the film, earning himself nominations for best actor at the Golden Globes (losing to Jack Nicholson in *About Schmidt*), the BAFTAs and the Oscars (losing both to Adrien Brody in *The Pianist*). Caine won awards from film critics in London and San Francisco. The Oscar nod was especially precious to the actor, making him one of only three men to have been nominated for acting Oscars in five consecutive decades; the others are Laurence Olivier and Jack Nicholson. 'This has made my day,' Caine said after hearing of his nomination. 'I am absolutely delighted, I couldn't be happier. It's been a long, long journey. I just wanted to see whether I could get a nomination. And I've got one, I'm happy now and my work is done.'

The Quiet American reached Britain in November 2002. The 15-rated film got strong reviews, especially for Caine's performance,

and grossed nearly $3 million. In America the R-rated picture went into wider release after the Oscar nominations were announced in February 2003. It had grossed nearly $13 million when this book went to press. Globally the picture has taken more than $25 million. A DVD and video release is expected in the UK and US before the end of 2003.

Caine told many interviewers he considered his performance in *The Quiet American* as the best of his long career. 'There are moments in everyone's life when everything comes together,' he told the *Dallas Fort Worth Star Telegram* in 2003. 'That's what happened here. I was experienced enough an actor. I was experienced enough as a man. I wanted to do something that I could really disappear into the character … rather than have a little of Michael Caine in there, like a movie star thing. I believe in this movie probably more than any other movie I've ever done.'

Does *The Quiet American* live up to all the hype? Surprisingly, yes – but don't expect a sweeping epic or some grand blockbuster. Noyce's film is subtle and intelligent, holding back from the sort of bombast that normally wins awards and critical kudos. The picture submerges you in the atmosphere of 1950s Vietnam and is all too aware of the cost of imperialist attitudes. The global crisis that threatened to sink this picture also made its subject matter more relevant. It remains to be seen whether this version of *The Quiet American* will retain its power once the current political climate has changed. But time will not diminish Caine's performance in this film, arguable the finest of his career. It's a masterclass in nuance and restraint, many emotions played out just in his eyes. Even in a poor film, such a performance would be worth watching. In this context it's essential viewing.

QUILLS (2000)

Cast: Geoffrey Rush (the Marquis De Sade), Kate Winslet (Madeleine), Joaquin Phoenix (Coulmier), Michael Caine (Royer-Collard), Billie Whitelaw (Madame LeClerc), Patrick Malahide (Delbené), Amelia Warner (Simone), Jane Menelaus (Renée Pelagie), Stephen Moyer (Prouix), Tony Pritchard (Valcour), Michael Jenn (Cleante), Danny Babington (Pitou).
Crew: Philip Kaufman (director), Nick Wechsler, Julia Chasman and Peter Kaufman (producers), Doug Wright (writer), Stephen Warbeck (music), Rogier Stoffers (cinematography), Peter Boyle (editor), Martin Childs (production designer).

The Marquis De Sade is held captive in the Charenton Asylum for the Insane. He writes pornographic novels and has the pages smuggled out to a publisher by laundry lass Madeleine. The asylum is run by the Abbé du Coulmier, who despairs of De Sade. Emperor Napoleon Bonaparte has De Sade's latest book *Justine* burnt and sends Dr Royer-Collard to cure the author. In exchange for his services, the doctor is given a grand chateau and an architect called Prouix to help him renovate it. Royer-Collard takes a teenage orphan, Simone, from a nearby nunnery as his wife.

"superb" "magnificent"

MICHAEL CAINE

Quills

BE BETRAYED

NOW AT CINEMAS ACROSS LONDON
OPENS NATIONWIDE FEBRUARY 2

De Sade hears about this and parodies the marriage in a graphic play performed by the inmates in public. Coulmier takes away the writer's quills and ink, so De Sade writes in red ink on his bed linen with a wishbone. Royer-Collard discovers this and has the scribe's cell stripped bare. So De Sade writes on his clothes, using his own blood as ink. The doctor has De Sade stripped naked and Madeleine flogged for her complicity. Coulmier becomes obsessed with Madeleine. Inspired by De Sade's writing, Simone seduces the architect Prouix. When they run off together, Royer-Collard discovers one of De Sade's books in Simone's bed. The doctor tortures the author.

But De Sade still finds a way to disseminate his words, whispering them to Madeleine through a chain of inmates. One of the insane sets fire to the asylum while another is inspired to cut out Madeleine's tongue and drown her. Coulmier has De Sade's tongue cut out as punishment. The writer uses his own excrement to write on cell walls. De Sade dies, opting to choke himself to death on a crucifix rather than receive absolution. A year later, the asylum gets a new Abbé. Royer-Collard uses the inmates to publish De Sade's writing, with the profits helping to rebuild Charenton. Coulmier is now an inmate, begging for a quill and ink to write his own story…

'THE FILM LACKS AN EDGE OF DANGER OR EXCITEMENT THAT MIGHT HAVE BROUGHT THE SUBJECT ALIVE IN MORE THAN A CEREBRAL WAY.'
VARIETY

'A COMPLEX, OFTEN FUNNY AND VIVIDLY-TOLD TALE, *QUILLS* ULTIMATELY CANNOT MAKE UP ITS MIND WHAT IT WANTS TO TELL US.'
EMPIRE

Quills was an award-winning play by Doug Wright. He spent five years developing a big screen adaptation, working with arthouse filmmaking studio Fox Searchlight. The script was offered to director Philip Kaufman, who was eager to work on the story. At the time America was gripped by a sex scandal involving then-US President Bill Clinton, turning censorship, pornography and sexual hypocrisy into hot topics. The project was approved by Fox Searchlight with a budget of only $14 million.

Kaufman and his four leading actors (Geoffrey Rush, Kate Winslet, Joaquin Phoenix and Caine) all agreed to take pay cuts to help the film stay within its limited resources. The film was shot in England, with the Bedfordshire estate of Luton Hoo appearing as Charenton asylum, while studio work took place at Pinewood. Unusually, *Quills* was filmed almost entirely in sequence

Caine was cast as the malevolent Dr Royer-Collard. 'I really, really enjoyed that character because very rarely do I play a total villain,' the actor told *Venice* magazine in 2002. 'I can usually find some redeeming feature, but that man had no redeeming features!' Caine was full of praise for the actor playing his on-screen nemesis: 'Geoffrey Rush was wonderful to work with, as well. One of the best movie actors around.'

Rush was just as enthusiastic about the experience of working opposite Caine: 'He's a legend,' Rush told *Rough Cut* in 2000. 'He tells you great stories about the absurdity of the profession that he's encountered over a 35-year period. But then, when the camera is on, it's like galvanising white heat that you've only got to respond to.'

Caine admitted to having been uncomfortable playing a sequence when Royer-Collard consummates his lust for teenage bride Simone. 'The only way we could accomplish that, her and I, was to laugh through the whole thing,' he told

FAR LEFT:
Dr Royer-Collard takes teenage girl Simone (Amelia Warner) as his bride in *Quills* (2000), but she exacts a costly revenge.

the *Toronto Sun* in 2001. 'At times when she grimaced [on screen], she [Amelia Warner] was holding back laughter. It's pretty embarrassing at my age to be doing that with a girl who's young enough to be my granddaughter.'

Quills had its world premiere at the Telluride Film Festival in September 2000, before getting a limited release in US cinemas during November, rated R. Critics were positive, and the film grossed $7 million over the next six months. Fox Searchlight pushed the film for recognition in the end-of-year awards. *Quills* won the National Board of Review's Best Picture award, but otherwise had to be content with Oscar nominations in technical categories and for Rush as best actor.

The film reached British cinemas in January 2001, rated 18. Reviews were muted, but Caine was nominated as British supporting actor of the year by the London Critics' Circle. The movie grossed just over $1 million in UK cinemas. It was released on video and DVD later in the year.

For a film brimming with sex, violence and pornography, *Quills* is surprisingly uninvolving. Visually the source material has been opened up to great effect, but the story remains stage-bound. Characters debate creative freedom and the hypocrisy of civilisation without ever appealing to your sympathy or intellect. Rush revels in his grandstand role as De Sade, gurning and gurgling with glee. By comparison the other characters are bland and lifeless, trapped in an inevitable escalation of horrors. Caine struggles to find a focus for his role, unassisted by spending much of his time in an irrelevant subplot involving his teenage wife. *Quills* looks great, but is altogether less than the sum of its parts.

BELOW: Caine played a supporting role in *Quills* (2000), a film about the later life and works of the infamous Marquis De Sade.

R

THE ROMANTIC ENGLISHWOMAN (1975)

Cast: Glenda Jackson (Elizabeth), Michael Caine (Lewis), Helmut Berger (Thomas), Michael Lonsdale (Swan), Beatrice Romand (Catherine), Kate Nelligan (Isabel), Nathalie Delon (Miranda), Rene Kolldehoff (Herman), Anna Steele (Annie), Marcus Richardson (David).
Crew: Joseph Losey (director), Daniel M Angel (producer), Tom Stoppard and Thomas Wiseman (writers), Richard Hartley (music), Gerry Fisher (cinematography), Reginald Beck (editor), Richard MacDonald (production designer).

Bored English housewife Elizabeth goes on holiday to Baden-Baden in Germany. She meets Thomas, a handsome young gigolo who smuggles drugs. Elizabeth's husband Lewis, a writer, imagines her having an affair. Elizabeth returns home but her attempts to reconcile with Lewis are always interrupted. Thomas sees a man called Swan looking for him and flees Germany. The gigolo writes to Lewis and mentions meeting Elizabeth. Lewis invites the German to dinner, to Elizabeth's annoyance. Lewis lets Thomas stay with them, employing the gigolo as a secretary. The writer bases a character in his new screenplay on Thomas. Lewis finds Elizabeth and Thomas having sex in the conservatory. The lovers flee to France, where Thomas resumes being a gigolo. He calls Lewis and tells him where Elizabeth is. Lewis drives to France, where he is followed by Swan. Swan finds Thomas and leads him away. Lewis takes Elizabeth back to Weybridge…

'THE MOST COMPLICATEDLY TRIVIAL FILM … A HIGHLY POLISHED HUMBUG.' ***THE OBSERVER***

'CAINE DOES WELL, VERY WELL INDEED, AS THE SARKY HUSBAND, CONSIDERING THAT HE'S FAIRLY WELL LIMITED TO LOOKING CONTINUOUSLY IRRITATED, EXASPERATED AND INFURIATED.' ***EVENING STANDARD***

Thomas Wiseman's novel *The Romantic Englishwoman* was first published in 1971. The author collaborated with American-born director Joseph Losey on adapting the book. Losey had helmed noted pictures like *The Go-Between* (1970) and *Accident* (1967). Playwright Tom Stoppard then joined the project at the director's request. 'He hardly changed the structure … but he largely rewrote the dialogue,' Losey told *Sight & Sound* in 1975.

For his leads the director cast Caine and two-time Oscar-winner Glenda Jackson. Caine told *Viva* magazine that he took the role to work with Losey and Jackson. He praised the latter as one of the most brilliant actresses in the world, but added: 'You only enjoy it professionally with Glenda. She's charming – but she doesn't go to lunch, if you know what I mean.' Losey proved even harder work. Caine bet £10 that he could make the director laugh at least once during filming. He lost the bet. The actor said the part of Lewis was unlike anything he had done

before. 'There was nothing of myself I could bring to that role, so I had to construct the character from the ground up. It was pure performance.'

The picture was filmed in England during autumn 1974, with location work in Germany and France. Because the movie was being made during the wrong season, Losey shot the middle section first, then the ending and lastly the opening, to get the environments he wanted. This created some discomfort for Jackson, who had to appear naked outside at night for one scene. 'A film set can be a very draughty place,' she said in the film's pressbook, 'and a garden in the middle of November isn't much fun either.'

In his autobiography Caine recalled that Jackson and her on-screen lover, Helmut Berger, seemed to hate each other on sight, with Caine acting as intermediary. The production was not a happy experience for him, nor was the end result: 'The film was not only very convoluted, it was also downright grim...'

Losey's first cut ran to 145 minutes, but the director removed nearly half an hour during editing. *The Romantic Englishwoman* was released in British cinemas with an AA rating in 1975. Critics were underwhelmed and the response was just as poor in America, where it was rated R. The movie was released on video in 1986 but has yet to make its DVD debut.

Near the beginning of this picture, a film producer describes a screenplay about a woman who goes off in search of herself. Michael Caine's character describes it as pretentious, derivative and very boring – neatly summing up the movie itself. *The Romantic Englishwoman* is a domestic melodrama that tries your patience beyond belief. The three central characters are people you would never want to meet – let along spend two hours watching. Caine gets to shout and play drunk but injects no life into the dull, tepid material. The film induces near-terminal ennui with its witless verbosity and drab visuals. Avoid.

SECONDHAND LIONS (2003)

*Cast: Michael Caine (Garth), Robert Duvall
(Hub), Haley Joel Osment (Walter).
Crew: Tim McCanlies (director/writer),
David M Kirschner, Corey Sienega and Scott
Ross (producers), Patrick Doyle (music), Jack
Green (cinematography), David Movitz (editor),
David J Bomba (production designer).*

In the 1960s young teenager Walter is left
with his eccentric uncles Garth and Hub for
the summer. They regale the boy with fantastic
tales about their own youth…

The screenplay for *Secondhand Lions* was
written by director Tim McCanlies a decade
ago, but his efforts to get the picture made were
repeatedly thwarted by its quirky subject matter.
'It took ten years to get this made,' he told
Variety in 2002. 'People always loved the
script, but it sort of defied easy categorisation.'
McCanlies had made a promising debut as a
writer/director with *Dancer, Texas Pop. 81*
(1998). He also shared a BAFTA Children's
Award for scripting the animated featured film
The Iron Giant (1999). Producer David M
Kirschner told *Variety* that McCanlies' script was
inspirational. 'If you look on the 'net, you'll see
these lists of the best scripts that have never been
made – this is one of them.'

The project finally got a green light to begin
shooting in 2002, thanks to financial backing
from special effects company Digital Domain
and New Line Cinema. For the uncles McCanlies
cast two highly regarded veterans, Caine and
Robert Duvall. The pair had worked together 26
years earlier on *The Eagle Has Landed* (1976)

and Duvall had won the best actor Oscar the year
Caine was nominated for *Educating Rita* (1983).
For the teenage boy, McCanlies chose Haley Joel
Osment, who became a child star thanks to his
performance in *The Sixth Sense* (1999). Osment
was Oscar-nominated for that role, but the best
supporting actor award went instead to Caine
for *The Cider House Rules* (1999).

Secondhand Lions was shot on location in
Texas at Duvall's insistence, beginning in
September 2002. Caine told *Premiere* magazine
that the film was life-enhancing and funny:
'There's even a secondhand lion. We buy one
because we didn't want a dog. It was cheap!'
He chose the role for the chance to work with
Duvall and Osment, and because of the script:
'It has to be one of the best endings I've ever
seen in a movie.'

The role required Caine to be convincing
while speaking in a Texan accent, something he
spent two months developing. 'It's a good accent
to be funny in, especially me. You see me with a
big cowboy hat, and I think I look funny right
from the start.' Caine told the *LA Times* about the
first time he used his accent on set, in front of an
all-Texan film crew: 'I was probably as nervous
as I've been in a long time. This role was a
tremendous departure, the most American
character I've ever played.' McCanlies admitted
worrying about Caine's accent before filming
began. 'A bad one is like nails on a blackboard to
a Texan,' the director told the *LA Times*. 'A week
out, I was bugging him to hear it.' But
McCanlies was happy with the results. During
shooting Caine performed an eight-minute
storytelling sequence in a single take.

Secondhand Lions is scheduled to
open at US cinemas on 26 September 2003.

SHADOW RUN (1998)

Cast: Michael Caine (Haskell), James Fox (Landon-Higgins), Matthew Pochin (Joffrey), Rae Baker (Julie), Kenneth Colley (Larcombe), Christopher Cazenove (Melchior), Rupert Frazer (Maunder), Leslie Grantham (Liney), Tim Healy (Daltrey), Emma Reeve (Victoria), Katherine Reeve (Zee), Angela Douglas (Bridget).
Crew: Geoffrey Reeve (director/producer), Desmond Lowden (writer), Adrian Burch and David Whitaker (music), Eddy van der Enden (cinematography), Terry Warwick (editor), Raymond Hughes (production designer).

Chubby schoolboy Edward Joffrey sees masked men trying to rob a van in the countryside. One of the men, Haskell, gives Joffrey cash to keep silent. Haskell meets Landon-Higgins, an upper-class civil servant. Landon-Higgins and Haskell plan to steal a high-security van containing £110 million of paper used to print English bank notes. Haskell enlists the aid of Larcombe, a terminally ill man who used to drive the paper van. The vehicle has radio-controlled security systems, using signals from mobile phone transmitters.

Larcombe discovers that restoration work on a cathedral has created a large shadow which no signals can penetrate. Haskell locates an abandoned airfield within the shadow where the van can be taken. His preparations are witnessed by Joffrey. The day before the heist, the shadow suddenly shrinks when scaffolding is removed from the cathedral. Haskell recreates the interference with a crane and help from Joffrey. The heist goes as planned. Afterwards Haskell is shot and fatally wounded by Landon-Higgins, but murders his own killer before dying…

Desmond Lowden's novel *The Shadow Run* was first published in 1989. Film rights were acquired by British producer Geoffrey Reeve,

who opted to direct the movie himself. Lowden was hired to adapt his book into a screenplay, with Robert Morgan supplying additional material. Reeve cast Caine in the leading role of murderous criminal Haskell. It was the pair's third collaboration, following on from *Half Moon Street* and *The Whistle Blower* (both 1986). *Shadow Run* also reunited Caine with James Fox and Kenneth Colley, both of whom had appeared in *The Whistle Blower*.

The production began in August 1997, shooting entirely on location in five English counties. Two months earlier Caine had told the *Times* that the project was a labour of love: 'It's a small English thriller, very quirky and quite strange. It's the kind of thing I pick up on and if I'm interested I do it. I play a Cockney again, a real London gangster, but there's a lot more to it than that. I started to read the script, it intrigued me and I thought, I've never seen anything like this before.'

Ironically, the film disappeared into its own 'shadow run' once shooting was completed. Unable to secure a theatrical release in Britain, the picture made its debut on video in various European territories during 1998. It finally appeared in the UK in September 2001, available only as a budget-price DVD. *Shadow Run* has not been released in the US to date.

During publicity interviews for *Shiner* (2000), Caine frequently said the role of Billy 'Shiner' Simpson was only his third appearance as a film gangster, following on from *Get Carter* (1971) and *Mona Lisa* (1986). *Shadow Run* didn't even rate a mention.

There's a good reason why this film took four years to be released in Britain – it's terrible. The main culprit is the risible script, made up of two disparate stories. One concerns a £110 million heist, while the other examines the bullying of a fat schoolboy at boarding school. Fusing these narratives together is a series of unbelievable coincidences and ludicrous leaps of logic. The children's acting is cringe-inducing, while the adults grapple with wooden, trite dialogue. Even Caine gives one of the most flaccid, lifeless performances of his career in this shockingly bad movie.

SHINER (2000)

Cast: Michael Caine (Billy 'Shiner' Simpson), Martin Landau (Frank Spedding), Frances Barber (Georgie), Frank Harper (Stoney), Andy Serkis (Mel), Danny Webb (Karl), Claire Rushbrook (Ruth), Matthew Marsden (Golden Boy), Kenneth Cranham (Gibson), David Kennedy (Chris), Peter Wright (D I Grant), Nicola Walker (D S Garland).
Crew: John Irvin (director), Jim Reeve and Geoff Reeve (producers), Scott Cherry (writer), Paul Grabowsky (music), Mike Molloy (cinematography), Ian Crafford (editor), Austen Spriggs (production designer).

Small-time boxing promoter Billy 'Shiner' Simpson is staging the biggest fight of his life. His son, Golden Boy, is contesting a world title at the York Hall in East London. Shiner accuses an old associate, Gibson, of skimming money from the event. Shiner has his two musclemen, Stoney and Mel, give Gibson a punishment beating. Golden Boy is nervous about the fight, but his father tries to boost his spirits. Police detectives want to arrest Shiner on suspicion of organising illegal fights. Such a bout left one fighter in a coma for 18 months; the fighter has since died. Shiner persuades the police to arrest him after the title fight.

After 30 years of struggle, Shiner has everything riding on Golden Boy. But his son loses in the second round. Shiner accuses Golden Boy of throwing the bout. The boxer is shot and killed by an unseen gunman. Believing there is a

conspiracy against him, Shiner charges around London, trying to find those responsible. Finally, Shiner is summoned to the roof of the boxing venue to face the gunman. It's Gibson – he was trying to shoot Shiner, not Golden Boy. Gibson, Stoney and Shiner all die in a bloody shootout…

'MICHAEL CAINE IS IN FINE FORM … THE VETERAN ACTOR REMAINS COMPELLING EVEN AS THIS SOMEWHAT HACKNEYED MELODRAMA BECOMES INCREASINGLY OVERWROUGHT.' *VARIETY*

'CAINE ADDS A BIT OF CLASS TO A STODGY CRIME FLICK … GREAT PERFORMANCE, FORGETTABLE FEATURE.' *EMPIRE*

Caine and British film producer Geoffrey Reeve had been frequent collaborators, working together on *Half Moon Street, The Whistle Blower* (both 1986) and *Shadow Run* (1998). In 1999 they conceived the idea for a modern reworking of Shakespeare's *King Lear*, relocating the story to the world of prize-fighting with Caine as the Lear-esque patriarch. 'I thought it's the nearest I'm ever gonna get to play it, so I'm gonna do it,' the actor told the *Times* in 2001. Scott Cherry was hired to turn the concept into a screenplay, with John Irvin attached to direct.

The $10 million production began shooting on locations around London in January 2000. York Hall in Tower Hamlets was used as the fight venue, having been home to boxing matches in the East End for decades. To add verisimilitude a dozen great British boxers from the past 50 years joined the cast, sitting ringside during the fight. In 2001 Caine told the *Big Issue* that making the film was like going home: 'I'd never shot such a Cockney picture, in which

every person has a Cockney accent. It was quite extraordinary. I've known so many characters and stories like *Shiner*. I've been to those boxing places. My dad used to take me to Manor Place Baths in Southwark, and in the film there are boxers I know from that time who'd fought in Bethnal Green.' Oscar-winning US actor Martin Landau appeared as a rival American promoter to help give the film some trans-Atlantic appeal.

Caine was suffering from arthritis in his hands during filming. That made shooting a scene where his character repeatedly punched a mirror particularly painful, but the actor said the entire role was just as tough. 'Playing a role so emotional was quite heart-wrenching and exhausting, but that's what I want to do now. As you get older, you look for characters that are more interesting. To see someone disintegrate is, although sad, very interesting to play. And as you begin to get older you begin to fall apart yourself.'

He rejected any suggestion that *Shiner* was just another British gangster movie, following on from the success of *Lock, Stock and Two Smoking Barrels* (1998). 'I've been an actor for 40 years and this is my third gangster movie,' Caine told *Empire* in 2001. 'I did *Mona Lisa* (1986), *Get Carter* (1971) and this. So I'm not exactly trying to corner the market on gangster movies here.'

The film got its world premiere out of competition at the San Sebastian Film Festival in September 2000, where Caine received a career achievement award. It didn't reach British cinemas for another year, when it was rated 18. Critics praised Caine's performance but felt the movie was nothing special. The picture attracted controversy for a scene where Caine's character holds a gun against a pregnant woman's stomach. A pressure group called Mediawatch-UK described the sequence as scandalous and unforgivable. The film got a brief theatrical release, grossing just over $50,000. *Shiner* was

LEFT: A photo call appearance to promote *Shiner* (2000).

more successful in Spanish cinemas, taking nearly $250,000.

The picture was released on DVD and VHS in Britain during 2002. US distributor Miramax had acquired North American rights to the feature in February 2001 but held it back for 18 months before releasing it on DVD, rated R.

Shiner may have drawn its inspiration from Shakespeare's *King Lear*, but the link is decidedly tenuous. Most of this film's problems stem from a script that tries too hard to out-think the audience. The 'who shot Golden Boy'

conspiracy is a massive misdirection that leaves you frustrated and underwhelmed when the killer's identity is finally revealed. It's a shame about the fumbled ending, as *Shiner* has much to recommend it. The film looks great, features an evocative Grabowsky score and a towering performance from Caine. He wrings every ounce of emotion from the material without ever going over the top. The supporting cast is strong too, especially *Shiner*'s two henchmen, played by Frank Harper and Andy Serkis. But Landau is wasted in a minor role, given just a handful of scenes despite his second billing. It's the flaws in the script that downgrade a potentially strong picture. There's nothing you haven't seen before in *Shiner*, but it's still worth a look.

A SHOCK TO THE SYSTEM (1990)

Cast: Michael Caine (Graham Marshall), Elizabeth McGovern (Stella Anderson), Peter Riegert (Robert Benham), Swoosie Kurtz (Leslie Marshall), Will Patton (Lieutenant Laker), Jenny Wright (Melanie O'Connor), John McMartin (George Brewster), Barbara Baxley (Lillian), Haviland Morris (Tara Liston), Philip Moon (Henry Park).
Crew: Jan Egleson (director), Patrick McCormick (producer), Andrew Klavan (writer), Gary Chang (music), Paul Goldsmith (cinematography), Peter C Frank and William A Anderson (editors), Howard Cummings (production designer).

Graham Marshall has a nagging wife and a house with faulty wiring. But he enjoys his job as a New York advertising executive and is looking forward to a promotion when his boss George Brewster retires. But George is pushed out early and one of Graham's staff, Robert Benham, is promoted over him to become head of

BELOW: Graham Marshall becomes a cold-blooded killer to enhance his career prospects in the mordantly humorous *A Shock to the System* (1990).

department. Later, Graham accidentally kills a homeless man in the subway and is shocked when he gets away with it. Suddenly, he feels powerful again.

When Graham's wife Leslie offers him no sympathy about missing the promotion, he decides she has to die. Graham tampers with a circuit so that she electrocutes herself while he is away at a conference. A local policemen, Lieutenant Laker, asks awkward questions about her death but can't prove anything. Graham sells his house in the suburbs and moves into the city. He begins dating his secretary, Stella. Benham, meanwhile, keeps undermining Graham, so the murderous executive decides to kill his new boss. He drugs Stella so she believes they spent the night together and then booby-traps Benham's yacht. But Graham leaves his distinctive gold lighter in a hire car he hired to plan the explosive device.

Laker believes that Graham may be responsible for Benham's sudden death and pressurises Stella for help. She discovers that Graham is lying about his missing lighter and realises he is a killer. Graham confronts Stella in the subway. She surrenders the lighter to him and he lets her live. The police have insufficient evidence to prosecute Graham who continues climbing the corporate ladder, murdering those who get in his way…

'PLEASANTLY MACABRE, AN OFFBEAT COMEDY ABOUT A HIGH-ROLLING PSYCHOTIC PLAYED WITH NASTY SAVOIR-FAIRE BY MICHAEL CAINE.'
WASHINGTON POST

'A SHOCK TO THE SYSTEM CONFOUNDS OUR EXPECTATIONS AND KEEPS US INTRIGUED, BECAUSE THERE'S NO WAY TO KNOW, NOT EVEN IN THE VERY LAST MOMENTS, EXACTLY WHICH WAY THE PLOT IS GOING…'
CHICAGO SUN-TIMES

Simon Brett's satirical novel, *A Shock to the System*, was first published in 1984. The story of a corporate executive who kills to get ahead was aptly timed in a decade of conspicuous consumption when greed was considered good. Five years later work began on a film version, following the success of Oliver Stone's *Wall Street* (1987). Andrew Klavan adapted the novel, with TV director Jan Egleson having his first crack at helming a big-screen film. Caine was cast as murderous executive Graham Marshall.

'It was the script that got me to take the part,' Caine said in the movie's promotional material. 'It's very strange and it captured my attention immediately. I'd been reading loads of scripts, one right after the other, and suddenly I read this one. I said, "Wait a minute." It's a very funny nightmare, quite frightening, but extremely funny. What attracted me to it more than anything else is I have never seen a movie quite like it.'

Caine described his serial killer character as a victim: 'They pass him over for a younger man. He's victimised and he knows it. I've played a lot of sympathetic villains, and Graham's certainly one of them. All psychotics – and Graham becomes one – are paranoid. They think of themselves as victims. And the reason they kill somebody is because they perceive that somebody to have done them a wrong.'

The picture began shooting with its sailing scenes in Montauk, Long Island, during May 1989. The production then moved into a vacant floor of a brand-new skyscraper overlooking New York's Wall Street for the office scenes. Other locations included an unused subway station near 42nd Street and Essex Falls in New Jersey as the site of Graham's suburban home. Future star Samuel L Jackson had a bit part as a street corner card hustler in a scene that appears during the film's opening credits.

Caine made his portrayal so sympathetic and charismatic that he created a dilemma for the filmmakers. In the original script Caine's character was supposed to die at the end of the movie. After five weeks of shooting it was decided that Graham had to survive and the finale was rewritten accordingly.

A Shock to the System reached American cinemas in March 1990. Review were generally positive but Egleson's direction suffered at the hands of the critics. The film was released amid a glut of similar tales about corporate machinations and greed, such as Brian De Palma's much derided adaptation of *The Bonfire of the Vanities* (1990), and *A Shock to the System* grossed less than $3.5 million. It reached the UK in October 1990 and took just over $20,000 at the box-office before being released on video. The movie is also available on DVD.

In 2002 Caine talked about *A Shock to the System* in an interview with *Venice* magazine. 'That was a lovely little film, but it was too small for its own good, really. It got lost. It was the sort of film, were it made today, that would be great as a film for HBO or something. But at the time, it just got lost in the system.'

The 'greed is good' mantra was old news even when this film was released in 1990, let alone now. That firmly dates *A Shock to the System*. But this is a dark and humorous satire on office politics, and also a wish-fulfilment fantasy for anyone who's ever wanted to see their boss meet a nasty end. The script overplays its many magical allusions and Egleson's direction is banal at best, but Caine gives a fine, edgy performance as the murderous Graham. The plot keeps twisting and turning, sustaining your interest to the end. This is an underrated movie, despite its flaws.

SILVER BEARS (1977)

Cast: Michael Caine (Doc Fletcher), Cybill Shepherd (Debbie Luckman), Louis Jourdan (Prince di Siracusa), Stephane Audran (Shireen Firdausi), David Warner (Agha Firdausi), Tom Smothers (Donald Luckman), Martin Balsam (Joe Fiore), Jay Leno (Albert Fiore), Tony Mascia (Marvin Skinner), Charles Gray (Charles Cook), Joss Ackland (Henry Foreman).
Crew: Ivan Passer (director), Arlene Sellers and Alex Winitsky (producers), Peter Stone (writer), Claude Bolling (music), Anthony Richmond (cinematography), Bernard Gribble (editor), Edward Marshall (art direction).

Doc Fletcher flies to Switzerland to buy a bank for Mafia boss Joe Fiore, taking Fiore's son Albert and a counterfeiter called Marvin Skinner with him. The $3 million deal is negotiated by Prince di Siracusa, an impoverished Italian aristocrat. But the bank proves to be just an office above a pizza restaurant in Lugano. Prince introduces Doc to siblings Agha and Shireen Firdausi. They show him a secret silver mine in Iran containing silver reputedly worth $1 billion. He loans them $20 million to fund exploitation.

American banker Henry Foreman wants to buy a European bank. He sends one of his staff, Donald Luckman, to find a suitable candidate. Meanwhile, in London, the world's richest man, Charles Cook, is worried when silver from the Firdausi mine depresses the market. He wants Luckman and Foreman to buy the Lugano bank for $60 million. Cook will then buy the silver mine from the Americans for $60 million, leaving them with a European bank acquired for nothing.

Doc seduces Luckman's ditzy wife Debbie to find out what is really going on. Fiore wants to sell the bank, but gives Doc a week to organise a management buy-out. Doc tries to foreclose on the mine but discovers it does not exist. The Firdausis are smugglers, recycling

The money is hot ... The tricksters are cool ... And the comedy is quick-silver fast !

Nat Cohen presents an Alex Winitsky and Arlene Sellers Production

MICHAEL CAINE · CYBILL SHEPHERD
LOUIS JOURDAN · STEPHANE AUDRAN · DAVID WARNER
TOM SMOTHERS and MARTIN BALSAM as Fiore

$ILVER BEAR$

Music by CLAUDE BOLLING · Executive Producer MARTIN C. SCHUTE · Based on the novel by PAUL ERDMAN
Screenplay by PETER STONE · Produced by ARLENE SELLERS and ALEX WINITSKY · Directed by IVAN PASSER · Technicolor ® Distributed by EMI Films Limited

Now available
in paper back
from ARROW Books

silver trinkets from India into ingots. Doc engineers a complex deal that leaves him with ownership of the bank, no one out of pocket and only one person going to jail – Luckman. Debbie moves in with Doc while her husband serves his prison sentence writing a book about his experiences...

'AMUSING PEOPLE. OPULENT HOUSES. VINTAGE CARS. GLORIOUS SETTINGS. LOVELY WOMEN. PITY ABOUT THE STORY.' *EVENING NEWS*

'DIRECTOR IVAN PASSER HAS ASSEMBLED A RATHER TALENTED SQUAD OF PERFORMERS, THEN MARCHED THEM THROUGH A MINEFIELD, LOSING ALL HANDS IN AN ATTACK ON AN UNCERTAIN OBJECTIVE.' *VARIETY*

Paul Erdman's novel, *The Silver Bears*, was a financial thriller set during the early 1970s' collapse of silver prices. First published in 1974, the film rights were snapped up and screenwriter Peter Stone commissioned to turn the book into a comedy; Stone had achieved great success with his work on several Cary Grant films including *Charade* (1963). Ivan Passer was brought on board to direct. He had been a leading figure in the Czech cinema's new wave of the 1960s, co-scripting all of Milos Forman's native films, but had left his homeland after the Soviet invasion of 1968.

In his 1992 autobiography, Caine recalled how he came to be cast in *Silver Bears*. The actor was planning to move from England to Los Angeles but his accountant told him he was virtually penniless, thanks to Britain's punitive taxes on high earners. 'Panicking, I accepted the first offer of work that came along, to make a picture called *Silver Bears*.' The picture reunited him with Joss Ackland, who had worked on *The Black Windmill* (1974). Making his film debut in *Silver Bears* was young comedian Jay Leno, who later became famous as the host of US TV's *The Tonight Show*.

The picture was shot in the final months of 1976, with locations in Switzerland, Morocco and England, and studio work at Twickenham. Caine was interviewed in Lugano for London's *Evening Standard*. The actor had a ready explanation when told he looked lean and fit: 'We were on location in Morocco. I had my usual cold and dysentery and lost 11 pounds.' Despite what he later wrote in his autobiography, in the 1976 interview Caine denied rumours about going into tax exile: 'You know, I took my decision and I'll pay my taxes and stay in England.'

Silver Bears was released in British cinemas in October 1977. Critics were unimpressed by the picture and it was not a hit at the box-office. The pattern was repeated in America. The film was released on video a decade later but has since been deleted and has yet to make its DVD debut.

This film is supposed to be a comedy but the laughs are few and far between. It takes nearly an hour to set up the first part of the plot before introducing a dozen new characters and subplots that merely muddy the already stagnant waters of this unremarkable tale. Most of the actors seem to be sleepwalking their way through, and Caine's performance is a strictly low-energy affair. He is upstaged by the frenetic efforts of Cybill Shepherd, who yelps and screams throughout as if being subjected to regular electric shocks. *Silver Bears* is proof that glamorous locations and a distinguished cast are not enough to overcome tepid direction and a yawn-inducing script.

RIGHT: Milo Tindle admires the jewels he is stealing in *Sleuth* (1972).

FAR RIGHT: Tindle fights back against his host's mind games in *Sleuth* (1972).

SLEUTH (1972)

Cast: Laurence Olivier (Andrew Wyke), Michael Caine (Milo Tindle), Alex Cawthorne (Inspector Doppler).
Crew: Joseph L Mankiewicz (director), Morton Gottlieb (producer), Anthony Shaffer (writer), John Addison (music), Oswald Morris (cinematography), Richard Marden (editor), Ken Adam (production design).

Milo Tindle accepts an invitation to visit the country estate of English crime novelist Andrew Wyke. Milo is having an affair with Andrew's wife, Marguerite, and wants to marry her. Andrew questions the younger man's background and financial circumstances. He says Milo

cannot afford to keep Marguerite, but the
problem can be solved. Andrew persuades Milo
to stage a burglary, stealing £250,000 of insured
jewels from Wyke's house. But afterwards
Andrew says this is all a ruse so he can murder
Milo and claim that the killing was in self-
defence. The writer shoots several bullets from a
revolver to prove he is serious before viciously
humiliating Milo. Finally, he fires the revolver
into the back of Milo's head.

Two days later, a policeman called Inspector
Doppler arrives, investigating the disappearance
of Milo. He interrogates Andrew and discovers

dried blood. The writer claims it was all an
elaborate double-bluff to humiliate Milo, but
insists that the final bullet was a blank. The
inspector arrests Andrew before peeling away his
own face to reveal that Doppler is actually Milo.
Andrew claims he knew all along and was just
playing up to Milo's game. Milo says he doesn't
want to play a game – he wants revenge.

Milo claims he has murdered Andrew's
mistress and has hidden four pieces of evidence
in the house linking the writer to the crime. The
police are due within minutes. Andrew doesn't
believe him, but when he tries to contact his

mistress he learns she is dead – strangled. Andrew frantically searches to find all the clues, eventually locating and destroying the murder weapon. Milo reveals that this, too, was just another game. Andrew's mistress is still alive. Milo taunts the author, telling him that Marguerite is never coming back to him. Andrew murders Milo but loses their final game, for the police are outside after all, waiting to arrest him…

'ALTHOUGH BRILLIANTLY PLOTTED, FLAWLESSLY CONSTRUCTED, GENUINELY THRILLING AND MORE THAN USUALLY ATTENTIVE TO CHARACTER, *SLEUTH* IS ESSENTIALLY A PIECE FOR THE THEATRE…'
MONTHLY FILM BULLETIN

'MR CAINE, WITH THE HELP OF SPECTACULAR MAKE-UP, SHOWS A RANGE WHICH ONE HAD NOT EXPECTED FROM THIS EXCELLENT PLAYER OF LAYABOUTS AND SECRET AGENTS.' **SUNDAY TIMES**

Anthony Shaffer's play *Sleuth* opened in 1970, with Anthony Quayle and Keith Baxter in the leading roles, and became a success in London's West End, running for nearly 2400 performances. The show was also a smash-hit on Broadway, winning a Tony award. But Shaffer, who was busy writing the screenplays for both *Frenzy* and *The Wicker Man* around this time, didn't want the play turned into a film, believing that any cinema version would stifle the play's future success. It would enjoy major West End revivals in 1978 and 2002, so he was clearly mistaken in this.

Shaffer was eventually persuaded to surrender the film rights and American director Joseph L Mankiewicz began working with Shaffer on an adaptation. Mankiewicz had won Oscars for writing and directing *All About Eve* (1950) and also for helming *A Letter to Three Wives* (1949). The two men added new material to keep *Sleuth* fresh for those who had already seen the play.

Sleuth only had a cast of two, so choosing the right actors was crucial. For the part of Wyke Shaffer favoured stage original Anthony Quayle, with Alan Bates as Milo. Instead Mankiewicz secured the legendary Laurence Olivier as Wyke, even though the actor had once dismissed the play as 'a piece of piss'. It was Olivier who reportedly chose Caine to be his co-star. The two actors rehearsed for a fortnight before filming began. In an interview on the *Sleuth* DVD, Shaffer recalled that the younger man was frightened of playing opposite Olivier. 'Michael Caine was really scared about working with Larry Olivier,' Shaffer says. 'He thought Olivier would overwhelm him.'

In fact, Olivier struggled for the first few days of rehearsals, having just been fired as director of the National Theatre. Caine talked about the turning point during a public interview at the NFT in 1998: 'One day he came in with a little moustache and he stuck it on, and suddenly it all went right. He said: "I can never act with my bloody face! I have to have some bloody nose, or something on, and this will do." But up until then he was floundering about, not know what he was talking about. Larry was crafty. He would do rehearsals, and he'd mumble away and then suddenly he could be this absolute giant of an actor, although he was shorter than me. Sometimes he'd come out of the bloody shadows, like a whirlwind at me, and take me completely by surprise, because he'd never do it in rehearsals. He was a very crafty bugger, Larry, and you had to hang on. The greatest review I ever got was after about a week [of filming with Olivier]. He said to me, "I thought at the beginning, Michael, I had a servant. I see I have a partner."'

Sleuth was shot during spring 1972. All the exteriors were filmed at Athelhampton House in Dorset, with production designer Ken Adam temporarily adding a hedge maze to the grounds. The interiors were shot on elaborate sets at Pinewood Studios. 'Ken Adam is a brilliant designer,' Caine told the *Evening Standard* when a reporter visited the production in May 1972. 'He's given a very weird feeling to the sets. And that's real oak, you know, in the hall, not a load of old plastic.'

In 1980 Caine told *Film Comment* that the 16-week shoot for *Sleuth* was the most exhausting he had worked on. 'Incredibly tiring. I'd have six-minute monologues at a time. I used to get home in the evening and say to Shakira, my wife, "I really can't talk now. I'm sick of the sound of my voice. I don't want to hear it again. You tell me everything, but don't ask me any questions. Let me just sit here and listen."' With a cast of only two, neither actor could take a day off. Mankiewicz had to shoot coverage of everything to give the editor sufficient footage to cut to.

Sleuth was released in American cinemas in December 1972, just in time for consideration at annual awards ceremonies. The picture attracted raves from critics and nominations for Caine, Olivier and best picture at the Golden Globes. At the Oscars Caine and Olivier were both nominated as best actor, but were beaten by Marlon Brando's performance in *The Godfather* (1972). Mankiewicz was nominated as best director for what proved to be his final film, while the score was also nominated.

Sleuth didn't reach British cinemas until August 1973. Reviews were strong, with many complimenting Caine for matching Olivier on screen in such a demanding part. The film eventually received four BAFTA nominations for Olivier, cinematography, art direction and

screenplay. Much later, a late-night TV screening of the film inspired a Manchester singer called Steven Morrissey to write 'This Charming Man', providing his band The Smiths with their first hit single in November 1983. The song borrowed a memorable line of dialogue from Shaffer's screenplay: 'A jumped-up pantry boy who never knew his place.'

Sleuth was released on video in 1987 and made its DVD debut in 2002. Shaffer died in November 2001, soon after recording his interview for the DVD. In November 2002 Caine told the *Hollywood Reporter* that he was hoping to remake *Sleuth* with himself in Olivier's role and British actor Jude Law taking over Caine's part. Six months later *Variety* confirmed that US filmmaking company Castle Rock had acquired the film rights to Shaffer's play as a vehicle for Law. Playwright Harold Pinter had been commissioned to write a fresh adaptation, having never seen the 1972 version.

Sleuth is a flawed diamond of a film – a priceless gem with sparkling dialogue, stunning production design and two bravura performances from Olivier and Caine. But it still has blemishes, never truly escaping its stage origin. The middle section fails to convince because Inspector Doppler is all too obviously Caine in make-up, especially when the wrinkles on his forehead abruptly stop at the 'hairline' of his bald cap. This distracts your attention and makes it difficult to discern whether or not Olivier's character believes in Doppler. But *Sleuth* overcomes these problems to deliver a compelling thriller riddled with sly asides about prejudice, the class system and gamesmanship. This film is among the finest of Caine's long career.

THE STATEMENT (2003)

Cast: Michael Caine, Tilda Swinton, Jeremy Northam, Alan Bates, Matt Craven, William

Hutt, Noam Jenkins, John Neville,
Charlotte Rampling.
Crew: Norman Jewison (director), Robert Lantos
(producer), Ronald Harwood (writer).

Pierre Brossard was a collaborator who sent
seven French Jews to be killed by a Nazi firing
squad. He escaped capture after the war and
lived a peaceful and anonymous life, sheltered by
right-wing elements within the Catholic Church.
Forty years later a new investigation into his
crimes is launched. Brossard finds himself
marked for death, being pursued across France
by the police and hit-men.

Brian Moore's thriller *The Statement* was first
published in 1995. Producer Robert Lantos
snapped up the film rights and veteran director
Norman Jewison came on board. Jewison's
movies have earned more than 45 Oscar
nominations and 12 awards. The director has
been nominated three times as best director, for
In the Heat of the Night (1967), *Fiddler on the
Roof* (1971) and *Moonstruck* (1987). At the 1999
Oscars he won the prestigious Irving G Thalberg
Memorial Award.

In 2003 Jewison told *Variety* that he had been
working for years to get *The Statement* made.
'Studios won't make a movie like this today,'
he maintained. Jewison chose Caine for the lead
role of Brossard ('I look forward to working with
Michael Caine, something that I have been trying
to do over the last 25 years') and expected to
bring the picture in for less than $10 million.

British playwright Ronald Harwood was
chosen to adapt the novel into a screenplay; he
had won the best adapted screenplay Oscar for
his work on Roman Polanski's Holocaust drama
The Pianist (2002). Shooting began in Paris on
31 March 2003. During filming Jewison had a
meal with Polanski, who had just won the best
director Oscar for *The Pianist*. 'This is a film the

French should have made years ago,' Polanski
told Jewison.

As this book was going to press a tentative
US release date was announced for *The
Statement*. The film is scheduled to receive a
limited release on 21 November 2003, making it
eligible for awards consideration. The response
of critics and its prospects for picking up any
trophies will determine how wide a release
it receives subsequently.

SURRENDER (1987)

Cast: Sally Field (Daisy), Michael Caine (Sean),
Steve Guttenberg (Marty), Peter Boyle (Jay),
Jackie Cooper (Ace), Julie Kavner (Ronnie),
Louise Lasser (Joyce), Iman (Hedy), Michael
Andrews (Hooker).
Crew: Jerry Belson (director), Aaron Spelling
and Alan Greisman (producers), Jerry Belson
(writer), Michel Colombier (music), Juan Ruiz
Anchia (cinematography), Wendy Greene
Bricmont (editor), Lilly Kilvert
(production design).

Sean Stein is a best-selling author who can't trust
women after losing much of his earnings to his

BELOW:
In *Surrender* (1987)
beleaguered author
Sean Stein vows
never to fall for
another woman,
to the bemusement
of his friend Jay
(Peter Boyle).

STARRING **MICHAEL CAINE**

ex-wife and a former lover in court. Daisy Morgan is an assembly-line painter who dreams of becoming an artist and is disenchanted with her boyfriend, a selfish but rich lawyer called Marty. When armed robbers force guests at a charity party to strip naked, Sean and Daisy are tied together. Next morning Marty flies off to deal with a case in a third world country. Smitten with Daisy, Sean persuades her to go on a date. The rich writer claims that he is broke, to discover if Daisy will love him for something other than his money. The pair fall for each other. Marty returns, a changed man after being held captive by pygmies. He is ready to commit to Daisy. She dumps Sean but goes back to him after discovering he is rich. They decide to get married, but Sean wants Daisy to sign

a pre-nuptial agreement. She wins $2 million at a casino. Sean has an epiphany, realising he alone is to blame for his problems, not women. Daisy decides love is more important than money. She and Sean are reunited…

'*SURRENDER* IS AN ASTONISHING CASE OF A MOVIE THAT CAN DO NO WRONG FOR ITS FIRST HALF AND LITTLE RIGHT THEREAFTER.'
CHICAGO SUN-TIMES

'A 1950s SITCOM DRESSED UP IN MODERN CLOTHES. MICHAEL CAINE AND SALLY FIELD ARE GOOD FOR A COUPLE OF LAUGHS ALONG THE WAY,

BELOW: Lovers Sean Stein and Daisy Morgan (Sally Field) are startled by an intruder during *Surrender* (1987).

BUT [THE] PRODUCTION RUNS OUT OF STEAM EARLY.' *VARIETY*

Comedy writer Jerry Belson had won awards for his TV work, but struck out with his feature film directorial debut, *Jekyll & Hyde ... Together Again* (1982). Five years later he returned to the big screen as writer/director of the romantic comedy *Surrender* (1987). The script lured double Oscar-winning actress Sally Field back to work after a two-year break. It also caught the eye of Michael Caine. 'I've always wanted to be in a real American screwball romantic comedy like they used to make before the war,' he told the *Scotsman* in 1987. 'I didn't want any concessions made to me as an Englishman, just to be accepted as an American star in an American comedy.'

Caine enjoyed his time on the picture, naming Field as one of the best actresses he had worked with. They had previously co-starred in the ill-fated disaster movie *Beyond the Poseidon Adventure* (1979). 'The great thing was to work with Sally and have a relationship with her which was so easy, playing off each other. I can only remember having that sort of relationship with one person before, Sean Connery. It's the happiest I've been with a picture for a long time ... I think it will be the biggest box-office hit I have done.'

But *Surrender* proved a resounding flop when released to American cinemas in October 1987. Critics were unimpressed and it grossed less than $6 million. There was also a backlash against the film in AIDS-conscious America because Caine and Field's characters had sex on their first date. 'The reaction was: how shocking, how irresponsible,' Caine told the *Daily Mirror* a month after the movie opened in America. 'Over there people are having blood tests before they even consider going on a first date. I'm middle-aged. It's a problem that hasn't really affected my generation.'

The picture reached Britain in December 1987. It was released on video in 1988 but has since been deleted and has yet to appear on DVD.

Surrender is like a living snapshot of the 1980s, a romantic comedy featuring only venal, self-obsessed characters. Belson's script probably looked hilarious on the page, but on screen it runs out of gas after only 45 minutes. During the first half of the film, Caine and Field sustain this limited material with the lightest of touches. But as soon as Steve Guttenberg reappears, love triangle dynamics overpower any attempt at sustaining or developing characterisation. By the finale, when the leads renounce their money-grubbing ways for love, you just don't care about them any more. Don't bother with *Surrender* unless you enjoy seeing two talented actors wasted on a trite, wafer-thin trifle.

THE SWARM (1978)

Cast: Michael Caine (Brad Crane), Katharine Ross (Helena), Richard Widmark (General Slater), Richard Chamberlain (Dr Hubbard), Olivia de Havilland (Maureen), Ben Johnson (Felix), Lee Grant (Anne MacGregor), José Ferrer (Dr Andrews), Patty Duke Astin (Rita), Slim Pickens (Jud Hawkins), Bradford Dillman (Major Baker), Fred MacMurray (Clarence), Henry Fonda (Dr Krim).
Crew: Irwin Allen (director/producer), Stirling Silliphant (writer), Jerry Goldsmith (music), Fred J Koenekamp (cinematography), Harold F Kress (editor), Stan Jolley (production design).

Soldiers at a missile base in Texas are killed by an unknown foe. Entomologist Brad Crane is already on the scene when US military investigators arrive, led by General Slater. Crane claims the base was attacked by a swarm of

ABOVE:

'Will history blame me – or the bees?' Dr Helena Anderson (Katherine Ross) and Brad Crane prepare to face *The Swarm* (1978).

African killer bees. His story is backed up by Dr Helena Anderson, one of the few staff to survive. The US President puts Crane in charge of efforts to stop the bees. Crane calls in experts from across the country, including America's top immunologist, Dr Krim.

The swarm attacks the nearby town of Marysville, killing 232 people. The rest of the townsfolk are evacuated by train, but this also encounters the bees. The train crashes

and burns – only 17 people survive. A massive airdrop of poison pellets fails to stop the swarm. Dr Krim dies after using killer bee stings to test a possible antidote on himself. The bees are flying towards the city of Houston, which is evacuated. The swarm attacks a nuclear power plant in its path; it explodes, killing more than 36,000 people. Slater gets presidential authority to replace Crane and uses a deadly pesticide against the bees without success.

The swarm attacks Houston and the military decides to set fire to the city. Crane discovers the missile base's sonic alarm system is identical to the vibrations of the killer bees' mating ritual – that's why the swarm attacked the base. He uses sonic lures to lead the bees away from Houston to an oil slick. When the bees converge on the oil, it is set alight, destroying the swarm. Mankind is safe – for now…

'KILLER BEES PERIODICALLY INTERRUPT THE ARCH WRITING, STILTED DIRECTION AND LUDICROUS ACTING IN IRWIN ALLEN'S DISAPPOINTING AND TIRED NON-THRILLER.' *VARIETY*

'IT SEEMS TO BE CAINE'S SAD FATE TO GO AROUND BEING INTELLIGENT IN DUMB MOVIES.' *TIME*

Irwin Allen produced the most successful disaster movies of the 1970s. He also directed several action sequences in *The Towering Inferno* (1974) and uncredited scenes for *The Poseidon Adventure* (1972). Allen decided he wanted to direct an entire film and acquired the rights to Arthur Herzog's killer bees novel, *The Swarm*, first published in 1974. Oscar-winning screenwriter Stirling Silliphant was hired to adapt the book and an all-star cast assembled, with Caine taking the lead as entomologist Brad Crane.

In 1978 Caine told *Film Review* that he had always wanted to work with Allen. 'I met him a couple of years ago and he said, "The next time I do a picture, I'll do it with you." You get lots of those sort of promises. But he's obviously a man of his word because the next time he did a picture, he did indeed cast me.' The actor said he used to dream about making a big Hollywood

LEFT: A star-studded cast could not rescue *The Swarm* (1978). General Slater (Richard Widmark) greets the arrival of Dr Krim (Henry Fonda), an old friend of Brad Crane. Observing them is Major Baker (Bradford Dillman).

movie and described what it was like working with screen legends like Henry Fonda, Olivia de Havilland and Richard Widmark: 'A bit nerve-wracking actually! But quite extraordinary!'

The Swarm was shot principally at Burbank Studios in California, with some location filming in Houston. The film had a reported budget of $15-21 million, but was a box-office disaster when it reached US cinemas in July 1978. The picture grossed less than half its budget. Critics had a field day deriding the script, acting and direction, amongst other things. The picture was just an unsuccessful in Britain.

'*The Swarm* was one of the most difficult pictures I've made,' Caine told *Film Comment* in 1980. 'Getting that dialogue and trying to make a reality for the character was an extraordinary exercise – like doing push-ups – and I'd recommend a picture like that to every actor. It's funny about films like *The Swarm* ... you're a sort of catalyst for a whole group of people, pushing, pushing, pushing. And it's very hard to do.'

Caine attributed the flop to the film's special effects. 'Everyone keeps threatening to show it to me,' he told the *Sunday Express* in 1978. 'And I will see it one day. But I can tell you one thing – if it didn't work, it was all the bees' fault. I always knew they couldn't act.' Surprisingly, the picture received an Oscar nomination for best costume design; the award went to *Death on the Nile* instead. In 1998, the film was reissued on VHS with 30 minutes of extra footage incorporated. The film is available on DVD, but only in its extended version. Recalling the film when interviewed by *Empire* in 1992, Caine observed that: 'It *looked* like it was gonna be good. If it were possible to know in advance how good a film will be, we'd all be in one box-office smash after another and I'd be as rich as Paul McCartney.'

The Swarm is so bad it's good. This film deserves to be included on any list of cult classic clunkers, such is the unbridled awfulness on show. In his single effort behind the cameras, Irwin Allen gave new meaning to the term disaster movie. Highlights in this unintentional comedy of terrors are a script packed with dialogue that beggars belief and a cast of stars performing away without a shred of irony. Caine appears to be taking a leaf out of William Shatner's book, such is the gut-wrenching intensity of his characterisation in this addle-brained endeavour. *The Swarm* is not just a cheesy delight, it's a quattro formaggi feast. Highly recommended, especially after excess alcohol.

SWEET LIBERTY (1986)

Cast: Alan Alda (Michael Burgess), Michael Caine (Elliott James), Michelle Pfeiffer (Faith Healy), Bob Hoskins (Stanley Gould), Lise Hilboldt (Gretchen Carlsen), Lillian Gish (Cecelia Burgess), Saul Rubinek (Bo Hodges), Lois Chiles (Leslie), Linda Thorson (Grace). Crew: Alan Alda (director/writer), Martin Bregman (producer), Bruce Broughton (music), Frank Tidy (cinematography), Michael Economu (editor), Ben Edwards (production design).

Michael Burgess is a history professor at a college in the small town of Sayeville. His prize-winning book about the American War of Independence is being turned into a Hollywood film. Michael is dating another professor, Gretchen Carlsen, but she doesn't want to live with him and he doesn't want to get married. The cast and crew arrives in town to begin shooting. Michael is horrified when he reads the script adapted from his book. Screenwriter Stanley Gould has turned historical fact into low-brow comedy. Stanley begs Michael to help him rewrite the script. The historian is smitten by lead actress Faith

Healy, mistaking her Method acting as her true personality. Michael and Gretchen split up.

Stanley and Michael feed their rewrites directly to Faith and the leading man, self-destructive womaniser Elliott James, who persuade the director to use the new material. Michael sleeps with Faith but is shocked when she then seduces Elliott to improve their on-screen chemistry. Frustrated with the director's disregard for history, Michael leads the local people employed as extras in a mutiny, sabotaging a day's filming. When the production leaves town, Michael and Gretchen get back together. Having learned to compromise, they decide to get married. At the film's premiere, Gretchen is pregnant…

'THE MOVIE WANTS TO JUGGLE A LOT OF CHARACTERS ALL AT ONCE, BUT IT KEEPS DROPPING THE MOST INTERESTING ONES.' *CHICAGO SUN-TIMES*

'ALAN ALDA … IS COMPLETELY OUTSHONE BY MICHAEL CAINE AS A DELIGHTFULLY FLIPPANT ENGLISH FILM STAR WITH A LECHEROUS DISPOSITION AND BOB HOSKINS AS A DIM EXTROVERT SCRIPTWRITER.' *DAILY EXPRESS*

Alan Alda became an international star thanks to his role as Hawkeye Pierce in the long-running TV series *M*A*S*H*. When that concluded in 1983, he created a short-lived television show called *The Four Seasons*. Alda's next project was the film *Sweet Liberty* (1986), which he wrote, directed and played the starring part in. The role of conceited, arrogant film star Elliott James was written especially for Caine, as he told *Films and Filming* in 1986. 'Alan Alda phones me up and said, "I've got just the part for you – a big-headed movie star." How could I refuse?'

Caine had just finished filming *Hannah and*

ABOVE: Flirtatious film star Elliott James tries to talk his way out of trouble in *Sweet Liberty* (1986), watched by his latest conquest Leslie (Lois Chiles).

Her Sisters (1986) in New York. In 1987 he told the *Scotsman* that both roles were chosen to prove his comedy skills: 'I wanted to change my image … I could get plenty of leads as gangsters and spies and lunatics and nutcases or in dramatic pictures, but I couldn't get a leading role in a comedy.'

Sweet Liberty was filmed in the summer of 1985, with extensive location work at Sag Harbor and Suffolk County in the state of New York. The leading actors were given the use of palatial mansions in the expensive Hamptons resort during filming. The picture also reunited Caine with Bob Hoskins, who had met and become firm friends while making *The Honorary Consul* (1983) in Mexico.

Interviewed by *Us* magazine in 1990, Hoskins said Caine tormented him during the filming of *Sweet Liberty*. 'I was setting up *Mona Lisa* (1986) at that point. And I really wanted him to play the villain in that, but … we couldn't afford him, really, so it would have been a big favour. And he kept saying, "I've got a script here, something called *Mona Lisa* – have you heard if it's any good?" And I'd just tell him to read it. I mean, I didn't want to say, "Yeah, it's great, you've got to do it!" He finally read it and said it wasn't bad. We … chatted about it and I thought, "Well, that's the end of that." Then on the first day of filming *Mona Lisa*, there he was: "You didn't think I'd be here, did you?"'

Sweet Liberty was released across America in May 1986. Critics gave it mediocre notices and the picture grossed just over $14 million. In Britain the BBFC required two seconds to be cut before classifying it as a PG. Reviewers were unimpressed but praised the comic talents of Caine and Hoskins. The film was released on video in 1987 but has since been deleted and isn't yet available on DVD.

Sweet Liberty could have been a good comedy, but a profusion of unfocused subplots restrict it to being just occasionally amusing. Alda's film keeps introducing new characters but never gives them room to develop. A subplot involving the elderly mother of Alda's character (played by silent screen legend Lillian Gish) seems to have wandered in from another movie altogether. There's plenty of fun to be had from Hollywood invading a small town – David Mamet made more from the concept in *State and Main* (2000) – yet Alda never gets beyond the obvious. Caine has great fun in his part, romping around as a latter-day Errol Flynn. But he gets too little screen time in a film that never succeeds in pulling all its threads together. *Sweet Liberty* is amiable and inoffensive, but nothing more.

T

TOO LATE THE HERO (1970)

Cast: Michael Caine (Tosh), Cliff Robertson (Lt Lawson), Ian Bannen (Thornton), Harry Andrews (Colonel Thompson), Ronald Fraser (Campbell), Denholm Elliott (Captain Hornsby), Lance Percival (Corporal McLean), Percy Herbert (Johnstone), Patrick Jordan (Sergeant Major), Henry Fonda (Captain Nolan), Ken Takakura (Major Yamaguchi). Crew: Robert Aldrich (director/producer/co-writer), Lukas Heller (co-writer), Gerald Fried (music), Joseph Biroc (cinematography), Michael Luciano (editor), James Dowell Vance (art direction).

Japanese-speaking US Navy linguist Lieutenant Lawson is sent to join a British operation on an island in the New Hebrides. An American Navy convoy will soon be passing the Japanese-controlled north coast of the island. The mission is to disable the enemy transmitter and have

ABOVE: Caine and his fellow actors spent months in the Philippines jungles filming *Too Late the Hero* (1970) with independent director/producer Robert Aldrich.

was shot at Aldrich Studios in Los Angeles and the production wrapped at the end of June 1969. As part of his promotional duties for the film, Caine featured in a photo-shoot for *Playboy* magazine. Dressed in character, he posed with half a dozen topless models for the October 1969 issue. Co-star Denholm Elliott appeared, looking somewhat bemused, in one of the pictures.

Originally scheduled for release in December 1969, *Too Late the Hero* reached US cinemas five months later. Critics gave the picture a mediocre response and it failed to repeat the success of *The Dirty Dozen* (1967). The film was released on video in 1987 and made its DVD debut in 2001.

Too Late the Hero is one of the many 'war is hell' films that got pumped out in the late 1960s and early 1970s like so many cynical celluloid bullets. Aldrich recycles plot elements from his own output, such as a suicide mission featuring a dozen scoundrels – just as in *The Dirty Dozen* (1967). *Too Late the Hero* is a decidedly humourless effort but the quality of acting helps overcome the stolid script. Caine is as reliable as ever, well matched by Robertson. The film's highlight comes at the climax with the duo running for their lives across the open plain, even if Aldrich telegraphs his finale in the movie's first 20 minutes. It still remains gripping viewing, waiting to see who survives.

UV

VICTORY (1981)
(UK title: *ESCAPE TO VICTORY*)

Cast: Sylvester Stallone (Hatch), Michael Caine (Colby), Max Von Sydow (Major Von Steiner), Pelé (Fernandez), Carole Laure (Renee), Daniel Massey (Colonel Waldron), Tim Pigott-Smith (Rose), Julian Curry (Shurlock), Bobby Moore (Terry Brady).
Crew: John Huston (director), Freddie Fields (producer), Evan Jones and Yabo Yablonsky (writers), Bill Conti (music), Gerry Fisher (cinematography), Roberto Silvi (editor), J Dennis Washington (production design).

Former England player John Colby runs a football league among the Allied prisoners at a German camp during the Second World War. A German officer, Major Von Steiner, recognises Colby and proposes an international match between prisoners and captors. Colby agrees on condition that his team get proper kit, rations and training facilities. Nazi officers turn the match into a propaganda event, pitting the Allies against the German national team with a Paris stadium as the venue. Canadian prisoner Hatch proves himself an able goalkeeper and joins the

team. The camp escape committee gets him to escape so he can travel to Paris and contact the French Resistance. A plan is formulated for all the players to escape at halftime during the match. Hatch lets himself be captured so he can go back to the POW camp and pass on the details.

The team is taken to Paris, where a crowd of French citizens is forced at gunpoint to watch the match. The Germans go 4-1 up, thanks to dubious decisions by the referee and superior fitness. At half-time the Resistance men break into the Allied team's dressing room from the sewers. Now is the chance to escape, but the team decide to go back and finish the match. By the final minutes the score is 4-4 and the crowd is going wild for the Allies. The Germans get a penalty but Hatch saves it. The match ends in a draw as the crowd storms the pitch. The players are swept out of the stadium with the crowd…

'*ESCAPE TO VICTORY,* THE MOST EGREGIOUSLY SILLY SORTIE INTO NAZI GERMANY THE CINEMA HAS YET GIVEN US, IS *MATCH OF THE DAY* MEETS *STALAG 17.*' **FINANCIAL TIMES**

'*VICTORY* AMOUNTS TO A FRANKLY OLD-FASHIONED WORLD WAR II MORALITY PLAY, HINGING ON SOCCER AS A CIVILISED METAPHOR FOR THE GAME OF WAR … SOME VERY GOOD PERFORMANCES FROM THE CAST, PARTICULARLY CAINE.' **VARIETY**

Victory was inspired by an article in the *New York Times* about a group of POWs who played the Germans at football in Holland during the Second World War. The prisoners won and were summarily executed. Screenwriter Yabo Yablonsky saw the potential for a film and began adapting the tale. The resulting story is credited to Yablonsky and Djordje Milicevic and Jeff Maguire, with the screenplay credited to Yablonsky and Evan Jones. The script kicked around Hollywood for years before being picked up by producer Freddie Fields. He had it substantially rewritten to incorporate a more upbeat ending.

The producer then went in search of a cast designed to meet three different markets. The star of the Oscar-winning hit *Rocky* (1976), Sylvester Stallone, was sought for his international box-office appeal. Stallone negotiated a percentage of the gross profits and a say in the shooting script. Caine and Max Von Sydow were hired for their acting ability. Caine told the *New York Times* about parallels he saw between himself and the character he played, Captain John Colby. 'He never believed he could become a captain, I didn't think I could conceivably be a famous actor. We're both men of humble origins thrust into situations far beyond our expectations.' A report in the *Guardian* said Caine likened his part to that of Alec Guinness in *The Bridge on the River Kwai* (1957).

More than a dozen football stars were cast for their ball skills, among them former England captain Bobby Moore and Brazilian legend Pelé. The latter also choreographed all the moves in the climactic football match. Helping to fill out the Allies team were half a dozen players from Ipswich Town, while the Hungarian national team played as the Germans.

Fields wanted director Brian G Hutton, whose previous credits included World War Two romps *Where Eagles Dare* (1968) and *Kelly's Heroes* (1970). But Stallone requested a director he could admire, so the job went to John Huston, then aged 74. Huston had been seriously ill since making *The Man Who Would Be King* (1975) with Caine. Hiring him cost an extra $250,000 for insurance. Huston told the *Times* why he took the job: 'It's a helluva good story. I only make pictures if I like the story or if they offer me a lot of money, and in this case it happened to be both. I see this picture as a definition of sportsmanship, of the male spirit at its very best – values which I subscribe to thoroughly.'

To help minimise other costs, the $15 million picture was shot entirely on location in Hungary during 1980. Budapest doubled for 1940s Paris, having similar architecture. The Hungarian government built the prison camp set at a riding stable outside Budapest. It took more than three months to construct and cost nearly £1 million. Caine was 47 when the movie was being made and not in the best physical shape of his life. He told one interviewer that the football scenes left him with a bad back, swollen ankles and pulled tendons. To another he described the shoot as an 'alcoholic miasma with lots of hot baths.'

The Allies versus Germans football match took a fortnight to film, with the MTK Stadium used in place of Colombe Stadium in Paris. Ipswich goalkeeper Paul Cooper was fitted with a mask of Stallone's face, in case he had to double for the actor in goal. Stallone lost 41 pounds for his role and trained as a goalkeeper for two months. At one stage the script called for him to run up the field and score the winning goal, but this was rejected by Moore and Pelé. Stallone had to be hero of the finale, so the script was changed to have him save a penalty and earn the Allies a 4-4 draw. Just as filming was concluding, an actors' strike in Hollywood shut down the production. Once the dispute was resolved, Caine had to fly back to Hungary from Los Angeles for a single day of shooting.

Victory was released in American cinemas during July 1981. The US did have a professional soccer league but the sport was still a minority interest at the time. Critics derided the film for being old-fashioned and it flopped at the box-office, grossing just over $10 million. In football-loving Britain (where the film was retitled *Escape to Victory*) reviewers had just as much fun laughing at it. The movie has achieved cult status in the past 20 years, however, with several websites devoted to it. You can even buy a football shirt in the strip worn by the Allies.

It's hard to think of many sillier films than *Victory*. The script may be loosely based on a true story, but reality flies out the window in the first five minutes. Caine is 20 years too old and several stone too heavy for his role, while the mixture of international POWs in the prison camp strains credulity to breaking point. But once you let yourself believe the unbelievable, *Victory* becomes an enjoyable romp. The unintentional humour is heightened by the fact that everyone plays their roles completely straight. Caine's efforts on the pitch are limited to shouting and pointing, while the real football stars show their skills. This film is top-notch tosh – if you don't take it seriously.

W

WATER (1985)

Cast: Michael Caine (Baxter),
Valerie Perrine (Pamela), Brenda Vaccaro
(Dolores), Leonard Rossiter (Sir Malcolm),
Billy Connolly (Delgado), Dennis Dugan (Rob),
Fulton Mackay (Eric), Jimmie Walker (Jay Jay),
Dick Shawn (Deke Halliday), Fred Gwynne
(Spender), Trevor Laird (Pepito), Chris
Tummings (Garfield).
Crew: Dick Clement (director/co-writer),
Ian La Frenais (producer/co-writer),
Bill Persky (co-writer), Mike Moran (music),
Douglas Slocombe (cinematography),
John Victor Smith (editor),
Norman Garwood (production design).

Baxter Thwaites is the pot-smoking governor of
Cascara, a wind-swept Caribbean island and one
of Britain's few remaining colonies. Cascara
receives no British aid but does have its own
liberation front, led by singing rebel Delgado,
who has refused to speak until the island is free.
Representatives from US oil company Spenco

visit Cascara to film a TV commercial beside
an abandoned rig. But when they restart the
rig, it hits a rich seam of mineral water.

A British civil servant, Sir Malcolm
Leveridge, tells Baxter that Cascara is being
abandoned and that all its inhabitants will be
relocated to another Caribbean island. Baxter is

outraged. When he hears that Spenco plans to turn the oil rig into a mineral water bottling plant, the governor sees a way to secure the island's future. Sir Malcolm agrees to sell the bottling rights, unaware of their value. When the error is discovered, he is sent back to redress the situation.

Foreign governments get involved, with US Marines, British SAS troops and French mercenaries all converging on Cascara. Baxter joins forces with the Cascara Liberation Front and negotiates for Delgado to appear before the United Nations, singing for Cascaran independence. This ploy works but the mercenaries drain the mineral water into the sea. A week later, Baxter is still trying to restart the rig. He succeeds but, instead of water, the drill hits oil. Cascara is rich and independent, after all.

'THE CENTRAL IDEA IS FRESH, THE PLAYING ENJOYABLE (MICHAEL CAINE AS THE SLOVENLY GOVERNOR AND FULTON MACKAY AS A ROGUISH PARSON ARE PARTICULARLY GOOD) BUT THE SCATTERSHOT OF COMIC INCIDENTS HAS NO REAL BITE.' **SUNDAY TELEGRAPH**

'*WATER* IS A FRENETIC MISHMASH. MICHAEL CAINE IS FINE … BUT HE CAN'T SALVAGE A PRODUCTION THAT'S TOP HEAVY WITH MULTINATIONAL PLOTS THREATENING THE ISLAND'S HARMONY.' **VARIETY**

Water was based on a story by US TV sitcom veteran Bill Persky, parodying the conflicts on Grenada and the Falkland Islands in the early 1980s. UK TV sitcom veterans Dick Clement

and Ian La Frenais had worked with Persky on a TV pilot and he told them his idea, whereupon the three men developed it into a screenplay. Clement became the director with La Frenais as producer and financial backing from Britain's

LEFT: Baxter Thwaites unites with the Cascaran Liberation Front leaders Garfield (Chris Tummings) and Delgado (Billy Connolly) to fight for the island's independence in *Water* (1985).

BELOW: Caine and co-star Billy Connolly take a break during location filming for *Water* (1985) on the Caribbean island of St Lucia.

Handmade Films.

The script attracted the interest of Caine, who agreed to play the lead role of rebellious diplomat Baxter Thwaites. Philip Judge's book *Michael Caine* quotes the actor on Baxter's appeal: 'The guy is crazy, but loveable. That's what I liked about him. He has his own sense of humour, but basically events just run him down like a steamroller.' The movie reunited Caine and British character actor Leonard Rossiter, who had appeared together in *Deadfall* (1968). In his final screen role, Rossiter played British civil servant Sir Malcolm Leveridge, a part originally offered to John Cleese. Several other roles were filled by American actors in order to improve the picture's box-office appeal in the US.

Water gave an early big-screen role to Scottish comedian Billy Connolly. He became good friends with Caine during a month of location work on the Caribbean island of St Lucia in May 1984, after which the production moved to Hartland Point in Devon for further location work. Shooting concluded with interiors at Shepperton Studios in June and July.

During filming Clement and La Frenais realised that the screenplay was flawed. 'We were rewriting the ending as we went along and that's never good,' Clement told Robert Sellers for the 2003 book *Always Look on the Bright Side of Life*. 'In hindsight, I always think you need to get those decisions out of the way before you get on the set. But, on the whole, it was a good shoot. Michael Caine was a fantastic trouper on the film, he was really a joy to work with, enormously supportive. I can't be more appreciative of his work on it and how professional he was.'

At Shepperton, Caine gave an interview to the *Guardian* during the final days of filming. 'This picture is very funny but it's not going to get anybody an Academy Award,' he said. 'It might get a $50-60 million gross, which to me is just as important. If they go broke on this picture they're not going to give me any more work.' The actor admitted to being a workaholic who couldn't go more than six weeks without a job. He said this helped explain why he had been in so many films. 'You don't go into a film thinking, "This is a load of crap but I need the money." I do things that I like and then make sure that I get the maximum amount of money out of it. I figure if I'm going to work someone's going to make massive amounts of money. One of the people is going to be me.'

Water was first released in Britain in January 1985, was savaged by most critics and failed at the box-office. Test screenings in America went so badly that the picture did not find a US distributor for more than a year, finally reaching cinemas in April 1986. It grossed less than $750,000.

A humourless comedy is a painful experience and *Water* certainly qualifies, with the slapstick visuals and staccato pace reducing most of the characters to one-note cartoons. Having Billy Connolly sing all his lines for the first hour might have seemed funny on the page, but any inherent humour in the idea drains away within minutes. Whenever the action drags, the script adds another group of antagonists, substituting complications for complexity. The editing doesn't help either. There is a pause after each sight-gag or punchline, as if the film is waiting for the intervention of a laugh-track. In the midst of this banality, Caine delivers a typically solid performance. *Water* aspires to be a 1980s equivalent to the classic Ealing comedies, but it lacks their wit, intelligence and charm.

THE WHISTLE BLOWER (1986)

Cast: Michael Caine (Frank), James Fox (Lord), Nigel Havers (Bob), John Gielgud (Sir Adrian Chapple), Felicity Dean (Cynthia), Barry Foster

(Greig), Gordon Jackson (Bruce),
Kenneth Colley (Pickett), David Langton
(government minister), Dinah Stabb (Rose),
James Simmons (Mark), Katherine Reeve
(Tiffany), Bill Wallis (Dodgson).
Crew: Simon Langton (director), Geoffrey Reeve
(producer), Julian Bond (writer), John Scott
(music), Fred Tammes (cinematography),
Robert Morgan (editor), Morley Smith
(production design).

A staff member at GCHQ Cheltenham, the surveillance centre for Britain's intelligence forces, is discovered to be a traitor. One of his friends is killed, the death made to look accidental. Frank Jones, meanwhile, visits Cheltenham for his son Bob's birthday, and is dismayed to find that Bob is seeing Cynthia, a married woman with a daughter. Cynthia's husband apparently commits suicide after learning of the affair, but Bob thinks this was faked. Bob himself later falls to his death from a roof terrace, and Frank begins to believe that his son was murdered.

Frank is then approached by Bill Pickett, a journalist investigating similar deaths. Bill is soon added to the death toll, however, dying in an 'accidental' car crash. Frank learns that Bob once met up with Greig, an old friend of Frank's who works for the Intelligence services. Frank gets Greig drunk and Greig says that Bob was killed by American agents, but that the real traitor is Sir Adrian Chapple. Frank visits Chapple and forces him to sign a confession. Chapple dies while trying to shoot his visitor and Frank realises that the confession could be seen as a suicide note. Perhaps the truth will emerge…

'MICHAEL CAINE … DOES MANAGE TO
LIFT THINGS OFF THE GROUND – THE
REST OF THE FILM IS MUTED AND
RATHER DULL.' ***THE GUARDIAN***

'CAINE DOES EVERYTHING RIGHT …
BUT HE'S STUCK IN A SLUGGISH
SCRIPT, FULL OF UNDRAMATISED
RESEARCH; A VAST AND TERRIFYING
SUBJECT TRAPPED IN A SMALL FILM.'
LONDON DAILY NEWS

John Hale's novel *The Whistle Blower* was first published in 1984. Producer Geoffrey Reeve acquired the film rights and hired screenwriter Julian Bond to adapt the conspiracy tale. The picture gave TV director Simon Langton his first cinema feature, having proved himself adept at handling similar material in the 1982 mini-series *Smiley's People*. Caine accepted the lead role of grieving father Frank Jones, having recently starred in another Reeve production, *Half Moon Street* (1986). The actor initially turned down the script, thinking he had been offered the role of 28-year-old Bob.

Caine told *Woman's Own* that his participation helped get *The Whistle Blower* made. 'I took short money on it and invested my time. I'm extremely proud of the result, especially as it's also a first film for the director. Every now and again I do a first film, and I must say I pick winners. I did Ken Russell's first, *Billion Dollar Brain*, and I did Oliver Stone's first, *The Hand*. I think *The Whistle Blower* is another winner.' [In fact, both Russell and Stone had previously directed films, *French Dressing* and *Seizure* respectively.] In a 1987 interview with the *Sunday Express* Caine said his big money role in *Jaws the Revenge* (1987) subsidised his 'no fee' participation in *The Whistle Blower*. He only received a percentage of the latter film's box-office profits.

The low-budget production was shot on location at the beginning of 1986 in and around Cheltenham and London. Staff at the real GCHQ were forbidden from appearing as extras in the film. The picture reunited Caine with Gordon

Jackson, with whom he had co-starred in *The Ipcress File* (1965) and *Kidnapped* (1971). It also gave him a chance to play opposite one of Britain's greatest stage actors, Sir John Gielgud.

In 1987 Caine told the *New York Times* that *The Whistle Blower* was timely. 'As soon as that picture was finished, we had Irangate [a scandal about covert US arms sales]. It always struck me that governments – not only yours – are doing a lot of stuff we didn't know about. It was Kafka-esque. How much are we being manipulated by the government … and how much do we know?'

The Whistle Blower was rated PG by the BBFC in October 1986 but did not reach British cinemas for another seven months. Caine was praised by many critics, but the film itself didn't fare so well. The picture reached the US in August 1987, grossing just over $1 million. It arrived amid a glut of Caine movies, including *The Fourth Protocol*, *Jaws the Revenge* and *Surrender* (all 1987). *The Whistle Blower* was released on video later that year and make its DVD debut as a budget-price release in 2001.

The Whistle Blower is a worthy but dull film about the dubious methods the Intelligence community uses to protect its own secrets. The problems stem from a script that takes far too long to get going, with nearly an hour elapsing before the central character faces any significant problem. Only after the death of Nigel Havers' character does the plot finally start to thicken. By then you will probably be too bored to care. Worse still, the ending is badly fumbled, with Caine's character left wandering around the empty streets of London. This sort of conspiracy thriller was tackled more convincingly in *Defence of the Realm* (1985). Despite these problems, Caine gives a powerful and subtle performance as the grieving father. He is easily the best thing in this mediocre effort.

THE WILBY CONSPIRACY (1975)

Cast: Sidney Poitier (Shack Twala), Michael Caine (Keogh), Nicol Williamson (Horn), Prunella Gee (Rina), Saeed Jaffrey (Mukarjee), Persis Khambatta (Persis), Ryk de Gooyer (Van Heerden), Rutger Hauer (Blane), Patrick Allen (District Commissioner), Joe De Graft (Wilby).
Crew: Ralph Nelson (director), Martin Baum (producer), Rod Amateau and Harold Nebenzal (writers), Stanley Myers (music), John Coquillon (cinematography), Ernest Walker (editor), Harry Pottle (production design).

In Capetown, political prisoner Shack Twala is released after ten years in a South African jail, thanks to his lawyer Rina Van Niekirk. But within minutes the police try to arrest Shack and attack Rina when she tries to stop them. The pair escape with help from Rina's new boyfriend, a British mining engineer called Jim Keogh. Shack and Keogh have to flee South Africa, but Shack insists on travelling via Johannesburg, 900 miles away.

The fugitives are stalked by Major Horn from the Bureau of State Security. He murders a white man who helps the pair and dumps the body in their car boot. Keogh realises that Shack is vice-chairman of Black Congress, a political group fighting against apartheid. The fugitives reach Johannesburg where Shack enlists the aid of Indian doctor Mukarjee to recover £750,000 of uncut diamonds. The stones will be used to further the Black Congress cause.

Keogh and Shack are reunited with Rina. She blackmails her estranged husband, Blane, into flying them across the border into Botswana. They land safely and are welcomed by Wilby, the chairman of Black Congress. But Horn arrives, intent on abducting Wilby and taking him back to South Africa to stand trial. Horn says that

Shack and Keogh were allowed to escape so they would lead him to Wilby. The uncut diamonds are just fakes. The Black congress members foil Horn's plan and kill all his men. Keogh realises he can no longer be neutral and murders Horn…

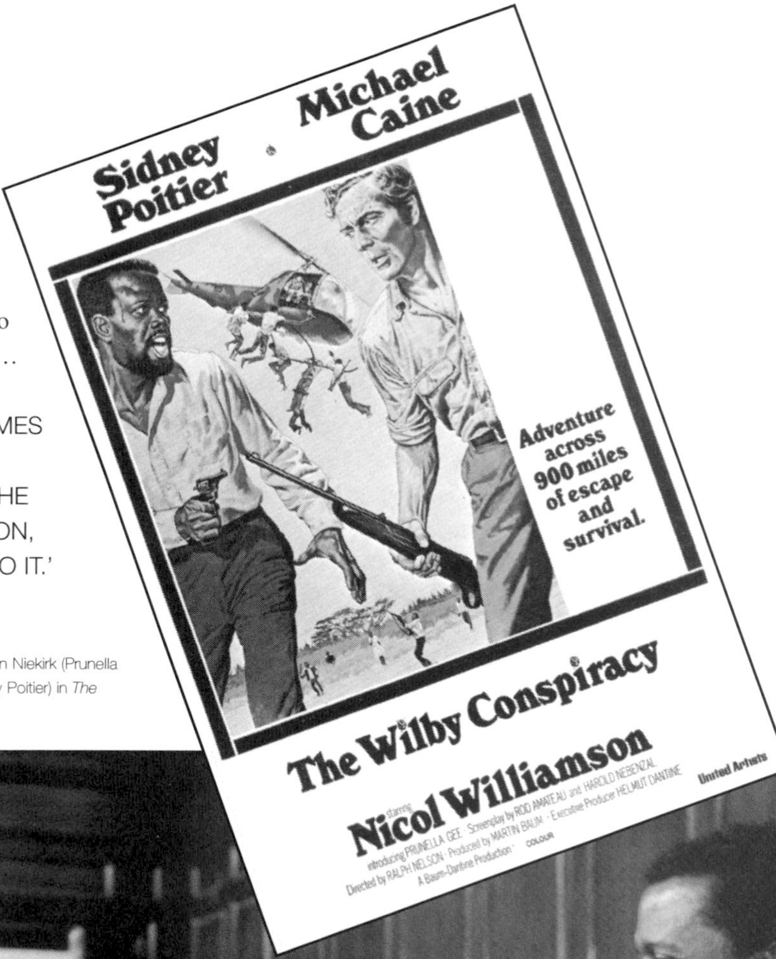

'SOMEHOW THE STORY COMES OUT TOO MUCH OF A POT-BOILER UNDESERVING OF THE FINE WORK THAT WILLIAMSON, CAINE AND POITIER PUT INTO IT.'
VARIETY

BELOW: Jim Keogh congratulates his lover Rina Van Niekirk (Prunella Gee) on securing the release of Shack Twala (Sidney Poitier) in *The Wilby Conspiracy* (1975).

SIDNEY POITIER • Michael Caine

Adventure across 900 miles of escape and survival.

The Wilby Conspiracy

starring Nicol Williamson

introducing PRUNELLA GEE · Screenplay by ROD AMATEAU and HAROLD NEBENZAL · Produced by MARTIN BAUM · Executive Producer HELMUT DANTINE
Directed by RALPH NELSON · A Baum-Dantine Production · COLOUR

United Artists

'MICHAEL CAINE HAS NEVER BEEN BETTER, CARRYING OFF HIS ROLE WITH A SENSE OF HUMOUR THAT NEVER INTERFERES WITH THE SERIOUSNESS OF THE ESCAPADE.'
DAILY EXPRESS

Peter Driscoll's political thriller about racism in South Africa, *The Wilby Conspiracy*, was first published in 1972. Screenwriters Rod Amateau and Harold Nebenzal adapted it for the big screen, downplaying the political content and heightening the more cinematic chase element. Ralph Nelson was hired to direct the film, having twice helmed films starring Sidney Poitier. Their first collaboration, *Lilies of the Field* (1963), had won Poitier a best actor Oscar – the first black actor to be awarded this accolade. Poitier was chosen for the role of political activist Shack Twala, while Caine came on board as British tourist Jim Keogh.

Caine had experienced apartheid while filming *Zulu* on location in South Africa in 1963, and soon learnt to abhor it. Several years later he also experienced the effects of racism while shooting *Hurry Sundown* (1967) in the US state of Louisiana. The actor had no time for such attitudes, as his mixed-race marriage to Shakira Baksh in 1973 showed. When the chance arose to star in an anti-apartheid thriller, Caine grabbed it.

The Wilby Conspiracy was unable to shoot in South Africa because of the film's political content. Instead Kenya and Nairobi were used for seven weeks of location work during 1974, with studio sequences lensed at Pinewood back in Britain. The picture was Rutger Hauer's first English-speaking role and gave English actress Prunella Gee her film debut. In 1975 she told *Film Review* about making the movie: 'As it was my first film, it was a bit of a strain. But Michael kept me doubled up with laughter most of the time. He is so funny. It was quite difficult to do some of the scenes for laughing.'

In Kenya Caine frequently found himself ignored while Poitier received all the adulation. But both actors almost made headlines for the wrong reason. They were filming a high-speed scene in a jeep with a camera mounted on the front of the vehicle. The £35,000 camera jolted loose and flew through the empty windscreen, narrowly missing them.

The Wilby Conspiracy was released in Britain in March 1975, rated AA. The picture got a mediocre reception from critics, uneasy at the mixture of politics and action. It reached America in July that year, rated PG. No DVD edition has yet been issued.

In his autobiography Caine said the picture was worthwhile, even without box-office success: 'This film was my first foray into that very risky realm of 'message' pictures, and as such proved to be a bit ahead of its time, but I am still proud that I made it anyway.' More than 20 years after *The Wilby Conspiracy*, Caine and Poitier were reunited to play the title characters in *Mandela and de Klerk*, a 1997 TV project about the end of apartheid in South Africa. The situation portrayed in their 1975 film had become part of history.

The Wilby Conspiracy is a curious mixture of chase film, buddy movie and political diatribe. It tackles the issue of racism with fervour, but loads the dice by portraying the white racists as evil sadists. There is also a certain crudity to the picture, with gratuitous nudity thrown in simply to titillate. But the strength of the three leads and a sardonically humorous script ensure that the film is never less than watchable. Nicol Williamson delivers a delightfully eccentric performance as the hunter Horn, while Caine and Poitier spark off each other well as the fugitives whose fates are inextricably linked. *The Wilby Conspiracy* is an enjoyable movie, even if it employs a sledgehammer to make its point.

WITHOUT A CLUE (1988)

Cast: Michael Caine (Sherlock Holmes), Ben Kingsley (Dr Watson), Jeffrey Jones (Inspector Lestrade), Lysette Anthony (fake Leslie), Paul Freeman (Prof Moriarty), Nigel Davenport (Lord Smithwick), Pat Keen (Mrs Hudson), Peter Cook (Greenhough), Tim Killick (Sebastian), Matthew Savage (Wiggins). Crew: Thom Eberhardt (director), Marc Stirdivant (producer), Gary Murphy and Larry Strawther (writers), Henry Mancini (music), Alan Hume (cinematography), Peter Tanner (editor), Brian Ackland-Snow (production design).

The great Victorian detective Sherlock Holmes foils an attempted robbery but, once the police have removed the perpetrators, Holmes' sidekick Dr Watson berates the legendary sleuth. Watson is the real genius – Holmes is just a character he created that enabled him to solve crimes anonymously. Watson turned each case into a story for top-selling magazine the *Strand* and, when people demanded to meet the great Holmes, Watson hired an actor called Reginald Kincaid to play the part. Alas, Kincaid is a drunk, a gambler, a womaniser and a buffoon. Watson sacks Kincaid but is forced to bring him back for one last case due to public demand.

The plates used to print the Bank of England's five pound notes are stolen and the chief printer, Giles, disappears. Watson deduces that criminal mastermind Professor Moriarty is behind the scheme and is apparently shot and drowned in a confrontation with his nemesis. Holmes finds a clue on a half-printed fiver and

225

RIGHT:
Director Thom
Eberhardt (right)
discusses the next
scene with his stars
Ben Kingsley and
Caine during the
filming of *Without a
Clue* (1988).

tracks Moriarty to an abandoned theatre near
the Thames, where the evil genius is forcing
Giles to print millions of bank notes. Watson
reappears, having survived his close encounter
with Moriarty. The printing plates are recovered,
the professor's thugs are arrested and Moriarty
is apparently killed in an explosion. Afterwards,
Holmes makes sure that Watson shares the credit.

'CAINE MANAGES TO BE … PEERLESS
IN HIS PRESENTATION OF THE
ACTOR'S PREENING VANITY AND SELF-
CENTREDNESS. BUT ONCE WE'VE
GOTTEN THE JOKE, WE'VE GOTTEN IT.'
WASHINGTON POST

'CAINE AND KINGSLEY ARE LEFT TOO
OFTEN WITH LITTLE TO DO EXCEPT
STAND ON EITHER SIDE OF THE

SCREEN AND CHEW OVER THEIR
RELATIONSHIP … ONCE REVEALED,
THAT PARTICULAR JOKE IS OVER, BUT
THIS MOVIE KEEPS CHEWING AT IT.'
CHICAGO SUN-TIMES

Screenwriter Gary Murphy conceived *Without a
Clue*'s role-reversal idea after watching a version
of the Sherlock Holmes story *The Sign of Four*
in which the great detective humbled Dr Watson
in front of Scotland Yard detectives. Murphy
wondered what would happen if Watson was the
genius and Holmes the lesser partner. From that
idea the script was born, co-written with Larry
Strawther. Thom Eberhardt was hired to direct
the picture, having shot three minor films. For
the roles of Holmes and Watson, producer Marc
Stirdivant cast Caine and Ben Kingsley. The
latter had won a best actor Oscar for playing the

lead in the biopic *Gandhi* (1982).

Shooting began in November 1987. A month earlier Caine mentioned the movie during an interview with the *Scotsman*: 'It's a comedy. It couldn't be anything else with me as Sherlock Holmes and Gandhi as Doctor Watson.' The picture was shot on location in and around London, Gloucester and the Lake District, with studio work at Shepperton and Pinewood. *Without a Clue* reunited Caine with Nigel Davenport, his co-star from *Play Dirty* (1968) and *The Last Valley* (1970).

'We've had so many laughs making this film,' Caine told the *News of the World* in June 1988. 'There have been over 100 Holmes movies, but never one like this. I knew the only way I could play Holmes was for some laughs. And this role has pleased me immensely. I don't think I've ever taken myself seriously and I do love doing comedy. Now I've proved that I can, I want to do more. It makes it much more fun going to work.' Quoted in the 1990 book *Candidly Caine*, Lysette Anthony, lead actress in the Holmesian spoof, remembered that 'Michael was brilliant in *Without a Clue*. He is such a professional, and he's very down to earth. The script stinks but he transcends all that in the way he dealt with the comedy. The director gave him a free rein...'

The film went through several name-changes during production (ranging from *Sherlock and Me* to *The Impostor of Baker Street*), eventually being released in America as *Without a Clue* in October 1988. Critics liked the combination of Kingsley and Caine, but found little else to recommend the movie. It grossed less than $9 million at the box-office. The picture reached Britain six months later, where it grossed less than $350,000. *Without a Clue* was released on video in 1989 and made its DVD debut 12 years later.

Without a Clue is a one-joke concept stretched out for more than 100 minutes. Turning Watson into a great detective and recasting Holmes as his stooge is a neat role-reversal, but the film foolishly delivers the punchline before the opening credits roll. Everything thereafter is just a pale imitation of material seen many times before. Caine excels as a witless, womanising buffoon and Kingsley makes a wonderfully uptight prig. But the script is strictly comedy-by-numbers with predictable plotting and flat, featureless direction.

WOMAN TIMES SEVEN (1967)

Cast: Shirley MacLaine (Paulette, Maria Teresa, Linda, Edith, Eve, Marie and Jeanne), Alan Arkin (Fred), Rossano Brazzi (Giorgio), Michael Caine (young man), Vittorio Gassman (Cenci), Peter Sellers (Jean), Anita Ekberg (Claudie), Elsa Martinelli (pretty woman), Lex Barker (Rik), Robert Morley (Dr Xavier).
Crew: Vittorio De Sica (director), Arthur Cohn (producer), Cesare Zavattini (writer), Riz Ortolani (music), Christian Matras (cinematography), Teddy Darvas and Victoria Spiri-Mercanton (editors), Bernard Evein (art direction).

A film compromised of seven vignettes. In *Funeral Procession*, a grieving widow is wooed by her dead husband's lawyer. *Amateur Night* sees an angry wife contemplate prostitution after catching her husband in adultery. *Two Against One* has two men competing for a disaffected woman's attention. *Super Simone* finds a quiet wife making increasingly bizarre attempts to catch the eye of her preoccupied husband, until he concludes she is going insane. A fight for an exclusive gown turns murderous in *At the Opera*. Two lovers contemplate killing themselves in *Suicide* but both change their mind.

Lastly, a handsome stranger follows two

women across Paris in *Snow*. Jeanne and Claudie decide to split up, so they can discover which of them their stalker is pursuing. He follows Jeanne, the meeker woman who has never found a man with whom she felt it was worth having an affair. The stranger follows her home in the snow and lingers outside for a while. Jeanne's husband Victor gets a phone call telling him what she has been doing all day. Victor is relieved to hear that she is not having an affair and thanks the private detective. The handsome stranger leaves a nearby phone booth, having completed his job. Jeanne watches the stranger walk away, intrigued by him…

'MOST OF THE BLAME … MUST FALL ON DE SICA, WHO HAS WASTED SUCH TALENTED ACTORS AS ARKIN, SELLERS, MICHAEL CAINE … IN A PONDEROUSLY DIRECTED, FLACCID WORK.' **TIME**

'EVEN MORE LABORIOUS THAN ALL THE REST OF DE SICA'S RECENT EFFORTS PUT TOGETHER, THIS IS OOH-LA-LA NAUGHTINESS IN GAY PAREE … AND ABOUT AS SOPHISTICATED AS SUET PUDDING.' **MONTHLY FILM BULLETIN**

Having chosen Caine as her leading man in *Gambit* (1966), Shirley MacLaine next decided to collaborate with the acclaimed Italian director Vittorio de Sica on a film made up of seven vignettes, each starring the actress as a different woman. MacLaine called in favours from friends she had made in the business, persuading several significant actors to appear in *Woman Times Seven* for a fraction of their normal fee. Caine was among those who grabbed the opportunity of working with De Sica.

Having just finished filming *Billion Dollar Brain* (1967), Caine travelled to Paris for his

wordless appearance as a private investigator stalking MacLaine in the final vignette, *Snow*. His part in the 12-minute sequence was shot on the city's streets, with De Sica using a hidden camera to capture footage without alerting the public.

Woman Times Seven was released in the US in June 1967 but did not reach British cinemas for a year, when it was rated X. Critics were underwhelmed by the picture, considering it a minor work for all involved. The movie was released on video in 1986, reclassified 15 in the UK. This has since been deleted and no DVD version is available.

Woman Times Seven is a vanity project for MacLaine, showcasing her comedic talents. The vignettes are slight and most outstay their welcome, underlining how dated the style and social commentary are in each. The highlights are a wry opening sketch with Peter Sellers and the suicidal couple played by MacLaine and Arkin in the penultimate piece. Caine's appearance is well handled but could have been played by any one of a thousand actors. This film is strictly for the most dedicated of Caine completists.

THE WRONG BOX (1966)

Cast: John Mills (Masterman Finsbury), Ralph Richardson (Joseph Finsbury), Michael Caine (Michael Finsbury), Peter Cook (Morris Finsbury), Dudley Moore (John Finsbury), Nanette Newman (Julia Finsbury), Tony Hancock (the detective), Peter Sellers (Doctor Pratt), Cicely Courtneidge (Major Martha), Wilfrid Lawson (Peacock). Crew: Bryan Forbes (director/producer), Larry Gelbart and Burt Shevelove (writers), John Barry (music), Gerry Fisher (cinematography), Alan Osbiston (editor), Ray Simm (art direction).

FAR LEFT: Caine paid back a favour to Shirley MacLaine by making a silent 12-minute cameo appearance with her in *Woman Times Seven* (1967).

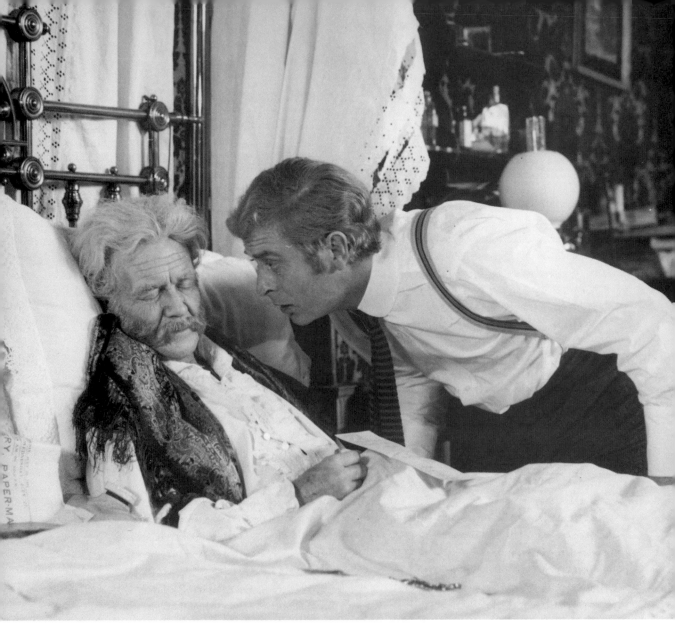

Elderly brothers Joseph and Masterman Finsbury are the last surviving members of a tontine. Whoever outlives the other will receive more than £111,000. The siblings live in adjoining houses but have not spoken for 40 years. Masterman believes he is dying and has his adopted grandson Michael send for Joseph. The other brother is in Bournemouth on holiday with his two adopted grandsons, Morris and John Finsbury. They have kept Joseph alive solely so that they can inherit the tontine. All three leave for London by train. En route, Joseph's hat and coat are stolen by a murderer known as the Bournemouth Strangler. The train crashes, killing the fiend. But Morris and John mistake the Strangler for their grandfather.

Fearful of losing the tontine, they hatch a scheme to secure the money with a fraudulent death certificate. The pair stuff the body in a barrel and post it to their home address. Confusion reigns as attempts are made to dispose of the corpse and of Masterman's still living body. The police, two firms of undertakers and a casket containing the cash from the tontine become embroiled in the chaos. Eventually everyone meets at a graveyard where the truth is revealed but the bickering continues…

'SOME VERY FUNNY MOMENTS … BUT THEY ARE JUST MOMENTS, BURIED IN A QUAGMIRE OF DAMP INVENTIONS WHICH DESTROY A STORY ALREADY QUITE INVENTIVE ENOUGH.' *MONTHLY FILM BULLETIN*

'THIS IS A FILM IN WHICH THE WHOLE IS CONSIDERABLY LESS THAN THE SUM OF ITS PARTS.' *THE OBSERVER*

Quirky comic novel *The Wrong Box* by Robert Louis Stevenson and Lloyd Osbourne was first published in 1889. More than 75 years later British director/producer Bryan Forbes chose the project as his next film, working from a script by Americans Larry Gelbart and Burt Shevelove. The pair had recently written the hit Broadway and West End musical *A Funny Thing Happened on the Way to the Forum*. The film attracted a cast of great British character actors, including distinguished thespians John Mills and Ralph Richardson. *The Wrong Box* gave comedians Peter Cook and Dudley Moore their film debuts and provided a final screen appearance for much-loved comic Tony Hancock. Caine was given third billing as the nervous, naïve Michael Finsbury.

He took the role as a way of escaping being typecast solely as a ladies' man. 'It was an antidote to *Alfie*,' the actor is quoted as saying in William Hall's biography, *Arise Sir Michael Caine*. 'I wanted to play a shy man with glasses. It was a scene-stealer film – every time you walked on, there was Wilfrid Lawson or Tony Hancock or Cicely Courtneidge or Ralph Richardson doing their number, and you didn't

stand a chance. That picture was so English it went well everywhere except in Britain!'

The picture was shot at Pinewood Studios with location work in Bath, London, Buckinghamshire and Surrey. Caine found himself wooing the director's actress wife, Nanette Newman, on screen. During filming Forbes told the *Evening News* he saw nothing wrong in casting his wife: 'Would I dream of putting her in a role unless I was confident that it was ideal for her? After the bad notices she'd divorce me immediately.' Caine and Newman had a narrow escape during shooting of the climactic chase sequence. Both were sitting atop a horse-drawn hearse when the animals suddenly bolted. It took Caine two miles to get the animals under control.

Forbes was full of praise for Caine's performance. 'Michael proved that he is an extraordinary actor,' the director was quoted as saying by Caine biographer Michael Freedland. 'He always showed up, no side, no temperament … just does it. There's too much preciousness surrounding acting. Most actors I've found, the greater the talent, the less the temperament. That's true with Michael, as with John Mills, Katharine Hepburn, Ralph Richardson and Dame Edith Evans.'

The Wrong Box was released in May 1966, rated U in Britain. Critics and the public were unmoved by the spectacle. But the film still won a BAFTA for its costumes and was nominated for two others – Richardson as best actor, plus art direction. Interviewed in 1999 by the reel.com website, Caine dismissed *The Wrong Box* in just four words: 'an obscure British comedy.'

The Wrong Box is a highly stylised mess festooned with mannered, over-the-top performances and laboured clowning. The script tries to turn a macabre comedy into a late-Victorian farce, but Forbes has over-egged the pudding with all manner of tricks and devices. Half the cast are playing their roles straight while the rest ham to their hearts' content, creating an ill-advised juxtaposition of acting styles. Caine gives a quiet, restrained performance among the eccentrics and makes little impression as a result. Unless you are a devotee of anyone involved, *The Wrong Box* is best forgotten.

YZ

ZEE & CO. (1972)
(US title: *X,Y & Zee*)

Cast: Elizabeth Taylor (Zee), Michael Caine (Robert), Susannah York (Stella), Margaret Leighton (Gladys), John Standing (Gordon), Mark Larkin (Rita), Michael Cashman (Gavin).
Crew: Brian G Hutton (director), Jay Kanter and Alan Ladd Jr (producers), Edna O'Brien (writer), Stanley Myers (music), Billy Williams (cinematography), Jim Clark (editor), Peter Mullins (art direction).
Swinging Londoners Robert and Zee Blakeley

BELOW: Robert Blakeley tests the limits of his open marriage when he embarks on an affair with Stella (Susannah York) in *Zee & Co* (1972).

X

X, Y & ZEE (1972)
See ZEE & CO. (1972)

have an open marriage and separate bedrooms. At a party Robert is intrigued by Stella, a beautiful young widow. They become lovers. Zee responds by insinuating herself into Stella's life. When Robert and Stella go away on holiday, Zee crashes her husband's car. He comes back to her again. Zee then tries to commit suicide. Robert saves her but considers letting Zee die to escape her mind games. Stella visits Zee in hospital and admits to lesbian tendencies as a teenager. Robert is due to spend the night with Stella but Zee drags him to a party and gets him drunk. Next day Robert argues with Stella, who wants to end the affair. Robert sleeps with his secretary. Zee visits Stella's new flat and seduces her. Robert arrives to find Zee triumphant…

'NOT IN YEARS HAVE THREE PEOPLE MORE DESERVED THE STAR BILLING THEY GET IN THIS *LOVE STORY* FOR ADULTS.' **VARIETY**

'THE FILM GRADUALLY SINKS INTO A QUAGMIRE OF REPETITION FROM WHICH THE ONLY WAY OUT IS THROUGH MELODRAMA…' **MONTHLY FILM BULLETIN**

Irish novelist Edna O'Brien wrote *Zee and Co* as an original screenplay in 1970 and the script's strong female lead attracted the interest of Elizabeth Taylor. American director Brian G Hutton was attached to the project and the role of Zee's husband was offered to Caine only after Peter O'Toole turned it down. In his autobiography, Caine maintained that the chance to work with Taylor was his main reason for accepting the role, but he never regretted making the movie. O'Brien had the opposite reaction after discovering her script had been extensively rewritten to include a lesbian finale. The enraged author claimed Hutton had butchered her screenplay.

The picture was shot predominantly on sets at Shepperton Studios with limited location work around London. The 14-week production began filming in January 1971. When Taylor was on set she arrived with at least three limousines to convey her entourage. During filming Caine told the *Evening Standard* about his early experiences on the picture: 'When we began this film both Elizabeth and I were nervous of each other. It was difficult because we had to go right into fights and love scenes rolling around the bed and we never even knew each other. But after the first couple of days we admitted that we were nervous. I gave her a bit of a hug – you know, not being familiar, but just to make human contact and we were fine after that.'

The actor discussed Taylor during an interview with the *Cranky Critic* website in 1998. 'She was the most extraordinary actress to work with. Elizabeth has a memory like a rat trap. She never flubbed a line. With Elizabeth, she had it in her contract that she didn't have to be in the studio until ten o'clock. I was always there at eight doing close-ups on my own with a continuity girl saying, "I love you, darling. Take your trousers off." I remember saying to Elizabeth, "I know for sure that you are a great star and a real professional." She said, "How do you know?' I said, "You are a great star because you don't have to get here until ten o'clock and I know you are a professional because you are never late!"'

The picture required Caine to perform love scenes, but he refused to be filmed naked. 'I think the public is sick of it,' the actor told *Photoplay*. 'I've never been fully nude on the screen because I don't believe I have anything that anyone would be interested in seeing. Nudity isn't interesting unless a girl is undressing for me, personally.'

Rated R, *Zee and Co* was released in January 1972 in America, renamed *X, Y & Zee*.

Critics praised the picture, with Taylor's volcanic performance getting most of the kudos. The film reached British cinemas several months later, rated X. It was nominated as the best English-language foreign film at the Golden Globes in January 1973, but lost to *Young Winston* (1972). A year later the picture was re-edited and reclassified as a PG for the US.

Few of Caine's films have dated as badly as *Zee and Co*. This hysterical, overwrought melodrama comes across like a Swinging Sixties hangover. Just imagine a cross between *Austin Powers* and *Who's Afraid of Virginia Woolf?* – then make it twice as bad. Taylor chews scenery like the world has run out of food while parading around in clothes that induce eye-strain in the viewer. Susannah York is both drippy and winsome while Caine is left looking angry or frustrated in equal measure. You can't care about the characters but you can laugh at their turgid, torpid love triangle. This film deserves to be enshrined as a camp classic – there's certainly no other reason to watch it.

ZULU (1964)

Cast: Stanley Baker (Lieutenant John Chard RE), Jack Hawkins (Otto Witt), Ulla Jacobsson (Margareta Witt), James Booth (Private Henry Hook), Michael Caine (Lieutenant Gonville Bromhead), Nigel Green (Colour-Sergeant Bourne), Ivor Emmanuel (Private Owen), Paul Daneman (Sergeant Maxfield), Glynn Edwards (Corporal William Allen), Neil McCarthy (Private Thomas), David Kernan (Private Hitch), Gary Bond (Private Cole). Crew: Cy Endfield (director/co-producer/co-writer), Stanley Baker (co-producer), John Prebble (co-writer), John Barry (music), Stephan Dade (cinematography), John Jympson (editor), Ernest Archer (art direction).

In January 1879 more than 1000 British soldiers

FAR RIGHT:
Lieutenant Gonville Bromhead shouts his orders to the British forces as they fight insurmountable odds in *Zulu* (1964), the film that gave Caine his first starring role.

are killed during a battle with the Zulu forces of King Cetewayo at Isandhlwana in South Africa. The next target for the 4000 Zulu warriors is a mission station at Rorke's Drift that also contains a hospital for British soldiers. Swedish missionary Otto Witt and his daughter Margareta hurry back to the station when they hear of the coming attack.

Lieutenant John Chard of the Royal Engineers is at Rorke's Drift to build a bridge. When word of the approaching Zulu horde arrives, Chard takes charge from the commanding officer, Lieutenant Gonville Bromhead. They have the same rank but Chard has three months' seniority. There are just seven officers, 36 sick and wounded soldiers and less than 100 fit infantrymen at Rorke's Drift. South African cavalrymen pass the mission station but refuse to stay and help. Chard is forced to send Witt and Margareta away after the Reverend causes trouble and gets drunk.

The Zulu send wave after wave of attackers against the station, but the Welsh infantrymen stand firm. The battle continues through the night and resumes next morning. Eventually the Zulu withdraw, chanting a salute to the brave British warriors. Eleven Victoria Cross medals for valour and extreme courage were given to the defenders of Rorke's Drift, the most ever awarded for a single battle…

'THE PRODUCTION IS DISTINGUISHED BY ITS NOTABLE ONSCREEN VALUES … TOP QUALITY LENSING … AND INTELLIGENT SCREENPLAY WHICH AVOIDS MOST OF THE OBVIOUS CLICHÉS.' *VARIETY*

'*ZULU* IS A TYPICALLY FASHIONABLE WAR FILM, PAYING DUTIFUL LIP SERVICE TO THE FUTILITY OF THE SLAUGHTER WHILE MILKING IT FOR THRILLS.' *MONTHLY FILM BULLETIN*

In the early 1960s journalist John Prebble wrote a series of articles about courage, using the true story of the battle at Rorke's Drift for one of his pieces. A shortened version of that piece appeared in *Lilliput* magazine. Film rights to the article were acquired by Diamond Films, a production company set up by Welsh actor Stanley Baker and American director Cy Endfield. They chose it as their first project, developing the screenplay with Prebble under the working title *The Battle of Rorke's Drift*. Originally budgeted at £2.6 million, finance was provided by US producer Joseph E Levine on condition the budget was cut to £2 million.

Baker was already attached as the star and cast people he had previously enjoyed working with, several of whom had appeared in *A Hill in Korea* (1956). Among the young actors Baker befriended on that picture was Caine, then struggling to make an impact in a succession of bit parts. During pre-production for *Zulu* Baker went to see Caine on stage in the play *Next Time I'll Sing to You*. Afterwards he invited Caine to audition for the role of Cockney malingerer Private Hook in *Zulu*. But the part had already been given to James Booth and Caine thought his chance had gone.

'Cy Endfield ... was convinced my face was that of a British aristocrat,' Caine told *Films and Filming* in 1969. '"It's long ... you've got a long face like a horse." He was never very complimentary towards me but he sort of talked himself, and Stanley, and me, into playing the aristocratic lieutenant. This was based on my 'horsey' face, longish blond hair ... and, of course, economics came into it.'

In a documentary on the *Zulu* DVD, Sir Stanley Baker's widow recalls Caine's screen test. 'Paramount were pressing for Terence Stamp,' Lady Ellen Baker says. 'There were only two tests made, Terry and Michael. Michael's

wasn't a good test, Terry's was very, very professional. But both Stanley and Cy knew it had to be Michael. Stanley said, "He's going to be a massive star."' Paramount and Levine reportedly fought against the casting of Caine and tried to have the actor sacked several times during filming. But Endfield and Baker stood by their decision.

Caine had fought in the Korean War as a soldier, but wanted to know more about how officers treated each other. 'I'd go to the Grenadier Guards' mess [in London] every lunchtime to talk with the officers,' he told *Film Comment* in 1980. 'I'd only been a private in the army, so my view of officers had been a private's view. I spent two weeks having meals with them, seeing how they spoke to each other.' The actor was also preparing to adopt the accent of an upper-class Englishman.

Location shooting took place over 14 weeks in Natal, South Africa during 1963, with subsequent studio work at Twickenham. During filming in South Africa each day's footage was sent to England for developing, then came back as 'rushes' so that it could be screened for the cast and crew. Caine was horrified by the results. 'This person came on, quite strange to me, completely awful-looking,' the actor said in a public interview at the NFT in 1998. 'Suddenly this terrible voice came out, and there was this terrible acting going on, and I threw up on the floor. I threw up and rushed out, and I've never been back to rushes.' The sole exception was *The Man Who Would Be King* (1975), when director John Huston insisted everyone attended the screening of rushes.

Zulu got its premiere (rated U) in Britain on 22 January 1964 – the 85th anniversary of the battle it depicted. Critics questioned the film's historical accuracy and considered the style old-fashioned. But it still found favour with audiences, grossing more than four times its budget at the box-office and becoming the third most successful general release of 1964, behind the James Bond blockbuster *Goldfinger* and the Beatles' movie debut, *A Hard Day's Night*. *Zulu* was BAFTA-nominated for best art direction. The movie reached US cinemas in June 1964, but failed to replicate its UK success. The picture was reissued to British cinemas in 1967, 1972 and 1976.

In a BFI poll to find the Top 100 British movies of the 20th century, *Zulu* was the second highest placed of seven Caine pictures, being voted 31st. It was issued on DVD in 2002, accompanied by a commentary track and two-part documentary about the film's genesis and production.

Zulu is a war film that still stirs the soul and compels the viewer 40 years on. The screenplay tweaks reality for dramatic effect, but the key features of this remarkable true story are accurate. There is a lot of time spent setting the scene, but this is more than repaid by the gripping battle that fills the second hour of the picture. Endfield extracts strong performances from his cast and the whole production looks fresh and new, aided by an evocative John Barry score. Caine creates an empathetic characterisation from limited material as the aristocratic Bromhead. His presence on screen belies the fact that this was Caine's first screen role of any note. He helps make *Zulu* a classic of its kind.

BELOW:
Lieutenants John Chard (Stanley Baker) and Gonville Bromhead contemplate the aftermath of the battle at Rorke's Drift in *Zulu* (1964).

FILMOGRAPHY

1950	Morning Departure	1975	The Wilby Conspiracy
1956	A Hill in Korea (aka Hell in Korea)		The Romantic Englishwoman
	Sailor Beware		Peeper
1957	How to Murder a Rich Uncle		The Man Who Would Be King
	The Steel Bayonet	1976	Harry and Walter Go to New York
1958	The Key		The Eagle Has Landed
	Carve Her Name with Pride	1977	A Bridge Too Far
	Blindspot		Silver Bears
	Passport to Shame	1978	The Swarm
1959	Danger Within (aka Breakout)		California Suite
	The Two Headed Spy	1979	Ashanti
1960	Foxhole in Cairo		Beyond the Poseidon Adventure
	The Bulldog Breed	1980	The Island
1961	The Day the Earth Caught Fire		Dressed to Kill
1962	Solo for Sparrow	1981	The Hand
	The Wrong Arm of the Law	1982	Victory (aka Escape to Victory)
1964	Zulu		Deathtrap
1965	The Ipcress File	1983	Educating Rita
1966	Alfie		The Honorary Consul
	The Wrong Box		(aka Beyond the Limit)
	Gambit	1984	Blame It on Rio
	Funeral in Berlin		The Jigsaw Man
1967	Hurry Sundown	1985	Water
	Woman Times Seven		The Holcroft Covenant
	Billion Dollar Brain	1986	Hannah and Her Sisters
1968	Deadfall		Mona Lisa
	The Magus		Sweet Liberty
	Play Dirty		Half Moon Street
1969	The Italian Job	1987	The Fourth Protocol
	Battle of Britain		The Whistle Blower
1970	Too Late the Hero		Jaws the Revenge
	The Last Valley		Surrender
1971	Get Carter	1988	Without a Clue
	Kidnapped		Dirty Rotten Scoundrels
1972	Zee and Co. (aka X, Y & Zee)	1990	A Shock to the System
	Pulp		Mr Destiny
	Sleuth		Bullseye!
1974	The Black Windmill	1992	Noises Off
	The Marseilles Contract		Blue Ice
	(aka The Destructors)		The Muppet Christmas Carol

1994	On Deadly Ground
1996	Bullet to Beijing
1997	Midnight in St Petersburg
	Blood and Wine
1998	Shadow Run
	Little Voice
	Curtain Call
1999	The Debtors
	The Cider House Rules
2000	Shiner
	Quills
	Get Carter
	Miss Congeniality
2001	Last Orders
2002	Austin Powers in Goldmember
	The Quiet American
	Quicksand
2003	The Actors
	Secondhand Lions
	The Statement

SELECT
BIBLIOGRAPHY

All publications are London unless otherwise stated.

Adams, Mark, *Mike Hodges* (Harpenden, Herts: Pocket Essentials, 2001)

Andrews, Emma, *The Films of Michael Caine* (Isle of Wight: BCW,1974)

Ashbrook, John, *Brian De Palma* (Harpenden, Herts: Pocket Essentials, 2000)

Billson, Anne, *My Name is Michael Caine: A life in film* (Muller, 1991)

Caine, Michael, *Acting in Film: An Actor's Take on Movie Making* (New York: Applause, 1990)

Caine, Michael, *What's It All About?* (Century, 1992)

Carlson, Michael, *Oliver Stone* (Harpenden, Herts: Pocket Essentials, 2002)

Catterall, Ali and Wells, Simon, *Your Face Here: British Cult Movies Since the Sixties* (Harper Collins, 2002)

Davies, Steven Paul, *Get Carter and Beyond: The Cinema of Mike Hodges* (Batsford, 2002)

Field, Matthew, *The Making of The Italian Job* (Batsford, 2001)

Forbes, Bryan, *A Divided Life* (Heinemann, 1992)

Freedland, Michael, *Michael Caine* (Orion, 1999)

Gallagher, Elaine, *Candidly Caine* (Robson, 1990)

Goldman, William, *Adventures in the Screen Trade* (Macdonald, 1984)

Hall, William, *Arise Sir Michael Caine* (John Blake, 2000)

Hodges, Mike, *Get Carter* (Eye, Suffolk: Screen Press, 2001)

Irving, John, *My Movie Business* (Bloomsbury, 1999)

Judge, Philip, *Michael Caine* (Tunbridge Wells, Kent: Spellmount, 1985)

Monk, Claire and Sargeant, Amy, (ed.), *British Historical Cinema* (Routledge, 2002)

O'Neil, Tom, *Movie Awards* (New York: Perigee, 2001)

Pendreigh, Brian, *The Pocket Scottish Movie Book* (Edinburgh: Mainstream, 2002)

Sellers, Robert, *Always Look on the Bright Side of Life* (Metro, 2003)

Thomason, David, *The New Biographical Dictionary of Film* (Little, Brown, 2002)